MW00333310

Virtue's Splendor

For Tracie

Tom Hibbs

MORAL PHILOSOPHY AND MORAL THEOLOGY SERIES
Romanus Cessario, O.P., and Joseph W. Koterski, S.J., series editors

Virtue's Splendor

WISDOM, PRUDENCE, AND THE HUMAN GOOD

THOMAS S. HIBBS

Fordham University Press
New York
2001

Copyright © 2001 by Fordham University Press

All rights reserved. No part of this publication may be reproduced, stored in a retrieval system, or transmitted in any form or by any means—electronic, mechanical, photocopy, recording, or any other—except for brief quotations in printed reviews, without the prior permission of the publisher.

Moral Philosophy and Moral Theology Series, No. 3
ISSN 1527–523X

Library of Congress Cataloging-in-Publication Data

Hibbs, Thomas S.
    Virtue's splendor : wisdom, prudence, and the human good / Thomas S. Hibbs.—1st ed.
        p.   cm.—(Moral philosophy and moral theology ; no. 3)
    Includes bibliographical references and index.
    ISBN 0-8232-2043-5 (alk. paper)—ISBN 0-8232-2044-3 (pbk. : alk. paper)
    1. Christian ethics.   I. Title.   II. Series.
BJ1249.H53   2001
170—dc21   2001042494

Printed in the United States of America
01   02   03   04   05   5   4   3   2   1
First Edition

Ut Tullius dicit, "ex justitia praecipue viri boni nominantur," unde, sicut dicit, "in ea virtutis splendor est maximus."

Thomas Aquinas, *Summa Theologiae,* II-II, 58, 3

In memory of
Monsignor Thomas Wells,
Priest, teacher, friend

During the fall of 1978, I had my first taste of philosophy at the University of Maryland at College Park, where as a freshman I had three avowedly atheistic professors. Not exactly a pleasant introduction to philosophy, it was, nonetheless, exactly what I needed to awaken me from the dogmatic slumbers of my unreflective youth. I had the good fortune at that time to meet Father Thomas Wells, a priest for the archdiocese of Washington, D.C. A gifted preacher and teacher with a relentless wit, Father Wells was the first priest, indeed the first Catholic, I encountered who could articulate the wisdom of the Catholic faith with intelligence, enthusiasm, and joy. In the midst of my intellectual unrest, he pointed me in the direction of St. Thomas Aquinas.

In the 1960s, Father Wells had attended Boston College, where I now teach. On the morning of June 8, 2000, I was at my desk at Boston College, working on yet another essay on Aquinas, when my wife called to give me the horrifying news that Father Wells had been murdered in his rectory in a robbery gone bad. Two thousand mourners attended his funeral at Sacred Heart Church in Bowie, Maryland, the first parish in which he served after his ordination and the place where in 1798 the plans were laid for the organization of the Roman Catholic Church in the United States and John Carroll was selected first bishop. In death as in life, Father Wells gives testimony to the transforming power of the Gospel, to the beauty of a life lived in imitation of Christ. To his memory, I dedicate this book.

CONTENTS

ACKNOWLEDGMENTS

The remote origins of this book date back to my graduate school days at the University of Notre Dame, where Ralph McInerny directed my thesis on the relationship between virtue and law in Aquinas. In addition to him, Mark Jordan, David Solomon, Stanley Hauerwas, and Alasdair Macintyre have over the years provided me with invaluable criticism and advice. My debt to their interpretations of Aquinas and to their approaches to contemporary ethics is evident throughout the book. To exonerate them of guilt, I should add that none of them read this manuscript, and only the first three have been my teachers in any official way. Although it would not be logically possible for all of them to approve equally of this or any other work on Aquinas, I consider myself enormously fortunate to have had such teachers and interlocutors.

After the dissertation, my work on Aquinas's ethics appeared in a number of published articles, some of which reappear in revised form in the book. I am grateful for permission to publish revised versions of the following articles: "Against a Cartesian Reading of *Intellectus* in Aquinas," *The Modern Schoolman* 66 (1988): 55–69; "Divine Irony and the Natural Law: Speculation and Edification in Aquinas," *International Philosophical Quarterly* 30 (1990): 419–29; "The Hierarchy of Moral Discourses in Aquinas," *American Catholic Philosophical Quarterly* 64 (1990): 199–214; "*Imitatio Christi* and the Foundation of Aquinas's Ethics," *Communio* 18 (1991): 556–73; "Principles and Prudence," *New Scholasticism* 61 (1987): 271–84; "The Revival of Prudence," in *Postmodernism and Christian Philosophy,* edited by Roman Ciapolo (Washington, D.C.: Catholic University of America Press, 1997); "A Rhetoric of Motives: Thomas on Obligation as Rational Persuasion," *The Thomist* 54 (1990): 293–309; and "Transcending Humanity," *Proceedings of the American Catholic Philosophical Association* 66 (1992): 191–213. I am also grateful to Hackett Publishing for allowing me to use parts of *Aquinas: On Human Nature* (1999).

Writing on the book began in the spring of 1995 while I was a Visiting Mooney Scholar at the University of Notre Dame Maritain Center, directed by Ralph McInerny. My debts to Ralph keep mounting.

I would also like to thank Joseph Koterski, S.J., and Romanus Cessario, O.P., the editors of the Fordham University Press Moral Philosophy and Moral Theology Series, in which this book appears. Romanus's comments on an early draft of the book were quite helpful. Thanks also to Anthony Chiffolo, managing editor of the Press, and to Annie Barva, a freelance editor who made many helpful corrections to the manuscript.

It is commonplace for an author to acknowledge a debt to his spouse and children and to thank them for their patience and forbearance during the process of composition, but I find myself equally grateful for their persistent interruptions. At least that's what impresses me now that the project is completed. My wife, Stacey, and our children, Lauren, Daniel, and Sara, provide constant reminders that writing about virtue is a paltry thing in comparison to the life of virtue.

INTRODUCTION: OBSTACLES TO THE RECOVERY OF AQUINAS'S TEACHING ON THE HUMAN GOOD

IN THE NOVEL *Love in the Ruins*, Walker Percy speaks of the "dread chasm that has rent the soul of Western man ever since the famous philosopher Descartes ripped body lose from mind and turned the very soul into a ghost that haunts its own house."[1] In his novels, Percy is preoccupied with the predicament of modern humanity; many of his characters are abstracted and detached from their bodies, desperately struggling to gain reentry into the bodily world by immersing themselves in alcohol, drugs, pornography, and violence. Percy combines the diagnostic skills of a psychiatrist with a novelist's flair for the dramatic implications of modern humanity's alienation from its own nature.

A more scholarly and more philosophical rendition of this thesis can be found in the writings of Pierre Manent, a contemporary political philosopher. Manent focuses on the modern antagonism toward a specific form of Christianity, namely, the catholic form, whose proclamation of an authoritative, public, and universal church is vehemently opposed by Machiavelli, Hobbes, and Locke, the founders of modern political thought. One of the peculiar, and often unremarked, features of the attack on the Roman Catholic Church is the accompanying repudiation of pagan philosophers such as Plato and Aristotle. We have to wonder why early modern philosophers did not continue the renaissance revival of pagan philosophy. One reason is certainly that the methods of the new sciences required a decisive break from the methods of ancient philosophy. But Manent detects another source for the attack on pagan philosophy:

---

[1] *Love in the Ruins*, 191.

in order to liberate himself from the "supernatural," modern man cannot rest content with becoming "pagan" again. It is not enough to affirm or reaffirm nature. This latter is henceforth exposed to being outbid or trumped by the supernatural. If nature is good, even very good, the supernatural is necessarily better, because it is infinitely good. If the earthly city provides natural goods, the heavenly city, which the church prefigures, dispenses supernatural goods that are incomparably superior to the former. . . . If the critique of the supernatural is going to achieve its political ends . . . it must entail a critique of nature. The critique of revelation implies the critique of pagan politics and philosophy.[2]

We need not enter here into the debates over whether and to what extent the West was Christianized during the Middle Ages. It suffices to note that the Catholic Church had penetrated the crucial and sovereign institutions of political and intellectual life. The result, according to Locke, of this strange and unnatural mixture of "things remote and opposite" is religious war and a debilitating confusion in the allegiance of citizens. Early modern political theorists, from Machiavelli and Hobbes through Locke and Rousseau, engage in a sustained battle against the Church, lord of the dark ages.[3] Manent explains, "To stop it [the Church] from immediately reconstituting itself, one must

---

[2] "Christianity and Democracy," in *Modern Liberty and Its Discontents*, 111. For Manent's comprehensive treatment of modern political thought, see *The City of Man*.

[3] Like Strauss, Manent is operating here with a rather undifferentiated conception of the Enlightenment. Perhaps the most important corrective to our understanding of the Enlightenment is found in the writings of Knud Haakonssen. In *Natural Law and Moral Philosophy from Grotius to the Scottish Enlightenment*, Haakonssen argues that in eighteenth-century Scotland, Enlightenment political theory is neither radically individualistic nor dominated by the language of individual rights (5–7). He speaks instead of a "conservative" Enlightenment, to which the thought of Hobbes is alien, which subordinates rights to duties and the latter to "historically given offices," all of which is derived from a "teleological and providentialist norm" (311, 327). Making "rights the primary feature" of a moral theory via autonomy and self-legislation marks the "death of natural law thinking" (62). Haakonssen cautions that the necessary opposition between religious natural law thinking and modernity is an invention of nineteenth-century liberalism and should not be read back into the eighteenth century (326). And yet he ends his book with the development in the United States of subjective rights (330 and following). Also of interest is *Enlightenment and Religion*, edited by Knud Haakonssen. Although it is certainly the case that nature and human nature retain their normative status for many writers in the modern period, Manent still captures both the roots and the ultimate trajectory of the distinctively modern flight from nature.

invalidate or at least decisively weaken many other ideas that appear to be unconnected with it, or that even seem to rival it rather than support it. I have in mind, for example, the idea of nature," which in Greek philosophy "had worked to deliver men from the fear of punitive gods."[4]

At the outset of the modern period, the Roman Catholic Church had much political power, even a kind of sovereignty. Yet, given the corruption of the late medieval Church and the harsh criticisms leveled against it by humanists and protestant reformers, the Church had little dialectical power. If the proponents of the primacy of the political were relatively weak in power, they possessed a significant dialectical advantage. We now stand on the far side of this grand conflagration, in which the Roman Catholic Church has seen its political sovereignty severely diminished, if not entirely eliminated everywhere. Yet, as Manent sees it, the original situation is reversed in another important respect. Although the Church now lacks sovereignty, it possesses a distinct dialectical advantage. How is this so?

> Democracy no longer in good faith, has any essential reproach to make against the church. From now on it can hear the question the church poses, the question that it alone poses, the question *Quid sit homo*— What is man? But democracy neither wants to nor can respond to the question. . . . On democracy's side of the scale, we are left with political sovereignty and dialectical impotence. On the church's side, we are left with political submission and dialectical advantage.

In its persistent affirmation that there is something determinate and normative to be discovered in the investigation of human things, the Catholic Church stands athwart the philosophy and the politics of the day. Manent comments, "What defines the Church as an agent in the human world . . . is that it bears a specific, proper thought or doctrine; it says something about man. It thereby . . . limits the arbitrariness of the democratic will, of democratic sovereignty, by reminding the latter that man cannot do whatever he wills."[5] Manent depicts our present moment as a time of tremendous opportunity for the Catholic Church, a time when it can recover its authoritative role as teacher. It does so at least in part by posing the fundamental question of humanity. Manent concludes, "The relation unleashed by the

---

[4] "The Truth, Perhaps," in *Modern Liberty and Its Discontents*, 41.
[5] "Christianity and Democracy," in *Modern Liberty and Its Discontents*, 113.

Enlightenment today is reversed. No one knows what will happen when democracy and the church become aware of this reversal."[6]

Manent is right to return us to early modern debates about human nature as initiating the flight from nature. Since the time of these classical modern debates over the state of nature and the human condition, philosophical investigations of human nature have been in steady decline. A number of reasons can be given for the demise of the philosophy of human nature. There is, first, the splitting up of the perspectives on human life into various disciplines: sociology, biology, economics, and ethics and religion. The suggestion that out of these disciplines might emerge a unified and comprehensive conception of human nature is dismissed as quixotic. Second, an influential scientific project consigns the study of human nature to the biological and chemical sciences and reduces human thought and volition to physiological processes. Third, philosophical reaction, especially prominent in certain strains of existentialism, against scientific reductionism denies the relevance of natural science to understanding the human world of freedom. Science is said to study natures; it tells us what something is, and it is capable of studying a person, a "who" not a "what." Finally, the project of modern political liberalism eschews any determinate conception of human nature as an impediment to democratic politics; instead of nature, the basis of politics is consensus and freedom. The extreme point in the flight from nature can be seen in the proclamations of so-called postmodern philosophers and deconstructionists concerning the vanishing of man, the evanescent self, that is our fate.

From the perspective of Aristotle and Aquinas, two of the most important and influential premodern philosophers, the break initiated in modernity consists precisely in the flight from nature, which itself reposes on the repudiation of the Aristotelian conception of soul and of human beings as composites of soul and body. The human soul, St. Thomas Aquinas writes, exists on the "confines of the spiritual and corporeal" (*Summa Theologiae* [hereafter *ST*], I, 77, 2). The human person is thus a microcosm of the whole universe, a little world, in whom the perfections of both the spiritual and the material orders coincide. St. Thomas adopts Aristotle's account of human beings as composites of soul and body, wherein soul is related to body

---

[6] "Christianity and Democracy," 113.

as form to matter. This is the so-called hylomorphic theory of human nature. Composed of matter and form, human beings are akin to all other natural substances. But because the highest capacity of the human soul is the intellect, which is an immaterial power, human beings are peculiar examples of matter-form composition. Nowhere else do we find an immaterial power united to a body.

St. Thomas's position eludes categorization in terms of the fundamental modern and contemporary alternatives of dualism and materialism. Nor does it help to depict hylomorphism as a compromise or middle position between dualism and materialism. The latter are closer to one another than either is to Aquinas. In his *Meditations*, Descartes's emphatic rejection of the body as constitutive of who we are as human beings provides a classic statement of dualism and sets the terms of debate over human nature well into this century.[7] What are the motives behind his project, the defining project for modern philosophy?

In the opening of his *Meditations*, Descartes laments the lack of certitude in all that he has learned. Except for some of the proofs of mathematics, his education has given him nothing more than probable knowledge, most of which rests on the opinions he has inherited from tradition and his elders. Even were the knowledge handed on to him without error, he would still be in a position of doubt, for he has accepted it on trust. If he is ever to arrive at absolutely certain knowledge, he will have to raze to the ground all the opinions that he has inherited from others and build his knowledge on a more secure foundation. He puts doubt in the service of certitude, as he sets out to establish indubitable knowledge by rejecting whatever admits of any doubt. Thus, he dismisses the senses, which are sometimes deceptive. The most radical proposal is that—because it is possible that some immensely powerful, malevolent being could deceive him about even such seemingly certain truths as those taught in mathematics—he must set these truths aside. It is important to note here that Descartes's doubt applies solely to thought, not to action; he admits that it would be absurd to try to live in accord with such doubt. But if one wants to provide an unshakable foundation for all of knowledge, the method is the appropriate means. Where then do we arrive at a certain basis for knowledge? We do so by unveiling the

---

[7] See *Meditations*, II.

necessary conditions of the possibility of the hypothesis of a deceptive evil genius: if he is deceiving me, it follows that I am being deceived, and if I am being deceived, I am thinking, and thus I must exist. Having reached this first certainty, Descartes asks: But what am I? "A man, of course. But what is a man? Might I not say 'rational animal'? No, because then I would have to inquire what 'animal' and 'rational' mean. And thus from one question I would slide into many more difficult ones." Rejecting as too complex the Aristotelian definition of "man," he proceeds to inquire whether he can affirm of himself anything bodily.

> But what about being nourished or moving about? Since I now do not have a body, these are surely nothing but fictions. What about sensing? Surely this too does not take place without a body. . . . What about thinking? Here I make my discovery: thought exists; it alone cannot be separated from me. I am; I exist—this is certain. But for how long? For as long as I am thinking. . . . I am therefore precisely nothing but a thinking thing. (*Meditations,* II)

The remainder of the meditations is familiar. Descartes offers an argument for the existence of an infinitely perfect being, thus eliminating the hypothesis of the evil genius and providing an avenue back to the external world. If God is infinitely perfect, he is not a deceiver, and trusting our senses is thus reasonable. It turns out not only that there is an external world but that we are somehow united to a body. But, like all physical things, the body is merely extended matter in motion. We can have clear and distinct—that is, certain—ideas about the physical world only insofar as we construe nature in mathematical terms.

As much as Descartes's thought breaks with the thought of Aristotle and Aquinas, it retains certain themes and assumptions. Descartes thinks that the basic truths about human nature and the world, even about God, are accessible to human understanding. Indeed, he is quite, perhaps inordinately, optimistic about the clarity of the knowledge we can achieve in these areas. He also refers to the intellect as a light of nature. But his writings unleash certain tendencies and raise certain problems that set the terms of philosophical reflection and debate for some of the most important thinkers after him. There seems no longer to be any natural goal or telos to human nature, and the place of human beings as parts of the whole is rendered

inscrutable. The relationship of mind and body is especially bewitch-
ing. The entire physical world becomes raw material on which we
exercise our control. Thus does the argument of the *Meditations* provide a basis for Descartes's mathematical physics, whose goal is to
render us "masters and possessors of nature."

The dualism Descartes espoused is often contrasted with materialism, which refuses to countenance a mind or intellect distinct from
the operations of bodily organs or physiological processes. In this,
dualism and materialism are indeed polar opposites. But a proponent
of materialism such as Hobbes is equally unsympathetic to the Aristotelian conception of the soul as animating principle of the body. On
this issue, it makes little difference whether one follows Cartesian
dualism or any of the many variants of materialism in modernity.
Hobbes writes,

> For seeing life is but a motion of limbs, the beginning whereof is in
> some principal part within, why may we not say that all automata (en-
> gines that move themselves by springs and wheels as does a watch)
> have an artificial life? For what is the heart, but a spring, and the
> nerves, but so many strings; and the joints, but so many wheels, giving
> motion to the whole body, such as was intended by the artificer?[8]

Human beings are merely complicated machines. Reason is simply a
complicated device of calculation; as he puts it, the activity of reason
is coextensive with the operations of addition, subtraction, multiplication, and division (*Leviathan,* chapter 5). For Hobbes, the consequences of banishing the soul as animating, organizing, and directing
principle of the body are immediate and striking. Freedom and coercion are indistinguishable, and reason is but a slave of the passions
(*Leviathan,* chapter 6). There is no ultimate end or natural goal to
human life and thus no shared common good in light of which ethical
reflection and political life might be conducted. We are isolated individuals, threatened at every moment by the potential attacks of every
other individual. Our only end is the "restless desire for power after
power." But even this desire fails to provide security, and we are
haunted by the fear of violent death. Because reason can discern no
goods or ends shared in common by all human beings, Hobbes turns
our attention away from properly human goods to the subrational, to

---

[8] *Leviathan,* introduction, 3.

the subhuman, to animal necessity, to the fear of violent death. The only way out of the natural state of war is by the establishment of a commonwealth, to whose leader we cede our natural right to do whatever we deem necessary to enhancing our prospects of survival. Much of modern philosophy involves an attempt to circumvent the seemingly endless debates over which goods are properly human and how a regime should be constituted so as to embody these goods. Even John Locke, who is often regarded as having a much milder account of the state of nature, grounds human government in the animal necessity of hunger, allied to the human capacity of labor.

In response to Hobbes's determinism and materialism, to his degrading depiction of the human condition, thinkers from Rousseau through Kant and up to the existentialists have sought to defend the dignity and freedom of human beings. Rousseau, the earliest and most powerful critic of Hobbes, counters that Hobbes simply imposes on the state of nature all the vices that accrue to human beings only after they have entered civilization. To arrive at the state of nature is to reach the childhood of humanity, a condition of humanity prior to the invention of language, reason, and imagination. By stripping away the adult capacities, whose invention accompanies the complexities of civilization, we can see that prior to civilization human beings would have had neither the motives nor the forethought to be combative in the way that Hobbes depicts them. "The same cause that prevents savages from using their reason . . . prevents them from abusing their faculties." [9] In this period before human beings develop self-consciousness, they lack the "egocentrism" of later humans. Their lack of reason and their limited conception of the future make it impossible for them to be burdened by a multitude of passions. Thus, the concern for self-preservation is hardly "prejudicial" to that of others. Rousseau compares us with our first parents in this way: "So much more profitable to these [primitive humans] is the ignorance of vice than the knowledge of virtue is to those [civilized humans]." [10] He provides us with a much more harmonious and pleasant picture of our first parents, but saddles us with other problems. Most of the capacities that we celebrate as properly human— such as reason, language, and will—are, for Rousseau, precisely the

---

[9] *Discourse on the Origin of Inequality*, pt. 1, 869.
[10] *Discourse on the Origin of Inequality*, pt. 1, 869.

instruments of our corruption and wickedness, of our alienation from nature, ourselves, and one another. In that sense, the comparison of the state of nature to the childhood of humanity is not apt. The transition from our original state to our present one is not the result of a natural development, the actualization of proper potencies present within our original state; instead, it is the result of a violent, revolutionary rupture. Indeed, we are so far removed from the state of nature that to call both precivilized beings and civilized beings by the name *human* is highly questionable. It is almost as if one species has replaced another.

From this all too brief survey of modern thought, we can see that the questions of human nature, human knowledge, and human freedom are intimately connected. Indeed, in philosophers such as Hobbes, Locke, and Rousseau, one finds a close correlation between their views about what human beings are and their views about ethics and politics. A similar correlation can be found in Aristotle and Aquinas. Indeed, we recover a severely truncated version of Aquinas's conception of human nature if we stop with questions of knowledge and freedom. For Aquinas, the study of human nature is the pivotal study; it provides crucial self-knowledge and urges us consciously to appropriate and actualize ends befitting our nature. It thus marks the transition from natural philosophy to ethics and politics. In fact, the discussion of human nature is, for Aquinas, finally inscribed within the investigation of the good life for human beings.

In recent years, there has been a remarkable resurgence of interest in classical conceptions of what it means for human beings to lead a good life. Although the primary focus of the return to classical thought has been Aristotle's account of virtue, the ethics of Aquinas has also received much attention. Our understanding of the integrity of Aquinas's thought has clearly benefited from the recovery of the ethics of virtue. Prior to that recovery, nearly all the work on Aquinas's ethics was on natural law. The teaching on law is an admittedly important component of his ethics, but it constitutes only a relatively small portion of his teaching about the good life. Thomas devotes most of his attention not to law, but to the virtues.[11] The recovery of

---

[11] Recent attempts to shift the balance from law to virtue can be found in Danial Mark Nelson's *The Priority of Prudence* and in Daniel Westberg's *Right Practical Reason*. Although these authors rightly emphasize the primacy of the virtues, they tend to underestimate the importance of precepts for Aquinas's ethics. Westberg is

the link between law and virtue is an important beginning, but both law and virtue need to be understood contextually, first, in light of a politics of the common good and, second, in light of the overarching theological structure of Aquinas's ethics. As Romanus Cessario, O.P., puts it, "In the final analysis, Aquinas understands the practice of virtue as nothing less than the full realization of evangelical glory in this life."[12] The complete recovery of Aquinas's ethical teaching must, then, reckon with his theologically informed account of the virtues, with the way nature is restored and elevated by supernatural grace.

Understood from either a natural or a supernatural perspective, the good life according to Aquinas involves the exercise not just of the moral virtues, but also of the intellectual virtues. Following Aristotle, Thomas divides the intellectual virtues into the practical, which have either doing (prudence) or making (art) as an end, and the theoretical or speculative, which are ordered to knowing for its own sake (understanding, knowledge, and wisdom). One of the intellectual virtues—namely, prudence—has received much recent attention. With few exceptions, however, contemporary discussions of Aquinas ignore the complex and nuanced relationships among and comparisons between the different sorts of intellectual virtue. Even more striking is the general neglect of the speculative, intellectual virtues and the role of contemplation in the good life.[13] Because Aquinas insists in a number of places that contemplation is superior to action and that the ultimate end of human life consists in the supernatural vision of God, the neglect is somewhat surprising. In fact, a number of difficulties attend our recovery of Thomas's account of the good life in terms

---

more carfeul on this score than is Nelson. For an exposition of Aquinas that unites precepts and prudence, see Ralph McInerny's *Ethica Thomistica* and Pamela Hall's *Narrative and the Natural Law: An Interpretation of Thomistic Ethics.* Long before the revivial of virtue ethics, Josef Pieper wrote his magnificent essays on the four cardinal virtues, published together as *The Cardinal Virtues.*

[12] *The Moral Virtues and Theological Ethics,* 6. Thomas O'Meara, O.P., argues for the primacy of a "graced anthropology" as the basis of Aquinas's reflections on the virtues. See his "Virtues in the Theology of Thomas Aquinas." By far the best account of the theological structure of Thomas's ethics can be had in Servais Pinckaers, *The Sources of Christian Ethics.* Also see the fine work by Stanley Hauerwas, *Character and the Christian Life: A Study in Theological Ethics,* and more recently Charles Pinches's *Christians among the Virtues.* Also of interest is Jean Porter's *The Recovery of Virtue: The Relevance of Aquinas for Christian Ethics.*

[13] The most noteworthy exceptions are Josef Pieper, to whose writings I refer later, and Servais Pinckaers, O.P., whose *Sources of Christian Ethics* is a magnificent corrective to the tendencies I am lamenting in this introduction.

of the practice of the virtues, intellectual and moral, acquired and infused.

The very complexity of Aquinas's teaching is perhaps the chief impediment to our recovery of it. He presupposes familiarity with the writings of his predecessors and uses in a highly supple way the various vocabularies at his disposal. The structure of his writing is dialectical in that each article in the *Summa* begins with a list of objections, which are inherited opinions about the matter at hand, and ends with a resolution of the objections. Although Thomas typically formulates an initial response to a question, a response adequate to that stage in the inquiry, he also refines and enriches his position at later stages in the inquiry. In the *Summa*, for example, he offers first a general consideration of the virtues and then later gives a more detailed treatment. Similarly, the opening consideration of law precedes a more specific examination of particular precepts and cases. The entire moral teaching commences with an argument for contemplation of God as the ultimate end of human life. The thesis receives clarification and determination in the later analyses of the intellectual virtues, the gifts, and in the culminating analysis of the relationship between the contemplative and the active lives. Thomas's text places unusual burdens on its reader.[14]

In addition to a lack of practice in reading certain kinds of texts, we face other impediments in our attempt to recover Aquinas's teaching on the good life. Even if we have begun to retrieve an appreciation for his fundamental question—the question about the best life for human beings—we have yet to revive his way of framing the question,[15] for he puts the question in terms of two rival candidates for the good life: contemplation and action. And we have inherited a number of modern teachings on human nature, on ethics and politics, on the nature of knowledge and philosophy, and on the nature of Christianity that stand between us and the successful articulation of Aquinas's question. What are these impediments?

The dominant philosophy of our times is a kind of crude pragmatic or utilitarian view of the good life as the maximization of wealth and

---

[14] Of course, the text provides its own correctives, and a successful reading of Aquinas will in part vindicate itself by its ability to show precisely where alternative interpretations have failed to appropriate fully Aquinas's pedagogy.

[15] For an introduction to the connection between philosophy and the good life in pagan and Christian authors, see Pierre Hadot, *Philosophy as a Way of Life*.

pleasure. Josef Pieper identifies the tyrannical modern tendency toward a world of "total work" as the chief opponent to the classical conception of leisure.[16] Even our so-called leisure time is often consumed with the restless accumulation of material goods and the uneasy cultivation of petty pleasures that fail to satisfy. In such a context, serious inquiry into the nature of the good life for human beings is apt to bring a derisive response. Behind these popular notions lie complex political and economic movements. The dominant modern views of politics and economics substitute a notion of subjective preferences for the ancient notion of excellences proper to human beings.[17]

Much of twentieth-century philosophy constitutes an attempt to circumvent the deleterious consequences of certain modern political and economic practices. The return to an ethics of the virtues must be understood in this framework. Influential representatives of the two dominant traditions in twentieth-century philosophy—continental and analytic—worry that an instrumental conception of rationality and of human action will result in human life being thoroughly subordinated to modern technology and its project of mastering nature. By contrast, Aristotle's ethical thought, at least that part of it that sees prudence as the centerpiece of the good life, points to an embrace of the particularity, contingency, and fragility of the human condition and to the virtues of "openness, receptivity, and wonder."[18] In spite of the enthusiasm with which some now turn to Aristotle in the hope of reviving one part or another of the classical conception of the good life, there is something odd and distorted about the Aristotle that has been revived. The contemporary focus severs what Aristotle ineluctably combines. Much is said about prudence, but little about the foundational analysis of human nature. Aristotle's consideration of the moral virtues culminates in a discussion of justice that links, as do many other passages in the *Ethics*, ethical to political matters. Yet

---

[16] *Leisure: The Basis of Culture*, 73.

[17] The construal of happiness in terms of subjective satisfaction is dominant in contemporary discussions. For a corrective to these modern misconstruals, see Pinckaers, *The Sources of Christian Ethics*, 230–33.

[18] Martha Nussbaum, *The Fragility of Goodness*, 20. For other contemporary discussions of Aristotle, see Hannah Arendt, *The Human Condition*, 206–7; Hans-Georg Gadamer, *Truth and Method*, 312–24 and throughout; Alasdair MacIntyre, *After Virtue*, 2d ed.; Charles Taylor, *Sources of the Self: The Making of the Modern Identity*, 3–107 and 143–76.

Aristotle is typically read as if ethics were autonomous from politics. He treats ethical philosophy not only as a part of politics, but also as one stage in a comprehensive philosophical education. But relevant teachings from the *Physics, De Anima,* and *Metaphysics* are rarely mentioned in contemporary discussions. As I have already noted, the most glaring omission concerns the contemplative life and its relationship to the active life.[19]

We have, then, a fragmented recovery and a divided estimation of Aristotle's philosophy, a division that mirrors to some extent Aristotle's own distinction between theoretical and practical reason. It is precisely this separation of practical from theoretical reason that attracts many contemporary thinkers to Aristotle. What features of Aristotelian practical reasoning are prominent in contemporary discussions? First, in place of abstract theory and general rules of conduct, Aristotle's practical philosophy underscores the singularity and contingency of the circumstances in which human acts are realized. Ethical reasoning has to do with the perception of concrete features of sense experience, features that cannot be captured in general rules or decision procedures of the sort put forth by Kant and Mill, the two most influential moral philosophers of the eighteenth and nineteenth centuries. Second, ethical deliberation and action, according to Aristotle, must be informed by rightly ordered inclination. On this view, we cannot isolate what we see and what we do from who we are. Put slightly differently, ethical knowledge is not like technical knowledge. It cannot be put at the service of whatever project we happen to have adopted; nor, once we have it, is our use of it optional. Because it informs our character, ethical knowledge circumscribes and directs our actions and, indeed, our very manner of perceiving and appraising the world. It cannot be instrumentalized in the way technical knowledge can. Third, both the formation and the exercise of practical virtue are situated within a social context, wherein we pursue excellence in concert with others. Given the situated nature of practical reasoning, it is not possible to gain a kind of autonomous control over all the contingent circumstances in which we find ourselves.

---

[19] Exceptions include Richard Kraut's *Aristotle on the Human Good,* which provides a thoroughly intellectualist reading of Aristotle's *Ethics,* and Aristide Tessitore's *Reading Aristotle's* Ethics: *Virtue, Rhetoric, and Political Philosophy.*

Considering the disparity between theoretical knowledge and productive knowledge, how are we to understand the former? Here again we face a number of impediments to the recovery of contemplation, impediments that can be traced to the works of Descartes, who radically altered the ancient conception of philosophy. A number of contrasts are striking. Instead of beginning, as do the ancients, from received opinions and working through them to get at the truth about a certain matter, Descartes initiates a radical break from received opinion and from tradition. Instead of sorting through the multiple senses of words and attempting to discern an order in them, he insists on a univocal conception of language, whose standard is the pristine clarity of mathematical discourse. Instead of a multiplicity of methods, in accord with the variegated ways in which things are and are understood, there will be one method; indeed, what things are, understood in terms of the different natural forms they exhibit, is subordinate to their susceptibility to "order and measure."[20] Instead of a vertical ascent from sensible things, the first things we encounter toward an understanding of the highest causes of sensible things— toward, that is, things that are first in the order of being—there is an endless horizontal project of mapping nature in mathematical terms. Finally, instead of the goal of wisdom as the good at which inquiry aims and that can be only partially realized by human beings and hence never can become a human possession, there is the anxious quest for a certitude that excludes all doubt. In his discussion of the difference between the modern view of the origin of philosophy in doubt and the ancient conception of its starting in wonder, Pieper writes,

> Does the true sense of wonder really lie in uprooting the mind and plunging it in doubt? Doesn't it really lie in making it possible and indeed necessary to strike yet deeper roots? The sense of wonder certainly deprives the mind of those penultimate certainties that we had up till then taken for granted—and to that extent wonder is a form of disillusionment, though even that has its positive aspect. . . . wonder signifies that the world is profounder, more all-embracing and mysterious than the logic of everyday reason had taught us to believe. The

[20] On Decartes's system and its foundation in a view of knowledge as constructive, of language as univocal, and of method as homogeneous, see Amos Funkenstein, *Theology and the Scientific Imagination*, 72–80, 179–92.

innermost meaning of wonder is fulfilled in a deepened sense of mystery.[21]

The passage captures nicely the premodern view of the roots of contemplation in wonder and suggests a number of ways in which the contemporary critique of speculative philosophy is off the mark. First, the contemplative aspiration is not one of mastery and control but of receptivity, which is not, however, to be identified with passivity. Second, instead of an exhaustive knowledge of its objects, the philosophic aspiration for knowledge is inherently limited and incomplete. Third, the result of the mind's awakening in wonder is not certitude but a heightened sense of mystery. Fourth, whereas many of the modern fields of knowledge tend toward specialization and fragmentation, philosophy aspires to know the whole, an aspiration that is less subject to any sort of control through techniques and methods. Finally, although philosophy puts in question the "penultimate certainties . . . of everyday reason," it is nonetheless oriented to an understanding of the shared human world and hence cannot be rooted in an individualistic conception of the mind. In fact, the pursuit of knowledge about our common world is a prime example of what the ancients meant by a common good, a good that is not diminished, but is instead increased by being shared.

Even if it marks an abrupt and unsettling break from the everyday, unreflective approach to the world, contemplation is to a large extent continuous with our prescientific experience of the world. For the ancients, contemplation requires neither the substitution of technical, mathematical language for prephilosophic speech nor the suppression of the question of the good at which inquiry aims. The teacher resists the temptation to develop a universal method that would obscure the distinctions among things inherent in our prescientific understanding of the world. Aristotle has an analogical view of human discourse, an account of the sciences as irreducibly plural, and a view of inquiry as anchored in the shared prescientific understanding of student and teacher. In his account of the hierarchy of the sciences, he distinguishes the different modes of defining and

---

[21] *Leisure*, 134–35. Against the view that philosophic wonder is a transitional state for the philosopher, Pieper writes, "Wonder is not just the starting point of philosophy in the sense of *initium*, of a prelude or preface. Wonder is the *principium*, the lasting source, . . . the immanent origin of philosophy" (135).

ways of proceeding appropriate to physics, mathematics, and metaphysics. By separating mathematics from physics and by subordinating the former to metaphysics, he repudiates the project of reducing nature to mathematical formulae. Although mathematics may be applied to natural phenomena, as was the case in the astronomy of Aristotle's time, the study of mathematics does not provide a more adequate account of the being of things, nor does it provide access to the study of the highest things.

I have mentioned, admittedly in summary fashion, a number of impediments to the recovery of the good life, as Aristotle and Aquinas understood it; some of these impediments obstruct our recovery of the theoretical component of the good life, and others are obstacles to our appreciation of the practical component. Another kind of impediment concerns the relationship between the two. Precisely because contemporary thinkers pay scant attention to the speculative, intellectual virtues, they have little to say about how these virtues might be incorporated into the good life. Indeed, this neglect tends to leave the speculative operation of the intellect to its own devices and thus invites an amoral conception of intellectual activity. Of course, some contemporaries see this amoralism as a reason for repudiating the very notion of speculative virtue. There is, however, something remarkably unreflective in this move, for most of those who advocate praxis and prudence over contemplation spend their time thinking, debating, and writing about the practical order. They are thus very often engaged in a theoretical examination of the practical order, but they have little to say about that very activity. What do Aristotle and Aquinas have to say about it and how it fits into their comprehensive teaching on the good life?

Let us begin with Aristotle. Although the philosophical and political are distinct ways of life, the consideration of one is incomplete without that of the other. The study of political things, of the aspirations indigenous to political life, leads to the recognition of ends that transcend the proper scope of politics. Political science raises questions—concerning the best regime, for example—that can be answered only by recourse to some of the teachings of speculative philosophy. Aristotle repeatedly urges the legislator to study the soul. The immediate consequence of that study is that laws should be instituted to succor salutary customs and to educate the passions. But there is another lesson. The perfection of the soul is not completed by harmonizing passion and reason, by habituation in the moral virtues. The intellectual virtues are necessary to perfect reason itself. There are human capacities higher and more comprehensive than those of the moral virtues. The best regime is one that would make room for philosophy, both because philosophy is a perfection proper to human nature and because politics in its full sense needs the guidance of philosophy. Even the most decidedly practical of philosophies will encounter questions that require it to develop a more comprehensive account or theory, one that moves beyond present particularities and that locates goods in relationship to one another, typically in some sort of hierarchy. In Aristotle's *Ethics* and *Politics,* the articulation of the human good, in light of which we deliberate about particular ends, is precisely such a theory. This is not to say that we can deduce particular conclusions from a theory, but rather that the theory provides the framework or horizon within which we deliberate and by reference to which we offer reflective criticisms of existing customs. We should not, however, conceive of the direction of influence as running solely from theory to practice, for encounter with and reflection on particulars will often help us to specify the more theoretical elements of our account and sometimes force us to alter those elements. The intellectual virtues play an important and peculiar role in this process, both in the articulation of theory and in mediating between it and existing regimes and customs.

Political philosophy does not, then, simply transform customs in light of some abstract ideal. Philosophers need prudence and an education in properly political things. They need this education not just to safeguard their precious activities from the irrational incursions of the political order, but also so that they may understand themselves and their activities, both speculative and practical, within the whole of human life.

There is a complicated relationship between philosophy and politics, contemplation and prudence. Although the life of contemplation is superior to that of moral virtue, the activity of contemplation cannot, strictly speaking, constitute a life in its entirety. One can be said to lead a contemplative life *(contemplativa vita)* in the sense that the most important activity in one's life concerns knowing, yet even those most blessed by nature can engage in contemplation only intermittently. Although Aristotle sometimes speaks as if prudence orders all of life's activities to the end of contemplation, we cannot discern in the theoretical teaching concerning the superiority of contemplation any guidelines for organizing the whole of human life. The point here is that the teaching on the superiority of theoretical pursuits is itself a theoretical teaching, not a conclusion of practical reason upon which one might act. Prudence must determine the part contemplation is to play in the whole of one's life and in the civil community. In this way, prudence is the comprehensive authority regarding practice, even the practice of the intellectual virtues.

What we have considered thus far are the salient impediments to the recovery of the Aristotelian and Thomistic account of the good life, an account that treats contemplation as an ineliminable component of that life.[22] The previous misunderstandings are impediments to a recovery of the philosophical portion of Aquinas's view. We now need to add a consideration of the impediments to the recovery of the distinctively theological features of Aquinas's depiction of the good life. Because Aquinas comments on nearly all of the relevant passages in Aristotle's texts and gives more attention than perhaps any other commentator to the unity and interconnections among various inquiries, his writings have much to contribute to the investigation of the reception of Aristotle's teachings in Christianity. Yet the chief obstacle has to do not with his interpretation of Aristotle but with the recovery of any theologically informed view of the good life. Certain tendencies in modern political theory and practice, which can be traced to John Locke, place inordinate and peculiar burdens of rational justification on believers and construe religious belief in essentially private terms as expressions of individual preference.[23] In such a context, Aquinas's project is apt to seem odd; not only does he treat religious belief as inviting theoretical reflection, but he also appropriates philosophy in a positive way and engages it critically. He never adopts a defensive, apologetic posture toward "reason."

Indeed, Thomas's positive appropriation of Aristotle evinces the view that religious faith is ordered to wisdom, a wisdom that encompasses, corrects, and completes the philosophic aspiration. Some would say that Thomas reads Aristotle not for Aristotle's own sake but in order to cull from his texts what might support the Christian

---

[22] Some of these issues in Aristotle have received careful attention. See Joseph Dunne, *Back to the Rough Ground.*

[23] See N. Wolterstorff, *John Locke and the Ethics of Belief.*

faith.[24] Aquinas's dual (some would say contradictory) role as Christian teacher and exegete of Aristotle is an impediment to our recovery of his view of the good life. Such a sweeping and negative generalization, whose verification would require detailed examination of the commentaries, runs counter to the explicit claims of Thomas, who often speaks of positions as true according to reasoned argument and according to the words of Aristotle. In the debates over the status of the commentaries, two strongly opposed views have dominated the literature. The first is that we are to take the commentaries both as expositions of Aristotle's teaching and as statements of what Thomas affirms to be philosophic truth. The second is that the commentaries are only expository. The latter view usually goes on to argue that on crucial issues Aquinas departs from Aristotle. My own view is that although Aquinas's views do not always coincide with those of Aristotle, it does not follow that there need be a necessary opposition between the two or that we should not take seriously his pervasive practice of showing that his own position can be traced to that of Aristotle. In reading Aristotle, Thomas is careful to read passages in relationship to their context and to locate individual doctrines as parts of specific sciences or arts with their peculiar modes of defining and proceeding. Where he confronts—either in Aristotle's texts or in the writings of his commentators—real or apparent conflicts and unresolved problems, he deploys Aristotle's own method of dialectical engagement. When he goes beyond Aristotle, he strives to show that passages over which commentators have disputed find their most complete explication in his own teaching.[25] Thomas's relationship to Aristotle, then, need not be seen as one of either fundamentalist fidelity or unprincipled transformation.

Theology does not simply supplement philosophy; rather, it engages it dialectically. Two features of Thomas's teaching—on contemplation and moral principles—provide useful avenues of entry into the dialectical character of his moral theology. The philosophic

---

[24] The most sustained attack on Aquinas along these lines is Harry Jaffa, *Aristotelianism and Thomism: A Study of the Commentary by Thomas Aquinas on* Nichomachean Ethics.

[25] For a summary of the literature in this debate and an argument for describing Thomas's relationship to Aristotle in terms of dialectical engagement, see John Jenkins, "Expositions of the Text: Aquinas's Aristotelian Commentaries." For my own understanding of the role of dialectic in Aquinas, see the first chapter of my *Dialectic and Narrative in Aquinas: An Interpretation of the* Summa contra Gentiles.

life of contemplation, which perfects what is best in human nature, culminates in a knowledge of God. Philosophic knowledge of the divine is inherently limited; we can know a great deal about what God is not, but our positive knowledge is oblique and imperfect, derived from reflection on the perfections present in God's effects. Although the philosophic contemplation of God partially meets the criteria for human happiness articulated in *Ethics* I, neither contemplation nor action completely satisfies the human longing for happiness. Aristotle himself acknowledges the gap between the aspiration for and the achievement of happiness. That none of the activities known to Aristotle fully meets his own criteria for the end of human life provides Thomas with an opening for a dialectical encounter between philosophy and theology. The vision of God, promised in Scripture, does meet Aristotle's criteria.

Thomas finds another opening for dialectical engagement in our experience of moral failure. The Ten Commandments overlap with the precepts of the natural law, the latter of which articulate goods congruent to human nature. There is an apparent redundancy in the dual revelation of the moral law, through nature and through Scripture. The scriptural revelation of the law is necessary because sin obscures our apprehension of the natural law. The convergence of the two laws evinces the reasonableness of a large portion of the moral teaching of the Jews. The ubiquitous experience of moral failure, of ignorance both of the good and of one's ignorance, constitutes a "probable sign" of original sin. Yet the latter doctrine cannot be known apart from divine revelation. Christian moral pedagogy locates human self-understanding within a comprehensive historical narrative, to which philosophy has no access. In that narrative, submission to divine law is not an end in itself; it prepares one for the coming of Christ. The education afforded by the law is dialectical in two senses: first, it restores our understanding of that which we, apart from sin, are able to grasp by reason, and, second, it points beyond itself to the need for a redeemer. The following of Christ consists primarily in the practice of the theological virtues of faith, hope, and charity. Even the divine law is ordered to the life of virtue, a life restored to us by the infused virtues of faith, hope, and charity.

The central teaching of Thomas's moral theology is that charity is the form of the virtues. Only charity secures our relationship to the ultimate end, which is contemplative union with God. So, although he affirms the contemplative character of the ultimate end, he appears to subordinate contemplation to action in this life. But this interpretation is simplistic, for Thomas's understanding of the relationship between action and contemplation transcends the Aristotelian opposition of them. Two contrasts between the intellectual virtue of wisdom and the gift of wisdom illustrate the difference. First, although the intellectual virtues can be possessed without the moral virtues, the gift of wisdom is inseparable from rightly ordered desire. Like the intellectual virtue of wisdom, the gift of wisdom is intellectual; it is a capacity of judgment and order. Yet it is also a result of love, rooted in charity, and is inseparable from an intimate experience of the divine; *sapientia* (wisdom) is etymologically related to *sapor* (taste). Second, the scope of wisdom is not limited to the speculative order; it judges all things, speculative and practical. It enables one to order all things in relation to God and appraises contingent, practical activities in light of "divine rules." Its mode of judgment, however, is not according to abstract principles and causes. Rather, it judges from connaturality, from an affinity to divine things, and is thus akin to the judgment of prudence.

The gift of wisdom arises from and overflows into love. In Christian contemplation more than in the exercise of the intellectual virtues, we become what we behold. The depiction of Christian wisdom accentuates Aristotle's description of wisdom as a gift, in which the soul is receptive. Because the gift of wisdom is rooted in charity, there is no possibility of separating what we know from who we are, a distinction that many see at the root of modern technological and instrumentalist conceptions of reason. Charity is not to be confused with Kantian-sounding imperatives of regarding others equally, impartially, or altruistically. Instead of violating the natural order of associations, charity orders all loves in relation to the ultimate end. It is inherently prudential.

Thomas describes our participation in divine wisdom and beauty not in terms of law, but in terms of the theological virtues of faith, hope, and charity. These virtues deserve more the name of virtue than do the natural virtues, for they have greater efficacy in attaining the end. They are also strikingly unlike the natural virtues. Charity both presupposes faith, which is rooted in the intellect, and issues in contemplative union with God. In both the origin and summit of the Christian moral life, we are receptive, although far from passive, before the transforming knowledge of Christ. Furthermore, friendship, which was an ancillary virtue in the moral life, becomes central to the Christian understanding of the good life. Individualism is thus not part of the Christian understanding of the human condition, nor is the aspiration to render ourselves utterly immune to contingencies outside of our control. Nothing could be further from the life of charity wherein, through the gifts of faith and hope, one participates with others in the redemptive suffering of Christ.

The link between the gift of wisdom and the infused virtue of charity undercuts many of the objections, already mentioned, to the philosophical understanding of the contemplative and the active lives. Thomas defends the superiority of the mixed life, wherein contemplation reaches fruition in a life of teaching and preaching, over the life devoted solely to contemplation. To see that this defense is more than an ad hoc adjustment of the Aristotelian schema, we need to consider Thomas's teaching on the nature of God and God's relationship to the world. Indeed, the metaphysical context, too often neglected in contemporary ethics, is crucial for a full appreciation of Thomas's ethics.

In pagan philosophy, there is a tendency to depict the divine life as an extension, amplification, and perfection of the life pursued by the philosopher. Thomas objects to this projection of the life of human excellence onto God. In fact, he does not engage in what some contemporary philosophers call "perfect-being" theology.[26] The very term *perfection,* derived from *per facere,* means "thoroughly made" and thus does not, strictly speaking, apply to God, who undergoes no indigent process to achieve excellence. The attempt to use human language about God not only is inherently limited, but also must deploy a jarring juxtaposition of terms. At the foundation of Thomas's theology is a description of God as subsistent being *(ipsum esse subsistens).* The description combines diametrically opposed modes of signifying: the concrete participle *subsistens* with the abstract infinitive *esse.* Although we typically use a concrete mode of signifying to speak of existing things, we use the abstract mode to refer to perfections. God resists conceptual articulation; God is not

---

[26] See, for example, Normann Kretzmann's *The Metaphysics of Theism: Aquinas' Natural Theology in* Summa contra Gentiles 1. Also see my essay, "Kretzmann's Theism vs. Aquinas's Theism: Interpreting *Summa contra Gentiles* I."

one being among many, not even the first and highest in a series. Nor is God to be confused with abstract ideas or perfections. The impossibility of conceiving of God as *a* being or as an idea points up the need to use both abstract and concrete modes of signifying. In God, the perfections that we signify in multiple and abstract ways are indistinguishable from God's concretely existing being.

God's relationship to the world is like that of an artist to an artifact. The comparison seems to confirm Christianity's anticipation of a technological ontology. But Thomas underscores the disanalogies between divine creation and physical or artistic production. On the side of God, there is no distinction between who God is and the model according to which God makes, a distinction that is essential to the instrumentalist view of fabrication. The divine essence is the pattern of created things. On the side of things made, God creates from nothing. God does not introduce forms into preexisting matter. Creation is instantaneous and hence cannot be properly conceived as a coming forth or a production. As the prominence of the language of the beautiful in the discussions of creation suggests, it is rather a manifestation of divine beauty and wisdom.

Another peculiar feature of Thomas's teaching on God's relationship to the world concerns God's knowledge of and providence over contingent and lowly singulars. Aristotle's Arabic commentators hold that to attribute such knowledge to God is unseemly. As we will see, Aquinas's rejoinder is that such a conception of God's relationship to the world presupposes an anthropomorphic view of God. Ortega y Gasset called the classical God a "philosopher admiring himself in the mirror." The perfection of human knowledge does indeed consist in moving from the singular to the universal, from the sensible to the intelligible, from the lowly to the exalted. Because we cannot know many things simultaneously, our attention to lowly things distracts from the contemplation of higher. But our mode of knowing is a result of the poverty of our intellectual power. God does not know by abstraction, nor does God know one thing at a time, but instead knows all things, low and high alike, without effort, at the same time, and in the same way. Christians thus teach that lowly singulars are not unseemly objects of divine knowledge and care. Thomas associates providence, both etymologically and substantively, with prudence, with the knowledge and temporal ordering of lowly singulars. Thus is resolved the difficulty in Plato and Aristotle concerning why the philosopher, once possessed of the vision of the highest things, should return to the shared human world of sensible objects. The descent from the contemplation of Beauty and Truth need not be an onerous task.

The Christian notion of transcendence, finally, is not so simplistic as it has seemed to some. The mixed life, advocated by Thomas, reflects the relationship between God and the world, and is an imitation of the life of Christ, who possessed the fullness of contemplative wisdom and voluntarily chose to communicate his surplus with lowly creatures. The ascent to the highest things now includes a descent to creatures. The final act in the drama of creation involves not the elimination of the world, but its transfiguration and elevation into a "new heaven and a new earth." The God, with whom we are to be united at the end of time, is not the self-thinking thought of Aristotle's God. Through revelation, Thomas understands God's thinking as a speaking that generates a word (*verbum*); from these two principles, the knower or speaker and the known or spoken, there arises a relationship of love. These relations in God are personal relations, and the divine life is a communal one of knowing, speaking, and loving. The doctrine of the Trinity supplies the strongest response to the objections, mentioned at the outset, to the premodern understanding of contemplation.

The distinctively Christian understanding of contemplation and action complicates the relationships among the theoretical, the practical, and the artistic. The model for our understanding of God's knowledge of the world is that of practical knowledge, especially the sort of knowledge had in the activity of making. God knows things in creating them. But from what we have just seen, the model of technical knowledge is seriously deficient as a model of divine creation. Indeed, because God at once makes and has providence over individual, created things, God's knowledge is as much akin to that of prudence as it is to that of a craft. The believer, whose loving encounter with God in contemplation overflows into acts of charity, imitates the relationship of God to creatures. As a result of grace, we thus participate in divine creativity. Thomas is careful to rule out the possibility of any creature creating autonomously. Strictly speaking, no creature creates at all, for we always presuppose something in our making. Yet Thomas speaks of the stages of salvation history as creation, fall, and re-creation. Although we could not have had anything to do with our initial creation, we can cooperate with God in our re-creation and in the providential re-creation of the natural order.

These final remarks about the metaphysical foundations of Aquinas's ethics return us to the impediment I mentioned at the outset concerning the difficulty of reading Aquinas. To avoid misunderstanding his texts, we shall have to read parts in light of the whole and to be open to the possibility that there is no easily isolated ethical teaching. Not only must we understand natural law in relationship to acquired virtue and both of these in connection with revealed law and infused virtue, but we shall also have to see the ethical teaching in light of metaphysical, anthropological, even Christological teachings. I mentioned at the outset that recent years have witnessed a gradual recovery of the integrity and complexity of Aquinas's position. Still, the remarkable complexity of his thought makes it enormously difficult to recover any large portion of it in a particular study. The present inquiry intends nothing even close to a comprehensive treatment of sources or issues. Instead, it approaches Aquinas's ethical thought in terms of a single issue: the great debate of antiquity and the Middle Ages concerning the rivalry between the active and the contemplative lives, between prudence and wisdom as virtues perfective of human nature. In this way, I hope to put before the reader the breadth of Thomas's vision of the good life.

1

Returning to the Human Things

From the perspective of Aristotle and Aquinas, the most striking feature of modern thought is the flight from nature, the eclipse of the soul, described in the previous chapter. In the tradition of Aristotle and Aquinas, the study of the soul is the primary avenue into the study of human nature. That study encompasses all living things and moves from the common to the particular; thus, the study of the peculiarly human is ensconced within that of the natural world. Consider the following striking passage from Aristotle's *On the Parts of Animals:*

> Every realm of nature is marvelous; and as Heraclitus, when the strangers who came to visit him found him warming himself at the furnace in the kitchen and hesitated to go in, is reported to have bidden them not to be afraid to enter, as even in that kitchen divinities were present, so we should venture on the study of every kind of animal without distaste, for each and all will reveal to us something natural and something wonderful. . . . The end for which those works are put together and produced is a form of the beautiful. If any person thinks the examination of the rest of the animal kingdom an unworthy task, he must hold in like disesteem the study of man. (I.5;645a17–30)[1]

There is no hint here of setting human beings in opposition to the order of natural substances. The intelligibility of what is highest and most noble in embodied nature—namely, the human soul—is in many ways akin to that of lower beings.

The study of the soul is the crucial, pivotal inquiry of philosophy,

---

[1] All translations of Aristotle's works are from *The Complete Works of Aristotle,* rev. Oxford trans., vols. 1 and 2. In some places, I have inserted portions of the original Greek text and, where noted, have modified the translation.

providing us with self-knowledge and urging us to realize and perfect our nature in pursuit of the goods of knowledge and virtue. Aquinas subscribes to Aristotle's teaching on the appropriate order of philosophical pedagogy. The student is to begin with the propaedeutic disciplines of logic and mathematics, and then move through natural philosophy to ethics and politics, and on, finally, to metaphysics. Where does the study of human nature occur? It is the culminating inquiry of the philosophy of nature, which investigates substances composed of matter and form. Because soul is to body as form is to matter and form is defined in relation to its proper matter, soul must be understood in relationship to body. The study of the soul pertains to natural philosophy from its mode of defining (*In Aristotelis* De Anima, Bk. I, lectio 1). In living things, soul is the animating, organizing, and directing principle of a body. Aristotle's approach is sometimes called *hylomorphism,* from the Greek terms for form and matter. This approach differs markedly from the mind-body problem of modern and contemporary philosophy.

In an essay that deftly deploys Aquinas's commentary on Aristotle's *De Anima* to explicate Aristotle, Martha Nussbaum and Hilary Putnam describe Aristotle's distinctive approach to the study of natural substances:

> The mind-body problem . . . starts from a focus on the special nature of mental activity—therefore from just one part of the activity of some among living beings. . . . Aristotelian hylomorphism, by contrast, starts from a general interest in characterizing the relationship, in things of many kinds, between their organization or structure and their material composition. It deals with the beings and doings of all substances. . . . It asks two questions in particular. . . . How do and should we explain or describe the changes we see taking place in the world? . . . What is it about individuals that makes them the very things that they are?[2]

For Aquinas, as for Aristotle, the study of the soul embraces all living things and investigates their natures by attending to their habitual modes of operation. Far from setting human beings in opposition to nature, it depicts them as part of nature, as one species of animal among many.

The study of human nature, then, presupposes some knowledge of nature in general, of its principles and causes. In the second book of

---

[2] "Changing Aristotle's Mind," 28–29.

his *Physics,* Aristotle investigates the principles or causes of nature. Most of his predecessors identify nature as the "first constituent or underlying matter" out of which natural things come to be. A common project among the earliest philosophers was to identify an element—say, water or fire—out of which all things emerge. As crude as these accounts may seem, they have the advantage of beginning with the most obvious fact about natural substances: their materiality. But how then do we distinguish different kinds of material substance from one another, say, a "cow" from a "man"? Aristotle suggests that the distinction between the two involves something more than a difference in constituent material parts. He calls that something more "shape or form." Although he holds that natural substances are composites of matter and form, and hence that the physicist must include both under the purview of his inquiry, he argues for the priority of form over matter. In the composite, matter is more receptive than active, whereas form is determining and actualizing. To take an example from art, a lump of clay is potentially a bust of Lincoln. It becomes an actual bust only after the sculptor has imposed a shape on it—that is, when the lump receives a determinate form. Indeed, we distinguish, identify, and name things from their forms—that is, not from the mere presence of matter, but from the specific way the matter is configured and organized. Even the lump of clay, which is potentially the bust of Lincoln, is more than mere matter; it has a certain composition, texture, color, and so forth that enable us to distinguish it from bronze. Matter may indeed be that out of which things come to be, but the form supplies the reason why the material constituents develop in the way they do. The formal cause is thus intimately related to the final cause, the goal, end, or telos of the process of growth. We implicitly acknowledge the authoritative standards of these causes when we refer to a given instance of a species as immature or defective. Just as the bust of Lincoln without a nose is either incomplete or defective, so too is an apple tree that bears no fruit.

The formal cause is evident, then, both when an organism is developing and when it is fully formed. Mature instances of species exhibit themselves as organic wholes, not as heaps of unrelated parts. The parts themselves are understood in relationship to one another—that is, in the complementarity of their functions and in the way they serve the survival and flourishing of the whole. There is, moreover, a directedness to living things, which is increasingly palpable as we approach the level of the human. To these two causes, Aristotle adds the initiating or efficient cause and the final cause. His description of the four runs thus:

> In one way, then, that out of which a thing comes to be and persists, is called a cause, e.g. the bronze of the statue, the silver of the bowl. . . . In another way, the form or the archetype, i.e. the definition of the essence, and its genera, are called causes (e.g. of the octave the relation of 2:1 . . .). Again, the primary source of change or rest; e.g. the man who deliberated is a cause, the father is a cause of the child, and generally what makes of what is made and what changes of what is changed. Again, in the sense of end or that for the sake of which a thing is done, e.g. health is the cause of walking about. (*Physics,* II, 1: 194b25–35)

Now, certain objections (most of which can be traced to early modern philosophers such as Descartes, Hobbes, and Bacon, who sought to supplant Aristotle's physics) are commonly raised against the appeal to formal and final causes. We will consider three. The first objection focuses on final causality and alleges that the attribution of these causes to subhuman beings involves personifying nature, an unwarranted projection of properly human traits onto subhuman beings. Only human beings deliberate about ends and consciously seek to realize goals. To say that plants or snails act for the sake of ends is to ascribe conscious intention to them. The second objection begins from an assumption, shared by Aristotle, that the subject matter of physics concerns material things in motion. Where Aristotle and some moderns part is on the issue whether an investigation of formal and final causes is integral to our understanding of material substances. Critics object that formal and final causes play no verifiable role in experience. The appeal to formal and final causes postulates the existence of "occult qualities," hidden causes that can never be verified by empirical, scientific inquiry. The third worry, which may well be implicit in the first two, is that the search for these causes is naive, superfluous, and unscientific. To focus on formal and final causes is to remain at the level of crude, unreflective common sense and to distract us from serious scientific analysis and experimentation. Besides, even if there are such causes, knowledge of them seems to add nothing substantive to what we derive from the exclusively quantitative accounts provided by the modern sciences.

By way of response, I should note first that nothing in Aristotle's description of formal and final causes eliminates the possibility, or at least diminishes the importance, of seeking explanations in terms of material causes. Indeed, his view is that a form cannot be understood apart from its material subject. Aristotle does not want to replace naturalistic explanations but to enlarge our sense of what it means to give such an explanation. In this sense, the second objection, the occult quality objection, is wide of the mark. The form is precisely the organization of the matter—which does not mean that the essences of material substances are transparent to human intelligence. Getting at the essence is difficult, but there is no gulf between the matter of a substance and its form. As I have already noted, the form is not some separate substance, unrelated to matter, but rather the very configuration and organization of the matter, exhibited in the process of growth and in the habitual activities of species. We come to know the essence by attending ever more carefully to the organization and activities of the substance in question. The first objection, concerning an anthropomorphic projection onto nature, also contains a kernel of truth. Final causality, for example, is clearest to us in our own consciously directed operations. The composition of form and matter, moreover, is most evident in examples from art, where the artist introduces from the outside a form into the matter. Thus, in the second book of the *Physics,* when Aristotle introduces the four causes, he begins with examples drawn from art , which is in keeping with the pedagogical principle stated in the opening of the work that we must begin with what is most evident to us and work toward what is most evident in nature (*Physics,* I, 1). But the fact that acting for an end is most obvious in conscious, human activity in no way diminishes the presence of final causality in dogs or apple trees. They, too, exhibit a process of development toward an end, although they are unaware of it. Not even in human development, which is directed to an end, is there always an imputation of conscious choice or intention. It is not as if a child chooses to grow.

If, finally, this view is naive, then there may well be some virtue in naïveté. Philosophy should never rest with the obvious, but it ought not to discount it either. Aristotle's approach has the advantage of fostering some level of continuity between our prescientific, commonsense experience of nature and our scientific inquiry into the principles and causes of nature. This prescientific experience is an ineliminable background for every inquiry and experiment. Can a doctor perform major surgery on a patient without an implicit acknowledgment of the proper functioning of organs such as the heart and the lungs? It is a minor point, perhaps, but nonetheless true. On a larger scale, if science is to give an account of its origin and purpose, it will have to recur to the prescientific familiarity with nature, or else its explanation will be merely an unreflective and dogmatic description of what it does and produces, not an account of how we might come to understand and value its inquiry in the first place.

Of course, one of the primary modern motives for rejecting formal and final causes is Darwin's theory of evolution. Although Darwin finally banished these causes, he himself was deeply ambivalent about whether his theory of evolution could do without them. In their absence, it is difficult to use terms such as *development* or *higher* and *lower,* terms that imply progress in the direction of what's better and higher and hence seem to involve the notion of a telos or final cause.[3] Classical evolutionary theory wants to concentrate exclusively on antecedent material and efficient causes, whose interaction is the explanatory nexus for change within and between species. But this focus gives us no ground for saying that one species is higher than another, only that one species is more fit for this or that environment. With regard to Aristotle, we may speak of one species' being higher than another in terms of levels of soul; higher souls contain the powers and capacities of lower-order souls and integrate them in service of whatever the highest power of the species may be. So animals have both the vegetative powers of plants and the sensitive powers proper to them, and human beings have both of these powers and rational powers as well.

Aristotle devotes the *De Anima* to a common and comparative analysis of these grades of soul. As Aquinas notes in his commentary, the inquiry of the *De Anima* is pivotal in three respects (*In Aristotelis De Anima,* I, lectio 1). First, the study of what human nature is and of what its proper activities are serves as a prelude to the study of the human good in the disciplines of ethics and politics. According to Aristotle, to be a wise legislator one must study the soul. One of the key arguments in the first book of the *Ethics*—the argument that

---

[3] For an attempt to align Aristotle and Darwin, see Larry Arnhart's *Darwinian Natural Right: The Biological Ethics of Human Nature.*

establishes that human happiness consists in activity of soul in accord with reason—appeals to the exercise of reason as the function peculiar to the human species. Second, metaphysics, the discipline at the pinnacle of philosophy, answers to the natural, human desire to know, an orientation disclosed in the study of the soul. The intellect, which is potentially all things *(potens omnia)*, is perfected by knowing material substances and their causes. As we learn in the *De Anima* and as is reiterated in the opening of the *Metaphysics,* human beings are located at the pinnacle of the animal world, in the very middle of the cosmos. Our intellectual capacity elevates us above all other animals, but the poverty of our intellect renders us inferior to the separate substances and God. Wonder, an openness to the whole, is the mark of human intelligence. Third, in contrast to the particular sciences, which examine parts of being, metaphysics investigates being as being. Unlike physics, it is not limited to mutable beings, composed of matter and form, but ranges over all substances. The wider scope of metaphysics presupposes that nonmaterial things exist. If only composite, material substances existed, then physics would be the fundamental and most comprehensive science. But how are we to begin to speak about immaterial things? Aquinas holds that we can do so by analogy to our knowledge of the immaterial operations of our own intellects. Thus, without the knowledge, established in the *De Anima,* of the immateriality of the human intellect and of the nature of its operation, we would not even be able to begin thinking about the nature and activity of the separate substances and God. We would not be able to study metaphysics.

If the study of human nature is for Aquinas crucial to the study of philosophy, it is also central to theology. We are already familiar with the order appropriate to philosophical pedagogy, which begins from what is most evident to us and first in our experience (natural philosophy) and proceeds toward what is first in the order of nature or being (metaphysics). By beginning from God, theology reverses this order and takes as its point of departure what is first in being and last in our experience (*ST,* I, 2).[4] Theology then treats the coming forth of things from God in creation and culminates in the return of all things to God through Christ and the sacraments. By far the largest seg-

---

[4] All references to and quotations from the *Summa Theologiae* are from the 1948 Marietti edition. Translations from all Latin texts are my own.

ments of Aquinas's theological writings are devoted to the created order of nature, in which human nature occupies a crucial place. Before Renaissance poets called "man" a microcosm, Aquinas, echoing a series of venerable Neoplatonic authorities, referred to human beings as existing on the horizon of the spiritual and the material. He traces the complexity of human beings (in contrast to the simplicity of lower embodied creatures and of disembodied angels) to their being situated at the juncture of the material and the immaterial. Human beings contain the perfections of both orders (*ST,* I, 77, 2).

One of the advantages of beginning with Aristotle's account of nature and human nature is that we gain some familiarity with the Aristotelian vocabulary that pervades the theological works, where Aquinas rarely pauses to explain the original context in Aristotle's own texts. Another reason is that the theological order of proceeding can mislead readers unaccustomed to Aquinas's complex pedagogical style. Because theology begins with what is prior by nature although last in our experience, the treatise on human nature in the *Summa Theologiae* begins with the soul and then turns to its union with the body (*ST,* I, 75–76). A reader might hastily infer from this procedure that we could know the soul prior to and in isolation from the body or that we could have some sort of immediate, introspective access to the nature of the intellect. Aquinas denies this inference explicitly in the same treatise (*ST,* I, 87, 1–4), but if the differences between the philosophical and theological modes of proceeding go unnoticed, readers might come away thinking that Aquinas has more in common with Descartes than with Aristotle. Because human beings are middle creatures, they must be understood in relationship not only to what is beneath them but also to what is above them. Thus, Aquinas pairs an ascending, philosophical approach that culminates with the human species as the zenith of animal life and a descending, theological approach that moves from God and the angels to humans as the lowest of intellectual beings.

But the theological descent presupposes a philosophical ascent, which has important consequences for the study of the soul. Its nature will not be demonstrated from causes as in mathematics, but rather from effects as in physics. That is, we cannot begin from what the essence of the soul is and demonstrate its properties, as we do in proving the Pythagorean theorem from the nature of a right-angle triangle. Instead, we approach its essence indirectly by seeing how it is manifest in its operations. As Thomas writes, the study of the soul "pertains to natural philosophy . . . from its mode of defining" (*pertinet ad naturalem . . . ex modo definiendi; In Aristotelis* De Anima, I, lectio 2, note 17). Because soul is always understood as the form of body, definitions in the study of the soul include sensible matter. One of the chief flaws in previous accounts of the soul, according to Aristotle, is that they all unite it to the body without explaining the union. Soul is to body as form is to matter and as act is to potency. Although natural things cannot exist without matter, they are named and defined not merely from their material constituents but from the specific way in which the matter is informed and organized, a pattern evident in their process of growth and in the activities peculiar to them. "The form indeed is nature rather than the matter; for a thing is more properly said to be what it is when it exists in actuality than when it exists potentially. . . . We also speak of a thing's nature as being exhibited in the process of growth by which its nature is attained. . . . Into what then does it grow? Not into that from which it arose but into that to which it tends. The form then is nature" (*Physics*, II, 1, 193b7–193b19, translation adjusted slightly). We apprehend the formal cause in apprehending the end or the term of growth of an organism. Thus, the formal cause is the basis of and is revealed by the final cause or that for the sake of which the process of growth takes place. Given this understanding of the relationship between form and matter, the question of whether the soul and the body are one is as pointless as the query whether an actuality and that of which it is the act are one. "Unity," Aristotle writes, "has many senses (as many as 'is' has), but the proper one is that of actuality." The primary sense of unity is the "relation of an actuality to that of which it is the actuality" (*De Anima*, 412b8–9). Actuality is said neither of form nor of matter but of the composite. Thomas comments, "form is essentially united to matter as its act; it is the same thing for matter to be united to form as for matter to be in act" (*In Aristotelis* De Anima, II, lectio 1, note 234).

The anchoring of human beings in nature and the refusal to conceive of the human intellect as offering direct access to an immaterial and spiritual realm has important implications for philosophy itself. In the very opening of the *De Anima*, Aristotle reflects on the goals and limits of philosophy. As creatures of open-ended wonder, human beings cannot by their own powers possess wisdom, but they can long for it and possess a portion of it. This is why Socrates calls himself a philosopher (literally a lover of wisdom) and not a sophist (one who claims to be wise). In modern philosophy, the desire for certitude and productive power supplants the aspiration for wisdom. At the very outset of the *De Anima*, Aristotle notes that knowledge is desirable for two reasons: *(a)* because of the certitude gained and *(b)* because of the nobility of the object known. When we cannot have both, we should prefer the dim knowledge of noble objects to the certain knowledge of less-dignified objects (*In Aristotelis* De Anima, I, lectio 1).

At least for Descartes, the quest for certitude requires initially dismissing the entire order of sense and bodily experience, even one's experience of oneself as a body. Putting into question the entire physical order allows the pristine intelligibility of the order of mind to come to the fore. We know ourselves better than other things, and we know our intellect better than our body. The intellectual self is known immediately and transparently. Following Aristotle, and in contrast to Descartes, Aquinas urges a methodological retreat in our pursuit of self-knowledge. There is no possibility of gaining immediate, introspective access to the intellect or the soul. The route to self-knowledge is indirect, oblique. To understand the essence of any species, we must begin with the objects naturally pursued by members of the species in question, then move back from these objects to examine the activities, powers, and, finally, the essence. The indirect route to self-knowledge follows from the fact that the intellect is a potency made actual only by knowing things. But a power is knowable insofar as it is in act. Thus, there is no possibility of knowing the intellect until it has been actualized by knowing something other than itself.

Elsewhere, Thomas quotes Aristotle's assertion that the soul knows itself in the same way it understands other things; things are knowable insofar as they are in act, and the intellect is made actual by knowing sensible things (*ST*, I, 87, 1). He then distinguishes two sorts of self-knowledge, particular and universal. For the former, the mere presence of the soul to itself suffices, as, for example, when "Socrates perceives that he has an intellectual soul because he perceives that he understands." For the latter, mere presence is not sufficient; something more is required in the form of a "diligent and subtle inquiry," in which the nature of the human mind is understood from the act of understanding (*ST*, I, 87, 1). The more subtle inquiry presupposes an apprehension of our own knowing through self-presence. Without this apprehension, there would be no experiential basis for our account of the powers and nature of the intellectual soul. Nonetheless, the sort of self-presence operative here is indirect, reflexive, and dependent on acts of knowing other things: "We proceed from things external to us, from which we abstract intelligible species and through which the intellect understands itself" (*In Aristotelis* De Anima, II, lectio 6, note 308). For evidence, one looks first to the public realm of sense experience. In attempting to define the nutritive soul, for instance, Aristotle focuses on the acts in which it manifests itself—namely, reproduction and use of food. The shift from essence to powers to activities to objects involves a retreat in the pursuit of self-knowledge; the human being is first understood within and as part of the natural world. The order reflects the nature of the human soul, which is a potency that must be actualized through interaction with the sensible world. Thomas expresses the neediness of the soul in this way: "Everything which is in potency to something and receptive of it lacks that to which it is in potency and of which it is receptive" (*In Aristotelis* De Anima, III, lectio 7, note 680). A certain view of the human soul thus underlies Aristotle's dialectical realism; the order of knowing is not to be confused with the order of nature or being.

In the movement from the sensible individual to the phantasm and from the phantasm to the intelligible species, what is grasped at the second or third stage is implicitly or potentially present in the previous one. As Thomas explains elsewhere, the process of abstraction involves a subtle and complex examination of sensible particulars and imagined phantasms. Consider, for instance, the following excerpt from the *Sententia super* Metaphysicam, where Thomas traces knowledge from sensible particulars to memory, experience, and understanding: "Experience arises from a collation of many singulars received in the memory. This kind of collation is proper to man and pertains to the cognitive power, which is called particular reason and which collates the intentions of individuals" (I, lectio 1, 15). The phantasm, thus prepared, has a dual role: as image of the particular whence it is derived and as potential bearer of the intelligible species. The phantasm exhibits itself to the intellect as both a "this" and a "such." For Thomas, the importance of abstraction is connected to the role of the agent intellect in Aristotle's account. The transition from phantasm to species involves a movement from the sensible to the intelligible, from the particular to the universal. Without some capacity to universalize the particular, to actualize what is potentially intelligible, there would be no knowledge. Abstraction is precisely the illuminating activity performed by the agent intellect.

The passages in Aristotle and Aquinas on the movement from the singular to the universal invite the following misunderstanding. It seems that we are to envisage the human mind as encountering an isolated object or set of individual objects and then going about the work of abstracting the universal nature from it. But it is difficult to see how we could arrive at the universal from a set of particulars without already possessing the universal in some way. This objection, of course, is the sort we would expect Plato to have brought to bear on Aristotle's alternative to his account of knowledge. Following Aristotle's statement in *Physics* I that we must "proceed from universals to singulars," Aquinas too asserts that in our cognition the universal has a certain priority (*ST*, I, 85, 3). We proceed from sense to intellect, singular to universal, but even at the level of sense, background knowledge is operative, a background that understands the singular in terms of what is more common: "first according to sense we judge the more common before the less common. . . . For example, when we see something from afar, we know it is a body before we know it is an animal, and an animal before we know it to be a human being, and a human being before Socrates or Plato." In this way, our intellect moves from potency to act, as an "indeterminate knowledge is a mean between potency and act" (*ST*, I, 85, 3). Because we are always already caught up in the activities of sensing, we are always actually or potentially in a state of understanding. The modern way of framing the question of knowledge in terms of bare objects of sense and clear and distinct ideas naturally generates skeptical difficulties. On Aquinas's view, the intellect is always already a participant in being, but that initial participation gives us nothing more than the penumbra of understanding.

In his treatment of human knowledge in the *Summa Theologiae,* Aquinas spends a good deal of time combating a view that he attributes to Plato and his followers. As Aquinas sees it, Plato confuses the mode of our understanding with the mode of the being of things. Aquinas is careful to locate Plato's view within its historical context, as a response to the position of the early natural philosophers. They held to one of two options: either there could be no knowledge because the objects of knowledge are sensible things, always in flux, or knowledge is a matter of the physical elements in us hooking up with the physical elements in things (*ST*, I, 84, 1). Wanting to save the character of knowledge as universal, immaterial, and immobile, Plato posits the existence of a separate order of Forms corresponding to our ideas. Aquinas objects that this view fails to salvage knowledge of sensible things, which are singular, material, and mobile, and that it renders the union of soul and body inscrutable. What is missing in Plato is a more radical reflection on the nature of our intellectual operation and its relationship to its proper objects, the natures of sensible substances. More specifically, what is missing is the intellectual operation of abstraction performed by the agent intellect (*ST*, I, 84, 6). For Aquinas, the intellect is both passively receptive of sensible things and active upon them (*ST*, I, 79, 2–3). Our knowledge of sensible things, which is at first vague and general, is made precise and specific by actively engaging with sensible things, by persistent questioning of them. In this way, what is potentially intelligible becomes actually intelligible.

Technically and precisely, Aquinas states that understanding is the result of the intellect's abstracting the intelligible species from the phantasm or image of the sensible thing. The language of abstraction can be confusing if we think of it in physical terms as a stripping away of a material surface to arrive at an intelligible or spiritual core. According to this view, the agent intellect's operation would resemble that of a construction crane, extracting the intelligible species from experience. Abstraction is no such mechanical process. It is an "active power to take under consideration the natures of sensible things without adverting to their individuating conditions"—that is, the conditions that pertain to them as this or that instance and not just as members of the species (*ST*, I, 85, 1, ad 4). Thus, we can consider the nature of a cow while disregarding the fact that this cow is here before us now and has a certain color, weight, and so forth. In knowing and defining natural substances, be they human beings or cows, we must include flesh and bones, but not "this flesh" and "these bones." The contrast is between signate matter—that is, the concrete matter to which we can point—and common matter. Physics includes common but not signate matter, and mathematics, which treats of abstract forms, excludes both signate and common matter, but includes what is called intelligible matter to account for there being numerically many instances of the same form—for example, triangles, squares, etc. Abstraction thus salvages what Plato's doctrine could not: knowledge of sensible things.

Two objections against abstraction may be considered at this juncture. First, does not abstraction involve falsity because it confuses the sensible singular with the immaterial universal? One response is that the universal corresponds to the nature of sensible singulars, a nature that is more than singular in that it is shared in by many. The deeper response is that the intellect never attributes its mode of understanding to the thing understood. It was this modal difference that eluded Plato. Second, in spite of what Aquinas says about the orientation of the mind to the sensible world, does he not in practice treat sensible singulars as mere means to universal knowledge, as starting points that are to be discarded once we have abstracted the intelligible species? Aquinas reiterates Aristotle's paradoxical expression: we both abstract from and understand in the phantasms (ST, I, 85, 1, ad 5). The key text for this issue is the article that asks whether we need to attend to a phantasm in every act of knowing, even after we possess the intelligible species (ST, I, 84, 7). By way of support for Aristotle's authoritative statement that the soul understands nothing without a phantasm, Aquinas adduces two arguments. First, if this were not the case, our understanding would not be hindered by damage to bodily organs in which our senses reside. Second, from experience, we see that the discovery of appropriate examples and the crafting of illuminating images are necessary for our act of understanding. Thus does the formation of phantasms—that is, appropriate examples—assist the facility of the intellect. The most important reason why we cannot sever the intellect's link to sensible singulars is the requirement of truth: the universal must correspond to the nature existing in singulars. Here we encounter once again that reflective act by which the intellect both knows and knows that it knows. In its reflection, the intellect extends to sense and judges that this singular in front of it is an instance of a certain natural kind. If we reflect on the activity of knowing sensible singulars, we can discover the experiential basis for Thomas's seemingly contradictory assertions about the human intellect—namely, that it cannot think without a phantasm and that thinking is an operation that resides in no bodily organ. In the very act of attending to sensible singulars, we apprehend them under a formality that transcends their mere particularity. There is no such thing as a bare singular. The commonplace act of judging that this singular before me is a tree reveals something not only about the thing known but also about the composite unity of the knower, who both knows what he senses and senses what he knows. In the acts of knowing and judging, we are simultaneously oriented to and independent of sense and singularity.

Here we have yet another illustration of how we come to know our own nature by reflection on our acts of knowing other things. Thus does Aquinas highlight something that Aristotle had merely noted—namely, the intellect's capacity of self-reflection and self-appropriation. With Aristotle, Aquinas describes knowledge as an identity of knower and known, but such an identity is also ascribed to sense in its relation to sensible qualities. Sense, however, does not sense that it senses. Self-reflection, then, is peculiar to the intellect. There is no private "I" or "Ego" for Aquinas because the intellect, as a potency, is nothing until it is actualized by things. Whatever self there is emerges in the very act of knowing the other-as-other. Emphasizing the identity of knower and known underscores the knowing of the other, but not as other. For the latter, reflection on and self-possession of our acts of knowing are necessary. They do not entail immediate introspection, but rather a mediated return to self in the very act of attending to things. Apart from this act of knowing the other-as-other, there is no conscious ego or self. As Frederick Wilhelmsen puts it, the "*ego* is rather known by being lived, not thought. . . . the *ego* is a dimension of spiritual act, not a thing but a spiritual doing." The ego is only in its performance of knowing.[5]

In a variety of ways, then, Aquinas underscores the intellect's natural orientation to sensible singulars. Indeed, he makes his own the Aristotelian teachings (*a*) that the intellect is a potency made actual only by its interaction with things, and (*b*) that knowledge is not by contact of knower and known or by the presence of a similitude of the latter in the former, but by an identity of knower and known. Some, however, see in the role of the intelligible species as mediator

---

[5] "The Dignity of the Human Person," in *Being and Knowing*, 248. As we shall see, another and perhaps more familiar sense of self comes from one's own narrative, which Wilhelmsen himself points out.

between intellect and thing an anticipation of the modern subject-object dichotomy.[6] In an article that asks whether the species is related to our intellect as what is understood or as that by which we understand (*ST*, I, 85, 2), Aquinas insists that the primary object of our knowledge is the nature of sensible things. The species is the means by which *(quo)* we know things rather than what *(quod)* we know. Aquinas's language might seem to imply that we first inspect the content of our consciousness and then look to the external world to confirm that the content accurately reflects external things. The most obvious problem with this procedure is that it traps us in an infinite regress. If what we encounter first is always the content of our consciousness, the way things have affected us, then the turn from the species to the world will always be frustrated by the fact that we will once again encounter an image or likeness of what exists outside us. One can see here how Descartes and Locke's view on the temporal priority of ideas in our coming to know external things quite reasonably generates both Hume's skepticism about whether we can know the external world at all and Berkeley's claim that "to be is to be perceived" *(esse est percipi).*

Descartes's quest for absolute certitude engendered the peculiarly modern enterprise of philosophical justification through epistemology. The framework for the enterprise is the subject-object split. It sets a mind over here in opposition to a world over there. The question is whether we can get from here to there. The task is to justify one's knowledge, to vindicate one's claims about the world in the face of skeptical doubts about whether the mind latches onto the world at all. From the perspective provided by Aristotle and Aquinas, the modern approach looks awfully contrived and artificial; instead of focusing on human beings actively engaged with things in the world, it offers us an abstract mind trying desperately to find entry into the world. Moreover, reasonable doubts are always local, never global; they are formulated against a set of background assumptions that could never all at once be successfully put in question. If doubt were to become truly global, it would be fatal. At the root of the modern

---

[6] See, for example, Robert Pasnau, *Theories of Cognition in the Later Middle Ages,* 11–27, 195–219, and 256–70. A corrective can be had in John O'Callaghan, "The Problem of Language and Mental Representation in Aristotle and St. Thomas."

problematic is an assumption that Descartes, Locke, Berkeley, and Hume share—namely, that what we know first are ideas, not things.

Aquinas nowhere asserts that we know the species and then through it know the thing. In terms of temporal order, the species can be known only after we have known the thing, by a reflective act that may accompany our knowing of things. In that reflective act, we simultaneously know the thing and know that we know it. In the latter, we acknowledge that our intellect has been informed by the nature of the thing, which is congruent with Aristotle's dictum that we know activities by first knowing the objects of those activities. If Aquinas does not anticipate the modern problematic, one might still wonder whether it would not be safer to eliminate the language of species altogether. Would it not be less misleading to speak simply of an intellect and a thing, or, better, of an intellect knowing a thing? Why posit the species or concept as a third thing? The response is that the concept is not a thing, but the informed activity of the intellect as it grasps the thing. Indeed, the Latin term *conceptum* can have our meaning of "concept," but it can also mean "thing conceived." The latter is more in accord with Thomas's use.

Perhaps the clearest indication that Aristotle does not conceive of the soul as constituting some private realm is that he is not at all troubled by the subject-object dichotomy that has haunted modernity. Because thinking is a passive affection and knowing involves the identity of knower and known, mind is nothing until it has actually thought. For Aristotle, there is no thinking without a thing thought, and no thing thought without a sensible phantasm. Throughout his discussion of thinking, he develops analogies to sense perception, wherein the sense in act *is* the sensible in act. The problem of moving from the private, interior inspection of images or ideas to their objective referents never arises for Aristotle. He assumes a certain connaturality between intelligence and the intelligible. If "to understand is to suffer," then there must be something common between the knower and known. As he argues in the *Physics*, between mover and moved, agent and patient, there is one actuality (see Aquinas's comments: *In Libros* Physicorum, III, lectio 5).

The indirect and mediated path to knowledge of the human soul does not diminish the importance of that knowledge. Indeed, the general investigation of soul culminates with an analysis of what is proper to human souls. Thus, we find Aquinas explicating Aristotle's comparison of sensation and understanding and his argument that intellect so differs from sense that it must be an immaterial power whose operation transcends every bodily organ. Like sense, the intellect is said to be passive with respect to sensible objects. It is a potency actualized by receiving the forms of things. But there are different senses of passivity, and a clarification of them is crucial to a comparison of sense and intellect. Aquinas writes:

> To be passive is spoken of in three ways. Most properly, something is said to be passive when from it is removed whatever is befitting to its nature or proper inclination, as when . . . a man becomes ill. Less properly, a thing is said to be passive when something, either suitable or unsuitable to it, is removed from it. In this sense, both he who is ill and he who is healed are said to be passive. . . . In a looser and more common sense, a thing is said to be passive when it receives that to which it was in potency without being deprived of anything. In this sense, whatever passes from potency to act may be said to be passive, even when it is perfected. And thus our act of understanding is said to be passive. (*ST*, I, 79, 2)

The primary sense of suffering or receiving entails a "certain corruption," the destruction of one contrary by another. This receptivity is the sort to which all natural substances are liable; it is the basis in the opening of the *Physics* for the discussion of change in terms of the displacement of a qualitative form by its contrary. If a natural substance undergoes a qualitative alteration—say, from white to black or from hot to cold—the contrary present at the beginning of the change is destroyed and replaced by the contrary that is coming to be and that is fully present at the end of the process of change. In another sense, one can speak of passion "commonly and less properly" insofar as it "imports a certain reception" (*importat quamdam receptionem; In Aristotelis* De Anima, II, lectio 11, notes 365–66). Thomas explains, "That which is receptive of another is compared to it as potency to act; act, moreover, is the perfection of potency. In this sense, it is called a passion not insofar as there is a corruption of the receiver, but as there is a certain health and perfection of that which is in potency by that which is in act" (*In Aristotelis* De Anima, II, lectio 11). Sensation can be called a passion according to the latter, extended meaning.

Knowing can be called a passion in only an even more extended sense than that which applies to sensation. The species informs without destroying the power of the intellect; the sort of receptivity operative here is that of an actuality perfecting a power. Thomas credits Aristotle with having realized that the mode in which sensibles are known differs from the mode in which they exist. To explain how this modal difference in the object arises, Thomas posits abstraction as the activity of the intellect whereby the natures of sensible individuals are understood in a universal way. Yet Aristotle does not use the term *abstraction;* he refers to two ways of knowing: induction and demonstration. Recent commentators have suggested that what is missing is not just the word, but the very operation that was to become the centerpiece of Thomas's psychology.[7] At least in the commentary, what Thomas means by abstraction is not controversial: it is simply the capacity for apprehending natures apart from their individuating conditions.

PROBLEMS OF SOUL AND BODY

The claims *(a)* that the intellectual soul is immaterial and *(b)* that it is a substantial form generate a number of problems. Some have supposed that the former assertion renders the latter impossible. If the intellect is immaterial, it cannot be the substantial form of a material body. They proffer a rival account of the relationship between soul and body, wherein soul is related to the body as mover to moved. This position has the apparent advantage of explaining the interaction of the soul with the body without immersing it in matter. Some who find this view congenial posit a number of souls as mediators between the body and the intellect (*ST,* I, 76, 3). An individual human being would be alive by the vegetative soul; animal by the sensitive soul; and human by the intellectual soul. Aquinas counters that the multiplication of souls has the awkward result of rendering any particular human being only accidentally one. "Animal" would be predicated of "human" accidentally, not essentially.

---

[7] The most forceful argument against the presence in Aristotle's texts of a doctrine of psychological abstraction is put forth by John Cleary: "On the Terminology 'Abstraction' in Aristotle." Cleary's essay is a response to Charles De Koninck's "Abstraction from Matter." On the tensions in Aristotle's account, see Deborah K. W. Modrak, *The Power of Perception,* 113–32. Also germane is Stanley Rosen's "Thought and Touch: A Note on Aristotle's *De Anima.*"

This returns us to Aristotle's definition of the soul as the "first act of a natural, organic body potentially having life." Aristotle follows the stipulation that in the definition of a form we must state its proper subject (*In Aristotelis* De Anima, II, lectio 1). The definition brings technical precision to the insight that the soul is the actualizing, animating, and organizing form of the body. We cannot understand one without the other. By "first act," Aristotle means the original act that gives being and unity to a substance. Subsequent acts, which involve the operation of its proper powers, are identified as "second acts." There are thus many second acts, but only one first act. Aristotle then refers to the subject of the soul as an organic body; a diversity of organs is appropriate to the complexity of operations of ensouled, living beings. Because the body is receptive of the animating soul, it is described as potentially having life. As Aquinas notes, it is the same thing for matter to be united to form as it is for matter to be in act. Aristotle remarks that it is as redundant to ask whether soul and body are one as it is to ask whether an act and that of which it is the act are one. The substantial form is derived from the highest power of the soul, which contains what belongs to lower souls (*ST*, I, 76, 4). Being contained by and ordered to the highest power in human beings, the lower powers are not the same in human beings as they are in inferior animals. They are transformed and elevated by their participation in the intellectual soul. One substantial form, the intellectual soul, gives being and unity to the whole.

Thomas finds grounds in Aristotle for two theses: first, that embodiment is constitutive of human nature, and, second, that the intellect is an immaterial power. He thus focuses on a difficulty that contemporary commentators on Aristotle have generally neglected. The difficulty is evident in Aristotle's asking the question whether the soul, or some part of it, is separable from the body. At least one contemporary scholar has addressed the issue. Deborah Modrak writes,

Aristotle seems to be fully cognizant of the tensions between two tendencies in his theorizing about the human soul—(*a*) the desire to give a unified treatment of all the faculties of soul such that the internal unity of the soul and the unity of the living being as ensouled is assured and (*b*) the desire to give an account of the intellect that captures its uniqueness and divinity. The first desire issues in the attempt to encapsulate the core concept of soul in the general definition and the second in the attribution of separability to active *nous* in 3.5.[8]

What is the basis for the assertion of the separability of the intellect? Unlike sense, intellect has no organ. If it had an organ, it would impede the reception of an unlimited variety of forms, as is true of the sensitive powers, which are limited to a specific set of contraries. For the mind to think all things and to think them in abstraction from the here and now, from the determinate material conditions of sensible objects, requires the presence of a nonmaterial power. Mind has "no nature other than potentiality." The intellect is not circumscribed by any organ and has no determinate nature. Thus, the intellect must be separable from the body. The conclusion follows from the coupling of the Aristotelian principle that whatever has a per se operation subsists with the fact that the intellect has an operation in which the body does not share. Aristotle couches his discussion of immateriality in guarded and negative language.

The ordination of human thought to the sensible world is evident even in Aristotle's consideration of the immateriality of human understanding. He establishes by negation the claim that thinking is a nonmaterial operation of human beings. Like sense, mind is a potency that is made actual only by interaction with the sensible world. The phantasm is necessary not just for the initial act, but for every act of knowing. The phantasm ensures that the universal knowledge is always a knowledge of the natures of sensible particulars. The universal is beheld in the particular, in which the intellect apprehends what is common to all individuals of a certain species. The capacity to transcend the realm of mere particulars in the very act of attending to it distinguishes knowing from sensing. Thomas frequently captures the human act of transcendence in the language of reflective self-appropriation; in the act of knowing, we appropriate the known-as-known and speak the known to ourselves and others.

The defense of the necessity of the phantasm for every act of knowing captures the essential activity of the embodied intellect, which must become "worldly" if it is to realize its natural perfection. Yet there appear to be tensions between this theme and the claim that the intellective soul has an operation per se separate from the

---

[8] "The Nous-Body Problem in Aristotle," 758.

body. Does the need for a phantasm belie the supposition that the soul has an operation independent of the body? Conversely, does the immateriality of the intellect compromise the rich description of the nature of embodied intelligence? As noted above, turning to the phantasm ensures that the intellect is true, that there is an adequation of the mind to the thing. The intellect orients its thinking with respect to the phantasm because its proper objects are the forms or natures of sensible substances. Although the body is not the organ of the activity of the intellect, it is necessary to provide an object. The intellect can consider the object apart from the here and now by abstracting the essence of the sensible particular from the sensible conditions in which it exists. Although the intellect cannot think without certain material conditions being present, thinking itself cannot be predicated of the body or of any bodily process.

Of all Thomas's claims about human knowledge and human nature, the assertion that the soul is a subsisting thing (*hoc aliquid*) seems most repugnant to Aristotle's teaching on the unity of soul and body. More damaging than the apparent contravention of Aristotle is the apparent contradiction at the heart of Thomas's thesis. On the one hand, what subsists is capable of independent existence; on the other hand, soul is the form of body, to which it is naturally united. How can we affirm both? The tension is most pronounced in Thomas's theological writings, especially in the second book of the *Summa contra Gentiles* (cited as *SCG*), which begins with a common consideration of human souls and angels as members of the genus of intellectual substances. Thomas proves that such substances are immaterial (*SCG*, II, 50), subsistent (*SCG*, II, 51), and incorruptible (*SCG*, II, 55). Some have supposed that these proofs apply equally to souls and angels. But this assumption overlooks the subsequent set of proofs for the immortality of the soul (*SCG*, II, 79). If the first proofs applied equally to souls and angels, why add a second set of proofs for the soul? The intervening chapters that clarify the nature of the soul as form of the body render dubious the applicability of the first set of proofs to the soul. Having concluded his inquiry into the union of soul and body, Thomas argues that angels and souls do not belong to the same species (*SCG*, II, 94) and that the soul is not, properly speaking, a member of the genus of intellectual substances. Critics, who hold that speaking of the soul both as subsistent and as form involves logical contradictions, have persistently overlooked

Thomas's carefully qualified use of language. He does not use univocal language when he calls the soul a *hoc aliquid*. To require him to use univocal language in speaking of the human composite and of other, natural substances is to demand that he violate the complex phenomena of human nature. The soul is a subsisting thing in only a diminished sense. He writes, "According to its genus, it befits the intellectual substance that it subsist through itself, for it has an operation proper to itself . . . ; it is, moreover, of the essence of what subsists through itself that it not be united to another. Thus, it is not of the essence of the intellectual substance according to its genus that it be united to a body, even if it is of the essence of the intellectual substance that is the human soul" (*SCG*, II, 91).

In Aquinas's last work, the *Summa Theologiae*, there is no common consideration of souls and angels. The order of inquiry, which treats angels before souls and which proceeds from the essence to the powers and operations of the soul, is the reverse of that Aristotle pursues in the *De Anima*. The reversal is a consequence of the theological method of Aquinas's work, which reflects broadly the order of being. Thus, it moves from God to creation, and within creation from angels to souls, and within souls from essence to powers. The theologian, Thomas notes, considers creatures, including human beings, in relation to God and thus focuses on that which is more spiritual—namely, the soul. Nonetheless, the structure of questions in the *Summa* highlights the disparity between angels and souls and affirms in multiple ways Aristotle's teaching on soul and body. The order of the questions on human knowledge runs thus: how the soul knows corporeal things (*ST*, I, 84), the mode and order of knowledge (I, 85), what the soul knows in material things (I, 86), self-knowledge (I, 87), and knowledge of immaterial beings (I, 88). There is an ascent from things to self-knowledge and on to the higher, separate substances. Compare the order of questions on angelic knowledge: cognition of immaterials (I, 56), cognition of material things (I, 57), and mode and order of understanding (I, 58). Angelic self-knowledge is subsumed under cognition of immaterial things. The descending order of consideration reflects the angels' immediate access to the immaterial and hence to self-knowledge. Contrary answers given to the same questions underscore the gap between the simplicity and immediacy of angelic knowledge and the abstract, mediated, and discursive character of human knowledge.

The limitations to human knowledge are evident in the prominence of negation in the entire discussion of human knowledge in the *Summa Theologiae*. The first five of eight articles on our knowledge of material things are answered negatively (*ST*, I, 84). The articles ask whether the soul knows sensible things through its essence, through innate species, from separate forms, or in the eternal ideas. The remaining articles affirm that the soul knows from sensible things, that it knows by conversion to the phantasm, and that the suspension of the operation of sense hinders judgment. Negation is also the initial approach in the study of self-knowledge. Having denied that the soul knows itself by its own essence (*ST*, I, 87, 1), Thomas acknowledges that the soul knows its own habits and acts by the indirect route Aristotle describes in the *De Anima* (*ST*, I, 87, 2–4). The darkness of our knowledge is also present in the subsequent question about our knowledge of higher things. The soul cannot understand immaterial substances in themselves (*ST*, I, 88, 1); material things are insufficient means of knowing immaterial things (I, 88, 2); and God is not the first thing we know (I, 88, 3).

Thomas moves back and forth without hesitation between descriptions of human beings as rational animals and as embodied intellectual substances. He speaks of human beings as the highest of animals and the lowest of intellectual substances. Against the supposition that the soul and the angel share the same species, he notes that the soul has of itself no integral species. It furthermore has "an aptitude and inclination to union with the body" (*aptitudinem et inclinationem ad corporis unionem; ST*, I, 76, 1, ad 6). To be the form of the body "pertains to the genus of animals" (*pertinet ad genus animalium; ST*, I, 90, 4, ad 2). "Animal" is predicated essentially of "human" because the form through which a being is a human is the same as that through which it is an animal. The limits to and analogous status of the treatment of the soul as a member of the genus of intellectual substances are clear from the statement that "forms by themselves are not placed in a genus or a species, but only the composites" (*formae non collocantur in genere vel specie, sed compostia; ST*, I, 76, 3, ad 2). The human being, then, is not properly in the genus of intellectual substances but rather in the genus animal; what leads Thomas to associate the soul, admittedly only a part of human nature, with intellectual substances is the capacity peculiar to human beings, a capacity underscored by Aristotle himself. As Thomas puts it in the commentary on the *De Anima*, "the soul is not a complete species, but is rather part of a species; thus, it is not wholly fitting to call it a subsisting thing" (*In Aristotelis* De Anima, II, lectio 1, notes 213–16).

What more can we say about the separability of the intellect? As Thomas notes at the end of his commentary, the scope of the *De Anima* is limited to a consideration of form insofar as it is related to matter. An answer to the vexing questions concerning the state of a separated intellect lies beyond the scope of natural philosophy.[9] Such a determination can be had in the response to the question whether "the separated soul can understand anything" (*ST*, I, 89, 1). The simple, affirmative response to the question is that the separated soul can understand because it has an operation proper to it. Nonetheless, "experience shows" that the soul understands by turning to phantasms. Hence, a difficulty arises, a difficulty that the Platonic view of the soul as merely accidentally united to the body dissipates. The consequence of that view is that union to the body is not "for the soul's good." The alternative, Aristotelian view, according to which soul is naturally and appropriately united to the body, seems to render the separated soul incapable of understanding anything because it will then have no access to phantasms. How are we to resolve the dilemma?

Thomas distinguishes between two modes of understanding: one in the body and according to phantasms, the other apart from the body with a turn to intelligible objects. The solution generates another problem, the difficulty of why the soul was not created so as naturally to understand intelligibles without recourse to phantasms. The response is twofold. First, the order of creation requires a hierarchy of beings, some of which understand intelligibles directly and others of which understand by recourse to phantasms. There is an order of perfection appropriate to each level. Second, given the first answer, if souls, although retaining their intellectual inferiority to angels, were to understand in a way akin to that of the separate substances, human knowledge would be "confused and general." Indeed, the separation of the intellect from the body is "outside the

---

[9] "*Quomodo se habeant formae totaliter a materia separatae et quid sint, vel etiam quomodo se habeat haec forma, id est anima rationalis, secundum quod est separabilis et sine corpore existere potens, et quid sit secundum suam essentiam separabile, hoc determinare pertinet ad Philosophum Primam*" (*In Aristotelis* De Anima, III, lectio 12, note 785).

essence of its nature" *(praeter rationem suae naturae)*. The separated soul has more than a muddled understanding only on account of the "influx of divine light," given through the "light of grace." Thomas resolves the question whether and how the disembodied intellect can understand only by deploying theological sources and principles. Aristotle's ambivalence concerning the separability of the soul is thus entirely understandable. He seems driven to its separability and perhaps incorruptibility by its capacity to exercise an operation in which the body does not participate. Given the natural union of soul and body as well as the dependence of the intellect on the body to supply it with objects of knowledge, what would the separated intellect know and how could it operate without a phantasm? The resurrection of the body, a doctrine of which Aristotle was blamelessly ignorant, illustrates how revelation solves the difficulties *(aporiai)* in which philosophy culminates.[10]

In spite of the limitations to the inquiry of the *De Anima* into the human soul, that discussion provides the indispensable means for our knowledge of separate substances. We cannot reason from the existence of the intellect to the existence of higher substances. Instead, their existence is established from reflection on the causal sources of sensible things. But when we come to describe the intellectual operations of the separate substances, we do so by analogy to that human operation in which the body does not share. In Aristotle's order of studies, the inquiry into soul marks the culmination of natural philosophy and precedes the study of ethics and politics, on the one hand, and the study of metaphysics, on the other. The study of the soul is thus pivotal.

Even if the study of soul does not rest primarily on introspective evidence, it does involve an appropriation of our own activity as knowers and of the immanent telos of our nature. The order of Aris-

---

[10] For some—namely, the Averroists—the supposition that there is one agent intellect for all human minds resolves the difficulties, both concerning human knowledge of universals and concerning the separability of the intellect. For Thomas's response, see the translation of the text and commentaries on it by Ralph McInerny, *Aquinas against the Averroists: On There Being Only One Intellect*. Thomas's adamant position against the unity of the intellect has been criticized for a too tidy interpretation of Aristotle and on some passages it may be guilty. Yet it has the effect of reestablishing the dialectical limits to philosophy and hence of correcting tendencies to excessive rationalism in the Averroist school. I return to this issue later.

totle's study of soul is instructive. He begins with a common consideration of the activities of all living things, with the soul as something in and of the world. When he describes the intellectual soul as a potency that is made actual through interaction with sensible substances and knowing as an identity of knower and known, he speaks of the soul's kinship to the whole; the intellect is *potens omnia*. The human soul's peculiar receptivity of the whole indicates that it is not merely a part of the whole, but is that part of the world in which and through which the whole is made manifest. There is a reciprocity between the increased interiority of the human soul and its increased openness to the external world. As Pieper puts it, "the higher a being stands in the order of reality, the wider and deeper its world. . . . The two together constitute spirit: not only the capacity to relate oneself to the whole of reality, to the whole world, but an unlimited capacity of living in oneself. . . . To have a world, to be related to the whole of reality, is only possible to a self, to a person, to a 'who' and not a 'what.' "[11]

If the union of the intellectual soul with a body has important ramifications for the nature of the human body, it also renders nearly philosophically inscrutable the question of the ultimate destiny of the human person. This does not mean that philosophy can say nothing positive about the possibility of life beyond the grave. We have seen Aristotle provide convincing arguments on behalf of the immateriality and subsistence of the intellect. Given the natural orientation of the intellect to sensible substances and of the soul to the body, whether the intellect could know anything in a separated state is problematic. In his response to that exact question (*ST*, I, 89, 1), Aquinas repeatedly uses the term *difficulty*. He begins with the Platonic denial that the soul is the form of the body; because on this view the soul's knowledge is not assisted but impeded by the body, there is no problem with whether a separated soul can know. But such a view suffers a more basic difficulty; it renders the original union of soul and body inexplicable because that union does not seem to be for the soul's good. Aristotle's position, by contrast, accounts for union but leaves us with the problem of how the separated intellect could know anything. Aquinas suggests two modes of being and knowing: one, united to the body, through phantasms, and another,

---

[11] *Leisure,* 110, 118.

separated from the body, through intelligible species. He adds: "To be separated from the body as well as to understand without turning to phantasms are beyond the nature of the intellectual soul." In fact, the knowledge of the separated soul is "general and confused" rather than "perfect and proper." How little we can complain of Aristotle's inability to resolve the issue is clear from Aquinas's statement that the separated intellect needs supernatural assistance. It knows "by means of participated species flowing from the divine light." This mode of knowing is not unnatural, but rather is supernatural because God is the "author of both illuminations, that of grace and that of nature" (*ST*, I, 89, 1, ad 3). But even this attribute does not alter the nature of the soul in such a way that it is no longer appropriately the form of the body. "The human soul remains in its proper mode of being even when it is separated from the body; thus, it retains a natural aptitude and natural inclination for union with the body" (*ST*, I, 76, 1, ad 6).

Throughout his reflections on human nature, Aquinas highlights the marvelous union of soul and body. The remarkable consequences of that union are clear from his discussions of the human body and of the passions, discussions that increase our appreciation of just how complex, rich, and supple his account is. In response to the query whether God gave the human body an apt disposition (*ST*, I, 91, 3), Aquinas focuses on the "upright stature" of human beings. The consequences for our relationship to the world are telling. In animals, the senses reside primarily in the face; because our face is not turned toward the ground, our senses are not confined to performing biological functions necessary for survival: pursuing food and fending off attackers. Our senses provide avenues for higher-level interaction with nature and other human beings. Beyond any pragmatic purpose, we take delight in the beauty of sensible things (*solus homo delectatur in ipsa pulchritudine sensibilium secundum seipsam; ST*, I, 91, 3, ad 3). We are open to and receptive of the whole: "The subtlety of sight probes the many differences of things . . . and enables us to gather the truth of all things, both earthly and heavenly." Our mouths do not protrude and are not primarily suited for self-defense and procuring food. If our mouths and tongues were like those of other animals, they would "obstruct speech which is the proper work of reason" (*ST*, I, 91, 3, ad 3).

It has sometimes been suggested that Western philosophical reflection about mind is wedded to an abstract and detached model of objectivity, with its penchant for comparing mind exclusively to sight. Aquinas's emphasis on the embodiment of reason in speech and on touch as the most human of the senses undercuts such a model. In response to the question whether the rational soul is united to an appropriate body, he highlights the importance of the sense of touch (*ST*, I, 76, 5). By comparison with the bodies of other animals, the human body is feeble—that is, less immediately equipped with powers serving the maintenance of life. Instead of a "fixed" set of bodily powers, it has reason and the hand, the organ of organs, able to craft limitless tools. Moreover, the human body is ordered to activities eclipsing that of mere survival: knowledge, communication, and love. For these activities, it requires an "equable complexion, a mean between contraries" (*ST*, I, 76, 5), giving it the ability to receive and discriminate an array of sensible qualities. Such a complexion is prominent in the sense of touch, especially in the hand, which actually grasps and takes on the form of the thing held. There is a striking analogy here between the hand's grasping of objects and the intellect's grasping of the forms of the things.

The link between touch and intelligence as well as the analogy between touch and thought illustrate from yet another vantage point the remarkable union of soul and body. The intellectual soul, we should recall, is the first act of the entire body, animating and informing the whole, which has important ramifications for the subrational powers of the human soul. For example, the participation of the lower, sensitive powers in reason is prominent in Aquinas's examination of the passions. Because the passions reside in the sensitive rather than the intellectual appetite, it might seem they could not be subject to moral appraisal. The faulty assumption here is that there is an unbridgeable gap between intellect and will, on the one hand, and the sensitive appetite, on the other. Aquinas counters with Aristotle's teaching that although the lower appetites are not intrinsically rational, they are amenable to rational persuasion and thus may participate in reason (*ST*, I-II, 24, 1, ad 2). Aquinas divides the passions into concupiscible and irascible passions. The former (which include love and hatred, joy and sorrow) pertain to sensible good and evil absolutely, whereas the latter (which encompass hope and despair, daring and fear) have a more narrow scope: the arduous or difficult good or evil (*ST*, I-II, 23, 1). The restricted scope of the irascible passions indicates their auxiliary and subordinate role; they are called into action when we encounter arduous goods or onerous evils. Because they concern a restricted good, they pertain to movement alone, as in struggle or flight, not to repose. Thus, the concupiscible powers are prior to the irascible, and among the concupiscible, the first is love, whose inclination to the good is the cause of all the passions (*ST*, I-II, 25, 2).

The positive appraisal of natural inclination and of the possibility of passion participating in reason underscores the dignity of the human body in Aquinas's account of human things, which we can see in two related ways. On the one hand, the human body is raised up, transformed by its union with the intellectual soul. On the other hand, the soul is naturally ordered to union with the body. We cannot disavow our bodies without courting self-misunderstanding. Leon Kass writes: "Thinking about the body is . . . constraining and liberating for the thinker: constraining because it shows him the limits on the power of thought to free him from embodiment, setting limits on thought understood as a tool for mastery; liberating because it therefore frees him to wonder about the irreducibly mysterious union and concretion of mind and body that we both are and live."[12]

Any view that treats nature and the body as "raw material for human activity and for its power," according to John Paul II, contravenes the Thomistic and Catholic teaching on the unity of the human person, "whose rational soul is *per se* and *essentialiter* the form of his body. . . . The person by the light of reason and the support of virtue discovers in the body the anticipatory signs, the expression and the promise of the gift of self, in conformity with the wise plan of the Creator."[13]

PERSON AND NATURE: THE DILEMMA OF FREEDOM

Thus far in my discussion of human nature, I have concentrated on the consequences of the unity of soul and body for the activity of human knowing. Yet the *De Anima* does not conclude with a discussion of the intellect, but with a consideration of thought and appetite

---

[12] *Toward a More Natural Science*, 295.
[13] *Veritatis Splendor*, 66.

as the two sources of movement in human animals (*De Anima,* III, 9–10). The description of mind as a potency and of the appetitive character of the human soul shifts our attention from the nature of the soul to the nature of the good that rational animals naturally desire. The resistance in various modern and contemporary camps to Aquinas's conception of human nature and knowledge is eclipsed only by the opposition to his account of free will. The chief impediment to recovering Aquinas's teaching on voluntary agency is the modern celebration of freedom that stands between us and the thirteenth century. The moderns themselves would describe their project not as a flight from nature but as a quest for freedom. Freedom has inspired nearly all the great political movements of the modern world, and modern philosophers have been preoccupied with the questions of whether human beings are free and, if so, how we are to characterize that freedom. By contrast, Aquinas not only devotes much less attention to the topic, but also develops a view of freedom at odds with modern understandings.

Some appreciation of modern conceptions of freedom is necessary if we are to uncover and appreciate the distinctive features of Aquinas's position. Just as with the question of mind and body, so too with the issue of freedom we find a basic set of options articulated very early in the modern period, in the writings of Descartes and Hobbes. The latter treats human nature and deliberation mechanistically and ends up denying the ascription of free choice to human agents. Choice is merely the last stage in deliberation, not a free rational judgment; it is always under the determining influence of antecedent passion. By underscoring the universal threat of violent death in the state of nature, Hobbes hopes to compel his audience to lay down their natural rights and to submit to a Leviathan, a governor with complete power over his subjects. By contrast, Descartes separates human understanding and agency from the realm of physical causality and urges us to adopt a posture of self-determination and self-regulation of our thought. Although he does not in the *Meditations* develop an ethical doctrine of freedom, the description of human nature that emerges from that work suggests a position distinct from Hobbes's.

When we compare the paucity of references to freedom in ancient philosophy with its centrality in modern philosophy, we can also note a corresponding shift in the modern period toward speaking of human beings as persons rather than as individuals with a shared human nature. Here the most important figure is undoubtedly Kant, who speaks of human persons precisely in order to distinguish them from nature. According to the Newtonian conception of nature that informs Kant's writing, nature is the realm of deterministic necessity, understood in terms of lawlike generalizations and mathematical formulae. The mechanistic flow of natural causes leaves no room for freedom. To make room for freedom, to carve out a niche for properly human agency, Kant appeals to the "fact of freedom," which is at least implicitly experienced in each individual's deliberation and action. How is this so?

In deliberating and acting, I must presuppose myself to be self-determining. Were I not to assume this capacity of free self-determination, I would undercut the very possibility of deliberation and choice: "Now I say every being that cannot act except under the idea of freedom is just for that reason in a practical point of view really free. . . . It must regard itself as the author of its principles independent of foreign influences."[14] More dramatically for Kant, the fact that in deliberating and choosing we find ourselves bound by a moral law is proof that we possess a rational independence from external causes. The moral law requires that, in cases where duty conflicts with inclination, we act against inclination—that is, against the deterministic realm of nature. We have experiential evidence to confirm our freedom whenever we experience conflict between the voice of duty and inclination. That it is possible for us to resist the pull of inclination and to act on behalf of duty testifies to our freedom from the realm of mechanistic necessity.

Another crucial characteristic of the moral law is that each individual gives it to himself or herself; in other words, only if I am self-legislating can I be autonomous and truly free. To accept a law from nature or human society or God is to act heteronomously—that is, to be enslaved to a force external to me. Our dignity consists in obeying a law we give ourselves. The rational self-determination that we discover in ourselves is present in each person, and it is the ground of the imperative that we treat humanity as an end, never merely as a means. Persons ought not to be instrumentalized; they have dignity, not price: "Man and generally any rational being exists as an end in

---

[14] Immanuel Kant, *The Metaphysics of Morals*, 280.

himself, not merely as a means to be arbitrarily used by this or that will, but in all his actions, whether they concern himself or other rational beings, must be always regarded at the same time as an end."[15] Although Kant uses the terms *man* and *humanity*, he resists grounding dignity and freedom on an anthropology or empirical study of the inclinations and propensities of human nature. To do so would be to return us to the realm of natural, causal necessity. Imperatives based on human nature could be the basis only of hypothetical imperatives (that is, commands that presuppose some contingent inclination in human beings: for example, if you want a Pepsi, you must get off the couch and go to the kitchen), not of categorical imperatives (that is, commands that we must obey regardless of our inclinations: for example, do not murder).

Kant presents a powerful defense of human freedom and of the distinctive dignity of human persons. At least in one respect, with his use of the term *person*, he is anticipated by medieval, Catholic thought. The notion of human beings as persons was originally coined in the course of the development of the doctrine of the Trinity. When Aquinas reflects on the three-personed God, he recurs to Boethius's classic definition of a person as an "individual substance of a rational nature" (*ST*, I, 29, 1). He notes that individuality belongs to concretely existing substances, especially to rational substances that have "dominion over their own acts." In the created order, *person* signifies "what is most perfect in all of nature." Especially in God, the term *person* connotes *(a)* incommunicability, because the divine persons are irreducibly distinct and unrepeatable, and *(b)* relationality, because the only possible ground for distinction in a simple divine being is the relation of origin. As we shall see, incommunicability and relationality are also characteristics of human persons, although for different reasons.

When we compare Aquinas with Kant, the chief modern proponent of depicting human beings as persons, we find some similarities. Both speak of the self-determination of rational agents and both underscore the individuality or incommunicability of persons, who are not merely parts or members of a common species. The person is a "who," not merely a "what." In both accounts, persons have a special dignity that sets them apart. These commonalities must, however, be

---

[15] Kant, *The Metaphysics of Morals*, 271.

set against quite different backgrounds. First, Aquinas nowhere sets persons in diametrical opposition to nature; instead, he refers to them as individuals of a rational nature and as most perfect in nature. We stand at the pinnacle of created, embodied nature; we thus recapitulate in ourselves the whole of nature and elevate bodily nature to a participation in our rational freedom. Thus, we can appropriate and direct the lower functions and capacities of nature in accord with the judgment of our reason. Second, Aquinas does not operate within the framework of a dichotomy between autonomy and heteronomy, at least in anything like Kant's formulation of the division. Aquinas would of course concur that if we are compelled by force to act or if we allow ourselves to be dominated by vicious rather than virtuous inclinations, we are no longer self-determined. But he speaks of human beings as "ruled rulers," whose self-determination is ensconced within and fostered by obedience to nature and God. The more we participate in the order established for us by God, the more free we are. This freedom is more than a liberation from an external and self-alienating law; it is, rather, a discovery of who and what we are as creatures. Indeed, to think of ourselves as utterly autonomous is to replicate the sins of pride and envy that undid the rebellious angels and our first parents.

In the whole order of embodied nature, human persons have an especially intimate relationship to the divine. The incommunicability of the person is underscored by the fact that each human soul is created immediately by God. Historically, the notion of the person as incommunicable is associated with the process of naming, whereby something stands forth as distinct from other things. We need only recall the importance of naming in the book of *Genesis*—for example, Adam's naming of the animals and God's renaming of Abram. If we are persons in our very origins, we are so by being called forth into existence in an especially personal way by our creator. Our very being is radically contingent, dependent on the free gift of a creator God. Our personal identity is realized not in autonomy but in being referred to the person who is our transcendent source. Aquinas observes that the human person is an *imago Dei;* our intellect and will reflect the divine. We are images of God insofar as we are dynamically and consciously ordered to the exemplar of the image, who is both source and goal of our life. Thus, community is in some sense prior to and constitutive of our individuality.

John Paul II's encyclical *Veritatis Splendor* concisely and eloquently addresses these issues of autonomy and heteronomy. To the
Kantian thesis, John Paul II responds that "obedience to God is not
. . . heteronomy, as if the moral life were subject to the will of something all-powerful, absolute, extraneous to man and intolerant of his
freedom. If in fact a heteronomy of morality were to mean a denial
of man's self-determination or the imposition of norms unrelated to
his good, this would be . . . nothing but a form of alienation, contrary
to divine wisdom."[16] Instead of heteronomy, we should speak of "theonomy or participated theonomy, since man's free obedience to divine law effectively implies that human reason and human will
participate in God's wisdom and providence."[17]

Aquinas's account of freedom is at odds not only with the classical,
liberal view of Kant, but also with the school of existentialism, whose
celebration of human freedom knows no limits. This school continues
the so-called humanistic reaction against the degrading determinism
of science and depicts all reliance on external standards as "bad
faith," a cowardly and immoral unwillingness to embrace our radical
freedom. In his *Existentialism and Human Emotions*, Jean-Paul Sartre traces our freedom to the absence of a God who creates and
knows natures. He echoes Dostoevsky's assertion that if there is no
God, all is possible.[18] The metaphysical doctrine of existentialism is
that existence precedes essence, that at first a human person is nothing and that whatever he or she becomes is the result of his or her
free self-fashioning. Thus, we are completely responsible for who we
are and cannot blame anyone (God, family, or society) or anything
(nature or law) for what we have become. Authentic experience of
our freedom involves anguish and the feeling of being forlorn. Thus,
Sartrean existentialism is fundamentally atheistic. If there were a creator God who made us according to some blueprint, then human
beings could be said to have a nature corresponding to a concept or
model in the divine mind. Because there is no creator God, "man
exists, turns up, appears on the scene, and, only afterwards, defines
himself. If man . . . is indefinable, it is because at first he is nothing.
Only afterward will he be something, and he himself will have made

---

[16] *Veritatis Splendor*, 57.
[17] *Veritatis Splendor*, 57.
[18] *Existentialism and Human Emotions*, 22.

what he will be. Thus, there is no human nature, since there is no God to conceive it. . . . Man is nothing else but what he makes of himself.[19]

Residual elements of Kant's conception of human dignity surface in Sartre's view that accentuating our radical self-creation evades any attempted articulation of human beings as objects possessing determinate, definable natures. Existentialism "gives man dignity" because it "does not reduce him to an object."[20] The universalist tenor of Kantian ethics perdures in Sartre's insistence that in creating ourselves we are creating an image of humanity as it ought to be. There is a tension, however, between the universalist thrust and the view of the moral life as a work of art.[21] Kant's conception of duty does not immediately invite comparisons with artistic self-creation. There is an unstated link between the two in the conception of autonomy as that which is free from all external restraint. If one gives up Kant's division between autonomy and inclination, then duty itself comes to seem an artificial imposition on autonomy. Here Nietzsche's remark that morality and autonomy are incompatible is prophetic. And once autonomy is construed as artistic self-creation, it is impossible to predict or limit the directions it might take: heroic sacrifice for the good of humanity or delight in the destruction of the innocent.

We might wonder, furthermore, whether existentialism liberates us from the shackles and dilemmas of modern science; it seems rather to entrench us more deeply in the dualisms we have inherited from Descartes. On the existentialist view, science can teach us nothing about what we are as human beings. Because the body is denigrated as merely biological, we lose any sense that we are animals. We are still lost in the cosmos with no proper place and without any clear limits on our use and manipulation of nature. Instead of safeguarding human dignity, existentialism deprives us of the ability to distinguish between an appropriate stewardship of nature and arbitrary tyranny over it. Indeed, there is an uneasy alliance between the emphasis on radical self-creation and the attempt to introduce moral limits by recourse to the notion that we are creating a universal norm. As I have already noted, the compatibility of these two asser-

---

[19] *Existentialism and Human Emotions*, 15.
[20] *Existentialism and Human Emotions*, 22.
[21] *Existentialism and Human Emotions*, 23 and 42.

tions is itself mere assertion. For Dostoevsky and Nietzsche, the denial of the existence of a creating and legislating God may well engender the aspiration for freedom understood as the raw exercise of power, exhibited in acts of spectacular destruction.

In its reaction against the degrading determinism of modern science, existentialism seems to recapture the sense of life as a drama. Its view, however, that we are nothing but what we make of ourselves at any moment dissolves the constituting continuity of a dramatic narrative. As Sartre puts it, we are "condemned at every moment to invent man."[22] If our choices involve at every moment the radical reconstruction of the self, then we are saddled with an atomistic view of human action and condemned to a paralyzing multiplication of possibilities. Habit could not be the basis of a virtuous character, but only an impediment to freedom.

There is, nonetheless, a sense in which Aquinas would subscribe to the priority of existence over essence. Created natures are dependent on their act of existence, which is a gracious gift of the creator God. This does not mean that nature or essence evaporates in the face of existence; nature remains the source of the intelligibility of substances. It means simply that our existence is contingent, dependent. What Thomas's existentialism unmasks is the false notion of the ego as self-constituting and self-sustaining. In itself, the self is nothing. Recall that it is only by wedding itself to the other in knowledge and in love that self exists in us at all. The fact that existentialism has given way to philosophical views that further dissipate the self, that treat it as a mere locus for the intersection of vectors of force and power, is not surprising. Having seen through the self, we encounter our nothingness. If we do not then encounter the person who is the creating and sustaining cause of our natures, we are left to the whims of our arbitrary and increasingly trivial choices.

The modern exaltation of freedom at the expense of nature and of our living relationship to a personal God begins by urging upon us the Herculean task of self-legislation but ends up reducing freedom to farce. If there is nothing either external to me or within my nature in light of which I might appraise my choices, then every choice validates (and thereby trivializes) itself. If Aquinas's view of the human person stands as an inviting alternative to the modern project, this

---

[22] *Existentialism and Human Emotions*, 23.

does not mean that his position can be easily understood or vindicated. Aquinas's emphatic statement that the will necessarily desires happiness (*ST*, I, 82, 1) sounds constraining to modern ears. According to Aquinas, the only sort of necessity that is repugnant to our voluntariness is that of force or coercion (*ST*, I-II, 10, 2). We are masters of our own actions by free choice of means not by determining ultimate ends for ourselves. We are who we are, ordered to goods appropriate to our nature, no matter what we may think or do. Aquinas is thus diametrically opposed to the popular view that our freedom consists in our capacity of radical self-creation. Of course, he does not mean that nature dictates one way of life for all; a variety of ways of life are compatible with the ends set for us by our nature. We can certainly act against our nature and frustrate its telos, or we can actively, consciously, and freely appropriate natural ends and in that sense "make" them our own. In what, then, does our freedom consist?

Some have wanted to see in Thomas's assertion that the will moves the intellect an inchoate acknowledgment of the autonomy of the will. Aquinas does indeed note that although the intellect moves the will by proposing ends to it, the will moves the intellect to the exercise of its own act (*ST*, I, 82, 4) and is even capable of moving itself (*ST*, I-II, 9, 3). He distinguishes between the specification of the act, which concerns the end and falls to the intellect, and the exercise of the act, which concerns agency and is under the control of the will. The role of the will in the exercise of intellectual acts is rightly seen as an important Augustinian contribution to Aquinas's generally Aristotelian view of human action. It allows Aquinas to reflect, in ways that Aristotle never does, on the ethical conditions of our exercise of our intellectual powers. Nowhere, however, does Aquinas countenance anything more than a relative and carefully circumscribed autonomy of the will. In fact, he derives freedom of choice from the "free judgment" of reason (*ST*, I, 83, 1). Every act of will is preceded by apprehension. The priority of the presentation of the good to the will underscores our dependence on an order of nature of which we are but a part. In its primordial relationship to things, the will does not act as an efficient cause moving things this way or that. Rather, it is drawn toward goods. Of course, the will is free to resist this attraction. To borrow a phrase from Yves Simon, we can say that the attraction undergone precedes the attraction freely chosen. Most defenders of Aquinas trace human freedom to the indeterminacy of reason, to its ability to consider a number of aspects of any object, its various desirable and undesirable features, and thus to revise its judgment about the goodness of any particular object.

What is common and deficient in these two approaches to human freedom is their essentially negative character. They accent the indeterminacy of intellect or of will or of both. Yves Simon coins the term *super-determination* as a more apt description of Aquinas's view of freedom. The indifference of judgment is rooted in the "natural super-determination of the rational appetite," which finds satisfaction not in any particular good but only in the universal good *(bonum in communi)*. The good in common or universal good is not an abstraction or an aggregate but the supreme good containing intensively all particular goods. Thus, the will's "inexhaustible ability to transcend any particular good" arises from its "living relationship to the comprehensive good." This relationship requires that the will "invalidate the claim of any particular good" to be the ultimate good.[23] To see the advantages of construing freedom as super-determination, one might ponder the difference between a virtuous and nonvirtuous, though not necessarily vicious, agent. We need to be careful here not to confuse Aquinas's conception of virtue as habit with our popular view of habit as the unreflective, mechanical, and rote performance of actions. Augustine thus speaks of sin as the "weight of habit" in his *Confessions*. A virtuous person will indeed possess a reliable character, but she or he will also act reflectively, be attuned to what is salient and peculiar in situations, and thus act in ways that could not be completely predicted, at least by those lacking the relevant virtue. With these caveats in mind, we do well to consider the following examples. In a situation that calls for the exercise of courage, someone who lacks the virtue of courage or possesses it imperfectly is likely to lack determination, to be torn between the options of courage and cowardice. The virtuous person by contrast will readily and with delight conform to what courage demands. Indeed, a perfectly virtuous person is incapable of knowingly acting otherwise. The question is, Who is more free in this circumstance? The one who lacks virtue and thus has an indeterminate will? Or the virtuous person whose will is super-determined?

---

[23] *Freedom of Choice*, 97–106 and 152–58.

One way to construe the shift from ancient to modern ethics is in terms of the accentuation of moral obligation in modernity, an emphasis accompanied by a greater reliance on law rather than on virtue. The emphasis is rooted in an early modern separation, which reached fruition in Kant, of the question of duty from the question of what is good for and perfective of the agent.[24] Although Kant was not the first to make such a claim, his texts have had the most palpable influence on modern moral discourse. Because Aquinas himself develops accounts not only of virtue but also of natural law, many contemporary moral philosophers find it difficult to locate him in the history of philosophy. Some see him as anticipating the modern turn to law. [25] What is his conception of law, and how does it affect his conception of human nature and human freedom?

LAW, FREEDOM, AND NATURE

To illustrate the distinctiveness of Aquinas's conception of law, it may help to compare his position with that of Francisco Suarez, one of his early modern commentators and critics. Throughout his writings, Thomas subordinates the question of duty to the question of the ends perfective of and naturally pursued by human beings. By modern standards, his conception of obligation seems impoverished, almost naive. He devotes no independent treatise, or for that matter no single *quaestio*, to the question of moral obligation. Suarez finds Thomas's relative silence on the issue discomforting. Yet although he criticizes Thomas's view, he fails to note that he and Thomas do not share the same universe of discourse. What Suarez is after—a theory of obligation—is not extant in Thomas's texts. In fact, Suarez contributes to the forgetfulness of the good in the history of ethics but is pivotal in the transition from Aquinas to Kant. A consideration, then,

---

[24] In his highly influential work, John Rawls states, "The two main concepts of ethics are those of the good and the right. . . . The structure of an ethical theory is . . . largely determined by how it defines and connects these two basic notions" (*A Theory of Justice*, 24).

[25] J. B. Schneewind and Alan Donagan think that Aquinas anticipates Kant, but these commentators import a modern, and therefore alien, conceptual scheme into their selective reading of Thomas. See J. B. Schneewind "The Divine Corporation and the History of Ethics," 173–91, and Alan Donagan, *The Theory of Morality*, 57–66.

of his theory will help elucidate the differences between Thomas and modern philosophers.[26] Having examined Suarez's position, we will consider Thomas's alternative view.

Francesco Suarez is often associated with the so-called late-medieval tradition of voluntarism. Although the divine will does play a decisive role in Suarez's theory of obligation, such a hasty classification does little to clarify the complexities of his thought. In *Natural Law and Natural Rights*, John Finnis attributes to Suarez a voluntarist view of obligation, a view that construes obligation in terms of "bonds created by acts of will."[27] Finnis dismisses voluntarism by saying that it leaves unanswered the question as to why we should obey God's will. Although Finnis's brief argument may successfully undermine the proponents of a radical voluntarism, it does not provide a sufficient refutation of every attempt to link obligation with divine commands or wishes. An adherent of the divine command theory of obligation might, for example, put forth convincing arguments concerning the nature of the divine attributes in an effort to circumvent the unwelcome consequences of a crude and arbitrary voluntarism. Clearly, theologians such as Scotus and Suarez, who are usually associated with voluntarism to one degree or another, would be at one with Thomas in their emphasis on the divine goodness. Though I will not elaborate on this point here, it certainly seems plausible that if God is necessarily good, one has sufficient reason to obey God's commands. This is but one possible rejoinder to the criticism Finnis has leveled against Suarez.

Still, one might wonder whether this approach does not commit Suarez to abandoning natural law altogether. That is, if divine commands are the source of moral obligation, is not all other moral knowledge spurious? Suarez does not think that the goodness or badness of an action is derived entirely or directly from God's will. His position is not so simple. Our knowledge of God's goodness presupposes a previous grasp of natural, human goodness. Suarez argues that only the obligation to obey the precepts is derived from God's will. That the precepts themselves can be known without any reference to revelation salvages the naturalness of the natural law. Accord-

---

[26] For a general comparison of Suarez and Thomas, see Walter Farrell, *The Natural Law according to St. Thomas and Suarez.*

[27] 45–49, 337–43.

ingly, Suarez makes a distinction between the knowledge of the precepts and the source of obligation. He writes, "This divine will, as either prohibitive or injunctive, is not the entire source of the goodness or evil which exists in the observation or transgression of the natural law, but necessarily presupposes in the acts themselves a certain fittingness or turpitude and adjoins to these the special obligation of divine law."[28]

What, then, does the divine volition add to the natural law? It clearly adds nothing to our knowledge of the content and the reasonableness of the natural law. Suarez says only that it adds a "special obligation." What does he mean by this? The divine volition introduces the authoritative force of sanctions that follow the transgression of the natural law—which, however, ironically returns us to the initial criticism John Finnis raised. Let me explain. In response to Finnis's objection, the divine command theorist had recourse to an argument for the goodness of God's commands. It turns out, however, that the reasonableness of the natural law is not derived from the reasonableness of divine intentions. The gap between goodness, which natural reason can apprehend without recourse to a commanding will, and obligation, which requires the intervention of the divine will, remains. Hence, the argument for God's goodness adds nothing substantive to Suarez's position regarding natural law.

Perhaps we should look elsewhere for the motivation behind Suarez's association of natural law with divine commands. Suarez holds that the judgment of reason regarding what is good or fitting does not in itself impose an obligation: "Law is that sort of authority that can impose an obligation. That judgment [of reason], however, imposes no obligation, but indicates what [obligation] should be supposed. Therefore the judgment, that it might have the form of law, should indicate a certain authority, from which such an obligation arises" (De Legibus, II, VI, 6). When Suarez refers to the judgment of reason (imperium rationis), he has Aquinas's view in mind, for Aquinas held that this judgment was a sufficient basis for the imposition of an obligation.[29] Suarez thinks it insufficient. His criticism is:

---

[28] I translate from the De Legibus ac Deo Legislatore, in Corpus Hispanorum de Pace, II, VI, 11.

[29] For a criticism of Suarez's action theory and a defense of the rational necessity of moral and legal obligations, see Finnis, Natural Law and Natural Rights, 297–343.

to judge that an action is good may well involve commending the action, but commending is not commanding. Law is truly obligatory only if there is an explicit connection between it and its origin in the will of a superior: "law in the rigorous sense . . . is said to be a general precept of a superior" (*De Legibus*, II, VI, 7). Thomas would certainly admit that the notion of a "command" involves the concepts of "superior" and "inferior." But Suarez goes further and seems to reduce obligation to the relationship between superior and inferior.

Suarez couples his analysis of command with the supposition that an obligation has some sort of efficacious force attached to it. In contrast to Thomas, who conceives of action primarily in terms of the final cause, Suarez construes human action in terms of efficient causality. He regularly refers to human action as the effect of a push or a force. Following Aquinas, Suarez asserts the reciprocity of intellect and will in human action, yet he fails to apply this teaching in his discussion of obligation. Instead, he distinguishes two elements of law as corresponding to the distinction between intellect and will. "If one attends to the power of moving in the law, then law is said to be that which in the ruler moves and obliges to action, and in this sense law is an act of the will. If, however, one focuses on and considers in the law the power of directing to that which is good and necessary, then law pertains to the intellect" (*De Legibus*, II, VI, 7). Suarez does indeed think that the goodness of an action is a precondition to its being obligatory, but his distinction between the judgment concerning the good and the fact of command foreshadows Kant's distinction between hypothetical and categorical imperatives. Suarez does not go so far as Kant; he thinks that the two categories converge, but that there is a modal difference between them. His view seems to be a hybrid of the Aristotelian and the Kantian. Reason can apprehend the good (Aristotle), but the apprehension of the good is an insufficient basis for obligation (Kant). In the end, Suarez must introduce the divine will as a sort of deus ex machina to ensure that the categories of the good and the right overlap.[30] The fortuitous convergence of obligation and goodness entails no intrinsic link between the two.

---

[30] The distinction between natural and divine law is tenuous indeed. As Suarez himself concludes, "natural law is true and proper divine law, whose legislator is God" (*De Legibus*, II, VI, 13). For a succinct statement of Suarez's position that locates him within the early modern debates over natural law, see Haakonssen, *Natural Law and Moral Philosophy*, 16–24.

It is precisely the absence of such a link that makes Kant possible. When one considers what one must do and not merely what it would be good to do, one adverts to the bare fact of command or to the fear of reprisal.[31] But the fact of command gives no reason for action, and sanctions supply only the most crude reason. And thus do we return to our initial dilemma.

The Suarezian disjunction of the obligatory and the good is not operative in Thomas's writings. On the contrary, the intrinsic link between the two permeates his discussion of law. In order to appreciate the difference between Aquinas and Suarez, it is necessary to consider the metaphysical and anthropological foundations of Thomas's position. Thomas's famous remark that the "natural law is a participation of the eternal law" (*ST*, I-II, 91, 2) has an Augustinian origin. This origin is clear from the frequent allusion to Augustine's *On the Free Choice of the Will*,[32] where Augustine argues that the eternal law is the rational pattern in the divine mind of all created things. The eternal law is the source of the natural law; as such, it is the ultimate ground for the intelligibility of the natural law. The eternal law, according to Thomas, is the locus of divine providence, and this rational governance of the universe has the character of law: "Granted that divine providence rules the world, . . . it follows that divine reason governs the entire community of the universe. The pattern itself of the governance of things, which exists in the divine mind as in the source of the universe, has the nature of law" (*ST*, I-II, 91, 1). Thomas describes God's legislative providence in this way: "the pattern of divine wisdom, as moving all things to their appropriate ends, has the nature of law" (*ST*, I-II, 93, 1). But divine causality does not erase or supplant secondary causality. God moves creatures by creating them and by endowing them with inclinations to ends congruent with their nature: "All things participate somewhat in the eternal law, insofar as from its impression they receive inclinations to appropriate acts or ends" (*ST*, I-II, 91, 2).

---

[31] These are the two modern alternatives; the former can be had in Kant and the latter in the tradition of legal positivism.

[32] See, for example, *ST*, I-II, 91, articles 1, 3, and 6, and I-II, 92, articles 1, 2, 3, and 6. This is not to say that Augustine is the sole or even the principal authority for the entirety of Thomas's teaching on law. Indeed, the question of sources is complicated by the presence of Isidore, Ulpian, and a host of medieval canonists. On the sources, see Odon Lottin, *Le droit naturel chez saint Thomas d'Aquin et ses predecesseurs*.

Thomas moves freely and with confidence from a vocabulary of laws to one of natures and inclinations. Indeed, he employs the latter to define the former. He does not, then, construe law in its initial or normative sense as propositional or deontological. He eschews any Kantian bifurcation of the natural and the rational. The natural law is an internal disposition toward what is good for and perfective of the agent. Misunderstood by many commentators, the force of the first principle—"do good, avoid evil"—is crucial. Daniel Nelson, for example, understands it as a factual comment about our always choosing apparent goods, not necessarily actual goods: "The standard version of natural law requires some natural pattern of love, some natural tendency . . . to a set of authentically good ends, to function normatively. The difficulty, however is that Thomas's statements about our . . . love of the good are regularly qualified by the observation that such a good is an *apparent* good. Whether or not actual goods appear good to us depends on right reason and virtue."[33] But it makes no sense to say that we desire anything under the formality of its being an apparent good. We always desire things as real goods, as perfective of our desires and capacities. As Ralph McInerny puts it, a "merely factual desire . . . does not exist."[34] The precept urges us to pursue what is truly good, to fulfill the formality under which we desire whatever we desire; thus, there is no illicit move from fact to value.[35] Because intellect and will are mutually operative in our natural orientation to the good, there is no way to separate out a pure apprehension of the good to which the will might be indifferent.

According to Thomas, the metaphysical foundations of moral obligation are not connected with divine commands in a Suarezian sense—that is, with an explicit revelation of moral precepts. Rather, God "commands" by inscribing tendencies within the natures of created beings. Creation itself involves the promulgation of the natural law (*ST*, I-II, 93, 5, ad 1, and I-II, 90, 4, ad 1). "God impresses the principles of proper acts on the whole of nature, and in this way God is said to command or to instruct [*praecipere*] the entire order of nature" (*ST*, I-II, 93, 5.). Law, as a directive principle of human acts, is woven into the natural orientation of human nature.

---

[33] *The Priority of Prudence*, 63.

[34] *Ethica Thomistica*, 38; see also 37–38 and 43–44.

[35] For a response to the accusation that Thomas commits the naturalistic fallacy, see Peter Simpson, "St. Thomas and the Naturalistic Fallacy."

One might object that I have exaggerated the differences between Suarez and Thomas, especially considering that Aquinas himself refers to commands as involving the relation of superior to inferior. The very definition of law, for instance, involves the notion that law must be promulgated by a proper authority. In his commentary on Aristotle's *On Interpretation,* moreover, Aquinas refers to the imperative mood as arising from the command of a superior. Yet in the *Summa,* he argues that, in expressing obligations, sentences in the imperative form are parasitic on those in the indicative form (*ST,* I-II, 17, 1). His grammatical observation is instructive. An ineliminable element in any command is its intelligibility. Even if the notion of command involves the relation of superior to inferior, it is not reducible to this relation. Instead, reason's apprehension that an action is one without which the good being pursued cannot be attained is sufficient to bind the agent. Aristotle's remark that we may call something necessary because without it a certain good could not be realized or some evil avoided (*Metaphysics,* 1015a, 22–26) helps clarify the sort of necessity operative here.

Contrary to Suarez, who envisions God as moving creatures by means of explicit commands, Thomas sees God as moving creatures through the avenue of creation by inscribing within them natural tendencies and desires toward certain ends. Obligation pertains primarily to what is rational and natural, and not to the commands of a superior. Or, rather, it is connected with the commands of a superior, but the construal of the mode of commanding is radically different from that in the Suarezian account.

Although Suarez does distinguish between God as first cause and God as the source of revelation, he associates moral obligation with only the second avenue of divine communication: "In one way is the natural law said to be from God as from the first cause; in another way it is said to be from God as from a legislator commanding and obliging" (*De Legibus,* II, Vl, 2). Thomas, on the contrary, grounds the obligatory force of God's explicit revelations in the natural and rational impulses of the original creation. Rational nature is, accordingly, the proximate source of obligation, whereas the pattern of God's creation, which Thomas identifies with the eternal law, is the ultimate source or ground of moral obligation. The primary sense in which God is said to command or to instruct (*praecipere*) creatures to follow certain patterns of behavior is through the act of creation.

The duality of the verb *praecipio* is crucial here—namely, its meaning both "command" and "teach." The superior thus simultaneously orders and instructs. God's commands clarify both the nature of the good and the means to attain it.

The sort of instruction that the natural law offers comes neither exclusively nor primarily in the form of propositions. Consider, for example, the problem of the sanctions accruing to the violation of the moral law. Sanctions are typically thought to be an important feature of the promulgation of a law; indeed, in a modern setting, where the natural intelligibility of law is put into serious question, sanctions come to occupy a more central and constituting role in law. On Aquinas's view, it is not clear what sanctions follow upon violations of the natural law; his position is that the crime is its own punishment, that vice deprives human beings of the virtues constitutive of human flourishing. Where, as is often the case, the deprivation of physical and material well-being does not follow vice, the punishment consists precisely in the vicious individual's being incited by success to sin further and thus to move further from her or his true good.[36] The sanctions of the natural law are thus more difficult to see than are those of the human law—and our obliviousness to them increases the more we violate the law. But this difficulty, which results from the intrinsic link between crime and sanction, has one advantage: we cannot separate crime from punishment and envision the latter as merely an extrinsic and arbitrary consequence of the former. This is the deeper meaning of the connection between command and instruction. To acknowledge the obligation of the natural law is to recognize and consciously to appropriate who and what we are.

Thomas's distinctive understanding of obligation is evident at the very outset of the treatise on law, where he defines law etymologically: "Law is a certain rule and measure of human acts on account of which someone is led [*inducitur*] to action or is held back from it. Law is so named from 'to bind' [*ligare*] because it obliges to action. The rule and measure, moreover, of human acts is reason, which is their first principle" (*ST*, I-II, 90, 1). Thomas highlights the intelligibility of law, which he associates with the rational apprehension of goods or ends. It is not merely that laws do in fact correspond to

---

[36] For a discussion of the sanctions accruing to the violation of the moral law, see Aquinas, *Summa contra Gentiles*, III, 141.

what is good and reasonable, but that this correspondence—or, rather, identity—is precisely what makes law normative and obligatory. Thomas stresses not only the rational character of law, but also the role of exhortation or persuasion: law is an inducement *(inducere)* to action.

Thomas's view of obligation reposes on a premodern conception of human action. Later, voluntarist thinkers criticize Thomas for identifying the command *(imperium)* of practical reason with an act of reason.[37] Thomas is uninterested, however, in the brute fact of command. He focuses instead on the fact that to command is always to command "something" and that this "something" is made known by an intimation or declaration of reason: "To command is an act of reason, presupposing an act of the will in virtue of which reason moves through the command to the exercise of the act" *(ST, I-II, 17, 1)*. The reference to an act of the will presupposed in reason's act of commanding evinces the close correlation of intellect and will in the practical order. The notion of presupposition is apt to mislead, however, because it gives the impression that the acts of reason and will are entirely separate and related only in a serial manner. When Thomas adds that "reason moves through the power of the will," he precludes such an interpretation. They are both simultaneously operative, although not in the same respect. This view of the mutual operation of intellect and will captures Aristotle's view of practical reason as "reasoning desire" or "desiring reason."

The discussion of human acts begins not with the *imperium* of practical reason, but with the *fruitio*, which marks the resting or complacency of the will in that which it sought *(ST, III, 11)*.[38] Practical reason, as Thomas puts it, begins from the future and reaches to that which is to be done now *(ST, I-II, 14, 5)*. The intention of the end precedes the securing of the end in execution. The account of intention as an act of the will is a mirror image of his account of *imperium* as an act of reason. Whereas the latter is an act of reason presupposing an act of the will, the former is an act of the will "presupposing

---

[37] Much of Harry Jaffa's criticism of Aquinas on natural law may be traced to his voluntarist assumptions about the nature of commands. See *Thomism and Aristotelianism,* 176–77.

[38] The discussion of human action has been influenced by Westberg, *Right Practical Reason,* and especially by Stephen Brock, *Action and Conduct: Thomas Aquinas and the Theory of Action.*

an ordinance of reason ordering something to an end" (*ST*, I-II, 12, 1, ad 3). As always, apprehension of an object must precede an intentional ordering of oneself to the object.

Once there is an intention of an end, there must be a choice of the appropriate means. In order to make a choice, which is an act of the will, an investigation of various possible means is often needed.[39] The *inquisitio* is an act of reason called *consilium*. The deliberative searching for an appropriate means to a desired end can also be understood in terms of universal and particular because deliberation involves the specification of an end in terms of a particular action. As I have already noted, precepts are as the ends to be realized in action; hence, deliberation also involves the movement from a precept to an instantiation of it in a particular act. This is not to say that there are two or three kinds of reasoning at work in deliberation, but that there is one sort of reasoning that is amenable to different descriptions. To counsel, Thomas adds another act preceding judgment and choice: *consensus*, which is an act of the will approving of or taking delight in appropriate means to an intended end. What seems superfluous is justified by the experience of taking counsel, which often ascertains many possible and appropriate means to a single end. In such cases, there is a clear distinction between consent, which approves of various means, and choice, which settles on one as that which is to be done (*ST*, I-II, 15, 3, ad 3).

In the movement from mere consent to choice, the activity of the intellect intervenes. Although choice is substantially an act of the will, it involves the activity of reason as well. The two concur in choice, which is materially an act of the will but formally an act of reason: "that act by which the will tends into something that is proposed as good, from which it is ordered to an end through reason, is materially an act of the will and formally of the reason" (*ST*, I-II, 13, 1).

The account of human action might naturally seem to terminate with choice. What could be left? As expressed in one objection to the postulation of an act of the will, which is called *usus*, subsequent to the command of reason, "after election nothing follows except execution" (*ST*, I-II, 16, 4, obj. 1). The distinction between choice and use arises from the will's dual relation to the thing willed. In the

---

[39] In *ST*, I–II, 14, 4, Thomas lists cases where deliberation and counsel are unnecessary, in which instances reason moves from intention to judgment and choice.

first, the thing willed is said to be present in the one willing it through a relation to the thing willed. But this procedure is to possess the end imperfectly, merely through intention. To possess the end perfectly and really, the will must tend to the thing willed so as to attain it. The tending of the will to the thing itself consists in an application of oneself to the action. The application, from which follows execution, is called *usus*. Once again, intellect and will are mutually operative: "use is primarily of the will as first mover, but it is of reason as directing the act" (*ST*, I-II, 16, 1). The rational act preceding and directing *usus* is *imperium*. Thomas's statement that the *imperium* sometimes (*aliquando*) precedes use in time indicates that its priority is not primarily temporal and that the two acts typically operate simultaneously (*ST*, I-II, 17, 3). As with all the other stages of practical reason, the separation of the acts of reason from those of the will leads to one of two unwelcome consequences: either the will is viewed as having no constitutive role in action, as thoroughly determined by the intellect, or the will is left "free" to choose whether to follow reason. Determinism or voluntarism, respectively, is the result. What, then, is the role of the *imperium* preceding *usus?* As Daniel Westberg puts it, "the function of the *imperium* is to be the rational link between *electio* and *usus:* to 'make sure' that the specific action chosen by the agent (and none other) is what is indeed carried out."[40]

The reciprocity between reason and will pervades the account of human action. As Thomas puts it elsewhere, "will and intellect mutually include one another" (*voluntas et intellectus mutuo se includunt; ST*, I, 16, 4, ad 1). On such a basis rests the explanation of the voluntary nature of human action. In order for something to be voluntary, it must be moved by an intrinsic principle to an end of which it has knowledge. The will is a "moved mover" (*movens motum*). The intellect moves the will not in the order of exercise but in the order of determination or specification. Whatever is in potency to many is reduced to act by that which is in act; the "object moves by determining the act in the mode of a formal principle" (*obiectum movet determinando actum ad modum principii formalis; ST*, I-II, 9, 1). Despite Thomas's consistent affirmation of reason as the source of the will's freedom, at least one recent commentator finds in the distinction between specification and exercise the grounds for supposing that

---

[40] *Right Practical Reason,* 181.

the will is autonomous.[41] James Keenan proposes that because the will moves the intellect, it must be autonomous: "as first mover, the will's movement is independent of and prior to reason's presentation of the object."[42] The thesis seems compatible with Thomas's claim that the will moves reason and suggests a way around the problem of an infinite regress of reciprocal acts of reasoning and willing. Thomas himself never makes this move, however. His account of how the act of reason can be commanded ultimately reduces not to the autonomy of the will but to reason's ability to "reflect upon itself" and "to order its own act" (*ST*, I-II, 17, 6). Reason does so through the mediation of the will, of course. Thomas explicitly poses the problem of an infinite regress. He gives a number of responses to the difficulty, responses that appear to be inconsistent. In a passage from the *prima pars*, he states that "it is not necessary to proceed into infinity, but it stands in the intellect as in a beginning. Apprehension must precede every motion of the will, but a motion of the will need not precede every apprehension" (*ST*, I, 82, 4, ad 3). In another passage, he states that "in its first movement the will proceeds from the instinct of some exterior mover" (*in primum motum voluntatis voluntas prodeat ex instinctu aliquius exterioris moventis; ST*, I-II, 9, 4). Some see the shift from the intellect as first mover of the will to an external first mover as introducing the possibility that the will can move immediately without the mediation of the intellect. Even were the first act of the will not directly dependent on reason, the will would nonetheless be moved by another.[43] A description of the movement of the will by an exterior and superior cause counts against the autonomy of the will because it depicts the will as a natural participant in goodness and being. A germane passage runs thus: "the first act of the will is not from the ordination of reason, but from the instinct of nature or a superior cause" (*primus autem voluntatis actus ex rationis ordinati-*

---

[41] James F. Keenan, *Goodness and Rightness in Thomas Aquinas's* Summa Theologiae.

[42] *Goodness and Rightness*, 47.

[43] The purported autonomy of the will undergirds Keenan's thesis that the *Summa Theologiae* introduces a distinction between the good and the right. Rightness concerns the conformity of one's actions to reason, whereas goodness consists in striving to attain rightness. Keenan sees charity as a striving, a matter of motivation and goodness, which seeks without necessarily attaining rightness. Virtue, then, has to do with rightness, not goodness. For a counter to this view, see James Doig, "The Interpretation of Aquinas's Prima Secundae."

one non est, sed ex instinctu naturae aut superioris causae; ST, I-II, 17, 5, ad 3). The will is always already in a position of being oriented to the good. The will's natural inclination to the general good is not, however, a sufficient cause of action; in order to act, the inclination must be presented with a specific object, which is done by reason.

The "root of liberty" *(radix libertatis),* then, is in the will as a subject, but in the intellect as cause because freedom presupposes the openness of the intellect to many different things and the ability to apprehend ends as suitable or unsuitable to one's nature. The philosophers, Thomas notes, associate "free choice" *(liberum arbitrium)* with the "free judgment of reason" *(liberum de ratione iudicium; ST,* I-II, 17, 1, ad 2). A similar line of reasoning provides the response to the question whether choice occurs freely or necessarily *(ST,* I-II, 13, 6). The will is called a rational appetite because it participates in reason's indeterminacy. It can wish or not wish; it can also wish this or that. Because reason can apprehend any of these alternatives as good, the will is not necessitated. No particular good, moreover, can determine the will, for every particular good can be regarded as defective in some respect: "If any good is not good according to all the particulars which can be considered in it, it will not move of necessity to the determination of the act. Someone can will its opposite."[44] Although reason determines the will by presenting it with an object, without which there would be nothing to be chosen, reason itself is not determined to any particular object. In the contingent order of practical reason, conclusions do not always follow of necessity from principles; that is so only in cases where a single mean is that without which an end cannot be realized *(ST,* I-II, 13, 6, ad 1).

Now it might seem to follow from the assertion that we deliberate only about means, not about ends, that a great deal of human action is thereby circumscribed or determined. Although intention is of the end alone and choice of the means alone, there is a certain relativity in their relationships. In arguing that intention is not only of the ultimate end, Thomas notes that the beginning of one part of motion is sometimes the end of another. What is an end in one respect and thus an object of intention can from another vantage point be a means to some other end and thus an object of deliberation and choice. Similarly, choice can be an end so long as it is not the ultimate

---

[44] Aquinas, *De Malo,* 6, 1, in *Quaestiones Disputatae,* vol. 2.

end, but one that is ordered to a further end (*ST*, I-II, 13, 3). Short of the ultimate end, there is ample room for deliberation concerning proximate ends that are subordinate to other ends: "It happens that what is an end with respect to some things is itself directed to a further end, just as the conclusion of one demonstration is the principle of another. What is an end in one investigation can be a means in another and thus there can be counsel about it" (*ST*, I-II, 14, 2). The contention that the same object of practical reason can from one vantage point be an end and from another a means is crucial to Aristotle's understanding of the unity of human life and of how the pursuit of a plurality of goods can be unified and ordered. In the *Ethics*, Aristotle speaks of three kinds of goods: those that are merely instrumental to other goods, those that are desirable for their own sake and serve no other end, and those that are both desirable as ends in themselves and as contributing to further goods (*Ethics*, I, 7, 1097a15–35). He speaks of the virtues as means to happiness and as ends in themselves. Expanding on Aristotle's point about the peculiar means-end relationship between the virtues and happiness, Aquinas notes that "wisdom or prudence is not compared to happiness as the medical art is to health, as health is to healthy activities. The medical art produces health as an exterior work brought about, but health brings about healthy activities by the use of the habit of health. However, happiness is not a work externally produced but an operation proceeding from the habit of virtue" (*In Libros* Ethicorum, VI, lectio 10, note 1267).

This alternative conception of means-to-end reasoning opens up the possibility of a richer understanding of freedom. Indeed, freedom understood as indifference or indeterminacy fails to account for a paradox at the heart of an ethics of virtue. Although the habit of virtue is not deterministic in a mechanistic sense, as if it involved mindlessly performing acts by rote, it is the case that one who possesses a virtue will not knowingly be able to act against the virtue. This, you may recall, is a salient difference between moral virtue and the virtues of art or skill. But how is such necessity compatible with freedom? Yves Simon responds that we need to expose "the fallacy of freedom conceived as indeterminacy" and explain "free choice as mastery over ends as well as the means leading to these ends."[45] What

---

[45] *Moral Virtue*, 78. This is what Pinckaers calls the "freedom for excellence." See *The Sources of Christian Ethics*, 327–99.

he seems to have in mind is Aristotle's conception of human excellence as a reflective appropriation not just of the ends or goods to
which one is naturally inclined, but also of the ordered interrelation-
ships among the goods. Such self-appropriation is not forced on the
agent, but it results in the cancellation of certain possible ways of
acting—namely, those incompatible with excellence of character. As
I have noted, Simon calls this alternative conception of freedom
"super-determination." Here is a more ample statement of his thesis:

> Freedom is super-determination rather than indetermination, . . . its
> principle is more highly and more certainly formed than that of deter-
> minate causality; freedom proceeds, not from any weakness, any im-
> perfection, any feature of potentiality on the part of the agent but, on
> the contrary, from a particular excellence in power, from a plenitude
> of being and an abundance of determination, from an ability to achieve
> mastery over diverse possibilities, from a strength of constitution that
> makes it possible to achieve one's end in a variety of ways. In short,
> freedom is an active and dominating indifference.[46]

A different sort of objection is sometimes raised against Thomas's
view of deliberation—that it has a sort of naive intellectualism in
overlooking the often egregious gap between deliberation and action.
But Aquinas does not divorce reason from volition; he is acutely
aware that the course of deliberation can be derailed in many ways.
His insistence on the intimate connection between intellect and will
allows for a complex and nuanced account of moral error. Emphasizing the crucial role of character in our apprehension of the good, he
quotes Aristotle: "as someone is, so does the end appear to him"
(*qualis unusquisque est, talis finis videtur ei; ST,* I-II, 9, 2). He adds,
"Something seems good and fitting from two causes, from the condition of what is proposed and from the one to whom it is proposed"
(*ST,* I-II, 9, 2). Because moral deliberation has to do with particulars,
the passions of the sensitive appetite, which concern particulars, directly affect the course of deliberation. Although the will is not
moved of necessity by the lower appetites, the passions can influence
the will on the part of the object. Such influence occurs when someone judges something to be good on account of passion, something
that in the absence of passion she or he would not deem good (*ST,*
I-II, 10, 3). Disorder can occur in each of the stages of practical

---

[46] *Freedom of Choice,* 152–53.

reasoning—intention, deliberation, judgment, and execution. Any sort of disorder involves not simply disordered passion or weakness of will but also error in the intellect, which is imprudence: "there is no sin without a defect, resulting from imprudence, in some act of reason directing" (ST, II-II, 53, 2). Weakness of will is not just a matter of the will being overcome by passion, wherein the sensitive appetite interrupts the movement in the practical syllogism from universal to particular. Instead, Thomas describes the weak as substituting a different major premise and thus reasoning "rationally" to an intemperate act. One can act for reason while acting against reason.[47] Insofar as reason is not wholly clouded over (obnubiletur) by passion, reason remains free to reconsider, to conquer the passion, or to keep itself from following passion (ST, I-II, 10, 3, ad 2). Describing the state of internal division and conflict resulting from disordered passion, Thomas writes, "in such a disposition, because man is disposed differently according to the diverse parts of his soul, one thing appears to him according to reason and another according to passion" (ST, I-II, 10, 3, ad 2). That passions and habits influence the entirety of the moral life is an important implication of Thomas's account of moral knowledge. Were it not for our natural inclination toward what is good, moral judgment would lose its hold on us.

This brief summary of the anthropological underpinnings of obligation enables us to describe the contrast between Thomas and Suarez in yet another way. Suarez explicates the moving force of moral obligation in terms of efficient causality, whereas Thomas places it under the category of final causality. The Thomistic schema runs thus: (a) human beings have at least an inchoate desire for the end; (b) the laws provide further instruction concerning the end; and (c) submission to these laws facilitates the achievement of the end. The last statement, which sounds as if precepts are merely instrumental, requires qualification. The role of the precepts can be clarified by adverting to the order of moral education. Often moral education is seen as starting with absolutes, necessary for unsophisticated youth, and then moving to a prudential appreciation of the merely instrumental and provisional character of the precepts. Thomas would describe moral development somewhat differently. Our initial understanding of moral precepts is likely to be primarily negative and

---

[47] See Westberg, Right Practical Reason, 207–15.

somewhat instrumental. We acknowledge that if we are to become persons capable of virtuous behavior, we need to avoid all actions that are destructive of the habit of virtue. In the process of becoming virtuous, we come to see more clearly the meaning and scope of the precepts, many of which are merely provisional. If we come to understand more fully what is required of us beyond conformity to rules, we also come to see that some precepts are more than merely instrumental or provisional, that they are constitutive of the goods that the virtues themselves aim at and embody. To distinguish among the precepts—to understand their relationships to one another—requires more than the knowledge provided by prudence; it also requires a knowledge of the institutional structures of our regime, of the way the common good is peculiarly embodied in our politics. Natural law needs not only the virtues but also political philosophy.

Thomas's vocabulary cuts across and is at variance with the Kantian categories. Thomas ties obligations to actions or pursuits necessary for, appropriate to, and perfective of human nature.[48] His view of obligation conforms to neither the hypothetical nor the categorical imperative, although it contains elements of each. Like the hypothetical imperative, it makes reference to desires or inclinations. Like the categorical imperative, it views certain obligations as nonnegotiable. The failure to conform to the Kantian division is hardly a disadvantage. Although Kantian theories of moral obligation can judge violations of the moral law in more severe tones, such an approach overlooks the resources of common moral language to appraise actions. Why is another sense of obligation necessary beyond the recognition that one must act and that natural law precepts are reasonable guides to action? Is obligation necessarily extrinsic to the recognition of what is good or best in a particular set of circumstances? Such a dichotomy is alien to our common manner of moral deliberation. As Peter Geach puts it, "Now what a man cannot fail to be choosing is his manner of acting; so to call a manner of acting good or bad cannot

---

[48] In his study of the sources of Thomistic natural law, Lottin concludes that the distinctiveness of Thomas's view is the emphasis on the intrinsic character of the law. He writes, "The law is nothing other than the rational expression of human nature. This is Aristotelian dynamism applied to the moral order" (*Le droit naturel chez Saint Thomas d'Aquin et ses predecesseurs*, 103). This emphasis is the key to one of the differences between Thomas and Suarez. Whereas Suarez nearly collapses the distinction between natural and divine law, Thomas refuses to do so.

but serve to guide action. . . . any man has to choose how to act, so calling an action good or bad does not depend for its effect as a suasion on any peculiarities of desire."[49] What is the difference between saying that an action is in all cases unreasonable or unjust and saying that the action ought not to be performed? Would it make any sense, moreover, to say that a certain course of action is the *right* one, but that another course of action is a *better* or the *best* one?[50]

Moral philosophers who create a chasm between the good and the right are bereft of the resources needed to make commands intelligible to moral agents. They are unable to provide a link between commands and the agent's desires and interests. From this omission, it might seem that Thomas would concur with Bernard Williams's statement that there are only internal reasons for action and "no external reasons for action." That is, there are no reasons or motives wholly independent of the desires that an agent presently has or can be led to have on the basis of desires she or he already has.[51] Thomas does indeed accept some such view, but he has a more complex account of the way we can come to have new desires than Williams's Humean account allows. Just as the disparity between Thomas's obligation and Kant's categorical imperative does not entail that the former is a kind of hypothetical imperative, so the repudiation of reasons utterly independent of desire does not entail that there is no sense in which reasons can be called objective. What is missing in contemporary attempts to revitalize Aristotle in the language of hypothetical imperatives and internal reasons is any serious reflection on the teleological view of human action—on action as directed not just to particular ends but to the inculcation of habits of character perfective of the agent. For Aristotle and Aquinas, moral training moves us from where we are now, with our partly formed and partly malformed character, to a possession and practice of the virtues. As I mentioned previously, participation in communal practice of the virtues and submission to mature practitioners of the virtues are indispensable to our progress in the life of virtue. Thus, we can have complicated sorts of desires, desires to have desires that we do not presently possess

---

[49] "Good and Evil," 71.

[50] It might make sense to say that an action is a good one, but that it is not the right one, even if the converse is false.

[51] "Ought and Moral Obligation," in *Moral Luck*, 123. For a critique of Williams, see MacIntyre's review of *Moral Luck*, "The Magic in the Pronoun 'My.' "

but that our exemplars do. Insofar as we understand our life to be a pursuit of the best life available to us, to the sort of beings we are, we aspire to a life that is universally and objectively the best. We can also accept on the basis of such a teleology of desire certain imperatives that cross over the Kantian divide. That is, such obligations are at once "categorical" or exceptionless and "hypothetical" or desire dependent; they inform us about activities that cannot be described as pursuit of the virtues.

If, in contrast to the quasi-scientific characterizations of obligation in modernity, Thomas's remarks should appear primitive, it is because his view presupposes a moral anthropology that had fallen into desuetude by Suarez's time. The consonance of obligation and virtue can be seen in Thomas's account of the way good is a moving force, something that obliges to action. This account lies behind the fundamental precept of the natural law: good is to be done and pursued, but evil is to be avoided. The principle has a status in the practical order similar to that of the principle of contradiction in the speculative order. Neither principle functions as a premise in a syllogism; instead, they are presupposed in every syllogism. Just as the principle of contradiction is the ultimate answer to the question why the basic principles of any science are accepted as true, so too the first principle of the practical order is the ultimate reason why any precept or act is considered desirable. "Do good, avoid evil" undergirds the intelligibility and desirability of all the practical precepts. In this way, all precepts result from *synderesis*, the habit of the principles of practical reason.

There is no divide between virtues and precepts. The precepts of the natural law command the acts of the virtues. Both are described as the ends of action. In an article that asks whether prudence establishes the end in the moral virtues, Thomas clarifies the relationships among prudence, *synderesis*, and the moral virtues. He writes, "the ends of the moral virtues preexist in reason . . . as principles naturally known; of this sort are the ends of the moral virtues because the end in action is as the principle in speculative matters" (*ST*, II-II, 47, 6). The identification of the ends at which the virtues aim with the principles of the practical order is explicit. The role of prudence concerns not ends but means, not primarily universals but particulars. If the ends are established by the first principles of practical reason, prudence assists in preparing the way for the realization of the ends "by disposing those things ordered to the end." Thomas concludes, "prudence, which is more noble than the moral virtues, moves them, but *synderesis* moves prudence, as the understanding of principles moves science" (*ST*, II-II, 47, 6, ad 3). *Synderesis* moves prudence, not in the sense that practical reasoning deduces its conclusions from the first principles held by *synderesis*, but in the sense that the principles of *synderesis* govern all precepts. The natural inclination to the good, articulated in the foundational principle of the practical order, moves the entire process of practical reasoning. As the habit of principles, *synderesis* is cognitive; as inclining to the good and recoiling from evil, it is affective (*ST*, I, 79, 12). Prudence must operate in light of some end, an end that operates in the practical order as a principle does in the speculative order. As we have just seen, Thomas describes these ends or principles of action alternately as the precepts of *synderesis* and as the virtues. The authoritative command of what is to be done in any action remains for prudence and not for *synderesis*.

Thomas's depiction of prudence gives content to the seemingly elusive image of the good person. Prudence is not only an ability to discern and apply the germane principle in concrete and variable circumstances. It also enables one to act as one ought: "Not only the consideration of reason pertains to prudence, but also the application to an action, which is the goal of practical reason" (*ST*, II-II, 47, 3.). The prudential link between perception and action presupposes rectified appetite, which ensures that practical reason will issue not in an option or even in a decision, but in an action. The various stages in human action are all at the disposal of prudence: "to prudence pertains rightly to counsel, to judge and to command of those things through which one reaches a due end" (*ST*, II-II, 47, 10). The chief act of prudence (*principalis actus prudentiae*) is to issue commands or to instruct (*praecipere; ST*, II-II, 47, 8). The dual meaning of the term *praecipio* surfaces once again. Prudence is prescriptive because its judgments are authoritative. This authority is not owing to some sort of calculative expertise, but rather is tied to its pedagogical power. Prudence is the mark of the morally educated human being; its concrete embodiment in human character presents an instructive example of practical wisdom.

The intertwining of the language of obligation with that of the virtues reveals the distance that separates Thomas from his modern interlocutors.[52] Whereas for Suarez a voluntarist theory of obligation explains the transition from perception to action, Thomas holds that virtue secures the link between the two. The moral precepts, according to Thomas, are impotent apart from some notion of human perfection and of the virtues constitutive of the human good. He wants to turn our attention from the enervating topic of obligation to the more interesting and more rewarding question of the good life for human beings. If we wish to know how we ought to live, we should begin by asking not what obligations we have, but what the good is for human beings. Only from this vantage point can we appreciate the Thomistic alternative.

---

[52] Stanley Hauerwas observes that "the language of commands tends to be inherently occasionalistic with a correlative understanding of the self as passive and atomistic." Thus, a moral theory that gives preeminence to the language of commands is apt to diminish the role of character and virtue. See *Character and the Christian Life*, 43.

2

Precepts, Prudence, and Politics

THE INVESTIGATION of the human things in Aristotle runs from the *De Anima* through the *Ethics* and *Politics* (and related texts such as *Rhetoric* and *Poetics*). In the preceding chapter, I have attended to the anthropological foundations of Aquinas's thought, but we have yet to consider the properly ethical portion of his work. Although the study of human nature remains dormant in contemporary philosophy, the study of ethics, especially the ethics of virtue, seems to be flourishing. Contemporary proponents of virtue draw freely on Aristotle and Aquinas, but they tend to isolate ethics from politics and thus to separate what Aquinas and Aristotle link. The consequence is that ethics itself is distorted. In this chapter, I hope to restore a bit of balance to the discussion of ethics in Aquinas by locating that discussion within a larger political context.

In most treatments of the history of ethics, Thomas still surfaces primarily as a proponent of natural law. Recently, more attention has been given to his discussions of the virtues, especially prudence, but most of these treatments suffer from an opposite defect: neglect of the role of moral precepts in practical reasoning.[1] Rarer still is the attempt to show how the precepts and the virtues are but parts of an encompassing theological ethics.[2] In this chapter, I focus on the moral precepts, on their relationship to the virtues, and on the political context in which Thomas situates both law and virtue. Then, in the final chapter, I turn to the theological elements of Aquinas's ethics.

---

[1] See, for example, Westberg's *Right Practical Reason,* which focuses on the neglected role of prudence in Aquinas. Ralph McInerny in *Ethica Thomistica* offers an account of the unity of precepts and prudence in Aquinas, as does Pamela Hall in *Narrative and Natural Law.* See also the recent essays by Maria Carls, "Law, Virtue, and Happiness," and Rev. Robert Gahl, "From the Virtue of a Fragile Good to a Narrative Account of Natural Law."

[2] Pinckaers's *Sources of Christian Ethics* is a noteworthy exception.

In spite of Aquinas's emphasis on prudence and because of his simultaneous emphasis on precepts, many commentators find his view to be un-Aristotelian and hence not fully appreciative of the role of prudence in the moral life. The typical view of Aristotle runs thus. Aristotle offers nothing like a system of rules, action in accordance with which would constitute rational behavior. He explicitly rejects the possibility of a systematic account in ethics (*Ethics*, VI, 8, 1142a23–4). The most Aristotle says is that there is a certain universal stability to moral matters. In his discussion of justice, for instance, he argues that natural justice "has the same force [*dunamis*] everywhere" (*Ethics*, V, 7, 1134b17–1135a5). Interestingly, in his commentary on the *Ethics*, Aquinas takes the passage as a point of departure for a discussion of the foundations of moral knowledge. He likens the structure of practical reason to that of speculative reason, wherein first principles are indemonstrable and naturally known (*In Libros* Ethicorum, V, lectio 12). Many see Thomas's comments as a fundamental betrayal of Aristotle's intentions, as a substitution of a geometrical model of reasoning for Aristotle's prudential approach.[3] Before turning to an extended examination of Thomas's view of prudence, we must confront a number of obstacles, the most notable of which is that the centerpiece of his ethics appears to be natural law, not virtue. Indeed, Thomas deploys an apparently un-Aristotelian analogy between moral reasoning and the deductive order of speculative reason.

Most treatments of Aquinas on law begin in the treatise on law in the *Summa Theologiae* and remain there. Our contention is that such a focus misses the extension of the moral teaching into the virtues. The problem is that the passages on the precepts of the natural law have typically been read in isolation from the rest of Thomas's moral teaching. Cut off from that whole, the discussion of law becomes problematic, if not unintelligible. Numerous difficulties in the account of law can be remedied by paying closer attention to the fertile discussion of prudence. Thomas here anticipates contemporary criticisms of exclusively rule-based ethical theories. Yet he does not neglect the important role of precepts and laws, and thus he is in a better position than are most contemporary virtue ethicists to re-

---

[3] See, for example, Jaffa, *Thomism and Aristotelianism*, 176. In contemporary virtue ethics, this is a standard objection to rule-based ethical theories. The supposition remains firm even in sympathetic readings of Kant, such as that in Nancy Sherman's *Making a Necessity of Virtue.*

spond to criticisms of virtue-based ethical theories. The amplitude of Thomas's ethics is best seen in his discussion of the virtue of justice, to which corresponds a determinate set of precepts. Justice not only unites law and virtue, but also links ethics and politics.

FROM LAW TO PRUDENCE

A careful reading of the discussion of law indicates that the so-called treatise on law is but a fragment of a larger whole. The articles on the natural law are dialectical in tone. Thomas appears to be at once asserting and qualifying the universal recognition of the precepts of the natural law. In 94, 2, he compares the order of speculative reason to that of practical reason. After he calls self-evident any proposition whose predicate is contained within the notion of the subject, he adds the following qualification: "It happens, however, that such a proposition will not be known through itself for one who is ignorant of the definition of the subject." He then offers an example. The proposition "man is rational" is known through itself according to its nature, but to one who does not know what a man is *(quid sit homo)* the proposition is not known through itself *(ST,* I-II, 94, 2). The phrase *quid sit homo* should call to mind the *Posterior Analytics* and its elaborate treatment of definition. The recognition of the necessity of a proposition hinges, then, on a precedent grasp of the definition in question. Because definition is a matter of understanding essences or natures, as we have seen, such knowledge can be had only empirically. As P. Hoenen puts it, "This cognition of the terms is a condition which is required but which is not sufficient, for beyond this it is necessary that the nature itself of the nexus be investigated in the concrete case."[4] *Intellectus,* like Aristotle's *nous,* operates on experience, not in isolation from it.

In *ST,* I-II, 94, 4, just two articles after Thomas introduces the comparison between the structures of speculative and practical reasoning, he qualifies it further. The article comprises a series of contrasts between the two modes of reasoning, the most notable contrast being that speculative reason has as its object necessary things, whereas practical reason operates in the realm of the contingent. The

---

[4] "De Origine Primorum Principiorum Scientiae," 180.

thrust of the argument is that although everyone equally knows the "common notions of the soul" *(communes conceptiones animae)*, the more we descend to particulars, the less helpful such an unqualified precept will be. There seem to be two sorts of difficulties here. The first concerns the common precepts, which are exceptionless but are somewhat removed from the level of particularity and hence rarely enter directly into deliberation. The second concerns the proper principles, about which Thomas writes, "Insofar as many particular conditions are introduced, the more likely it is that a principle will fail" (*ST*, I-II, 94, 4). He adds, "If in common matters there is a certain necessity, the more one descends to proper matters, the more a defect is found" (*ST*, I-II, 94, 4). Why is this so? The weakness here is the opposite of that accruing to the common principles; with the proper principles, the more conditions one adds, the more specific the principle becomes and the narrower is its scope. Consequently, the more useless the precept is as a guide for action because it covers fewer cases.

The analogy between the structures of speculative and practical reasoning, then, is not nearly as strict as one might initially have thought. At one point in this article, Thomas explicitly contrasts moral and mathematical knowledge (*ST*, I-II, 94, 4). From this contrast, we can infer that demonstrative knowledge will be rare in ethics. Suggesting a different sort of analogy, he likens the defects in moral principles to the way in which things in nature occur in most cases, but not in all. We must be careful not to overstate the qualification. There is necessity operative even in contingent matters, and practical reasoning has truth as its proper object. It is simply that the truth of practical order differs from the truth of the speculative order. How so?

Behind the qualification of the universal applicability of the natural law lie three Aristotelian motifs, each of which illustrates the reciprocity of law and virtue. First, because ethical judgments are of particulars, we cannot deduce the judgment of particulars from universal precepts. Not only the particular, in which action terminates, but also the precept is derived from experience. The image of mapping abstract ideas onto unformed matter, which is dominant in the account of art or *techne*, is misleading in the realm of action. Instead, the precepts emerge from reason's reflections on and judgment about the goods to which human life is ordered. Second, the recognition of the precepts of the natural law has much to do with proper education. Thomas echoes Aristotle's conviction that only those who have been well brought up will profit from ethical instruction (*Ethics,* II, 3, 095a1–10). It follows that a knowledge of general precepts, such as the natural law provides, cannot ensure that one will behave ethically. There can be a gap between the knowledge of precepts and action—a gap not possible between the knowledge of a virtuous character and action, or between the virtuous person's possession and use of the knowledge. This is but one important implication of the definition of virtue that Aquinas borrows from Augustine: virtue is that "by which we live rightly of which no one can make bad use" (*ST,* I-II, 55, 4). Third, laws are to be understood in terms of the ends of human action, which we are already at least implicitly pursuing as individuals and as members of communities: "the order of the precepts of the natural law corresponds to the order of the natural inclinations" (*ST,* I-II, 94, 2). Where we as individuals and communities fall short of meeting the standards of the moral precepts, there is still the possibility of a dialectical engagement because we cannot choose any action except under the formality of the good. In the same passage where Thomas asserts the connections between precepts and inclinations, he also lists a hierarchy of goods on which the precepts are based. There are, first, goods such as self-preservation that humans share with all substances; second, there are inclinations to goods such as sexual intercourse and the raising of offspring that humans have in common with other animals; finally, there are the goods proper to the human species—for example, to live in society and to know the truth about God. Because these goods are general and positive, there is an endless variety of ways in which they might be fulfilled; although Aquinas holds that there are specific ways in which humans can utterly fail to pursue these goods, he does not suppose that they can derive a set of absolute, positive precepts from the list. Yet the list of inclinations, upon which repose the precepts of the natural law, suggests a background for all of human action and thus provides various avenues of entry for the dialectical engagement of particular customs and practices.

The fundamental precepts are inviolable, but—because of their generality—they remain in need of further clarification. In this way, the precepts become amenable to practical application. The consideration of additional or unforeseen circumstances may engender a reformulation of the secondary precepts, which "can be changed either in some particular case or in rare occurrences on account of special causes impeding its observance" (*ST*, I-II, 94, 5). Such passages on the mutability of the secondary precepts and on the difficulty of applying them to concrete circumstances have perplexed many commentators.[5] Thomas himself posits this relation between primary and secondary precepts: "to the natural law pertains, first, certain most common precepts, known to all, and, second, certain secondary and more proper precepts, which are like conclusions following closely upon primary principles" (*ST*, I-II, 94, 6). Thomas associates the derivation of detailed precepts from the natural law with the promulgation of human law. This association occurs in two ways: "in one way, as conclusions from principles; in another way, as certain determinations [*determinationes*] of common principles."

The procedure appropriate to the first way is similar to that of demonstrative science. There are instances when derivations from the natural law can be made in a straightforward way. The precept that we must not kill, for example, can be derived from the principle that evil should be done to no one (*ST*, I-II, 95, 2). Even in these cases, an assessment of the particular is necessary, an assessment that the precept itself cannot provide. In many other cases, however, natural law will provide only an important background to the prudential artistry of the legislator. The second method is comparable to that operative in the arts wherein "common forms are determined to something specific" (*ST*, I-II, 95, 2). As I have noted, the passage raises certain difficulties about the distinction between action and art. The passage might tempt us to think of abstract, general principles as forms and of particular circumstances or customs as matter. Given such a relationship, the job of the legislator would be to induce abstract forms into unformed matter. Thus, we would reduce ethical and political reasoning to *techne*. This conclusion is misleading, however. Except hypothetically, there is no such thing as mere matter; all matter is informed. In the legislative or political realm, precisely what form is to be introduced is not evident apart from a prudential assessment of circumstances or customs—that is, of what forms are already

---

[5] Thus, John Finnis wonders about the "principles which prudence uses to transform the first principles of natural law" (*Natural Law and Natural Rights*, 51), and Daniel O'Connor's astringent critique of Thomas's doctrine of natural law focuses on this lacuna. See *Aquinas and Natural Law*.

operative. Prudence involves not simply the subordination of particulars to appropriate universals, but the appraisal of concrete, contingent circumstances. Certain general principles of justice or of the virtues are indeed desirable in every society and at all times; the legislator should judge in light of these natural standards. Precisely how one is to introduce these standards, what concrete form they are to take, will largely be determined by antecedent conditions and circumstances. As Thomas observes, custom, evident in both speech and deeds, declares the judgment of reason about things to be done: "custom has the force of law, abolishes law, and is the interpreter of law" (*ST*, I-II, 97, 3). Finally, we should note that wherever there is an artistic determination of the natural to the human law, the culmination of the determination is not an action, but the specification of common to proper precepts. In the negotiation between proper precepts and the singular circumstances of action, prudence is once again preeminent—both for individuals and for regimes. A politics of virtue requires prudential mediation between an account or theory of the human good and particular customs, laws, and mores.

What emerges from the passages on the importance of custom is the need for the legislator or political theorist to deploy a complicated strategy that makes use of theory, art, and prudence. The same complicated strategy was operative in Aristotle's political theory. We may take the content of the natural law to be Thomas's attempt to specify Aristotle's remarks about natural right. Natural law is, of course, ultimately a practical teaching, meant to inform action, but it is also in part a theoretical account of the goods appropriate to human life and of the evils discordant with it. The move toward a theoretical account of the practical is salutary. As Salkever puts it, "The theoretical enterprise is . . . at its inception both evaluative and explanatory; it begins with the sense that there is a human need for a universal perspective on the basis of which the local and particular things take on a new and better meaning."[6] Some scholars, including Salkever, insist that Aristotle never attempts to codify the theoretical insights that guide political evaluation. Even if this is so, it is not immediately evident that Thomas's codification is as threatening to an Aristotelian approach as it has seemed to some. The basic precepts often operate at some distance from the level of immediate deliberation and choice,

---

[6] *Finding the Mean: Theory and Practice in Aristotelian Political Philosophy*, 16.

and the legislator must exercise a prudential and artistic flexibility in applying them.

This flexibility in applying the precepts of the natural law constitutes an important disparity between the speculative and the practical orders. There are other contrasts. In an article that asks whether the natural law can be abolished from the human heart (*utrum lex naturae possit a corde hominis aboleri*), Thomas has this to say: "As for the other, secondary precepts, the natural law can be deleted from the hearts of men, either on account of evil persuasions . . . or because of depraved customs and corrupt habits, just as among some theft and even vices contrary to nature are not considered to be sins" (*ST*, I-II, 94, 6). The prohibition of theft is among the fundamental precepts of the natural law; the reference to it here reveals the degree to which the natural law is mutable. Aquinas does not discount cultural and educational influences. There is, nonetheless, according to MacIntyre, "evidence of the work of *synderesis*" in the "continuous reappropriation" of certain rules and in the "recurring resistance to discarding them." These precepts, "to which cultural degeneration can partially or temporally blind us," can "never be obliterated."[7]

There is, finally, another way in which Thomas indicates the limitations to a deductive conception of morality. This limitation concerns the intelligibility of the fundamental precepts of the natural law. We have already seen that knowledge of first principles is not intuitive or a priori. They are derived from reflection on experience. First principles in the practical order arise from reflection on the character of human action. Rules are intelligible in light of an overarching conception of the goals of human life or of a particular community. And law is "nothing other than an ordinance of reason for the common good" (*ST*, I-II, 90, 4). Thomas most often adduces the precepts against murder and theft as examples of inviolable and absolute principles of the natural law. The violation of these precepts destroys the very foundation of the human community (*ST*, I-II, 96, 2). The prohibition of theft, murder, and so forth safeguards those practices and institutions that are constitutive of the common good. For Aquinas, universal, negative precepts describe types of action, the performance of which can be described in no other way than as a repudiation of the virtues constitutive of the common good. This view

---

[7] *Three Rival Versions of Moral Enquiry*, 281.

is certainly a possible extension of Aristotle's understanding of law as an articulation of the fundamental goods or virtues necessary for the sustenance of communal life. The precepts have an intrinsically social dimension to them, not only in their initial formulation but also in our coming to understand concretely and precisely what they do and do not entail. In order for the precepts of the natural law to have an efficacious influence on action, we must "engage with others" in such a way that we can become "teachable learners."[8] In brief, living in accord with natural law requires a politics of the common good.

The integrity of Thomas's ethical teaching is usually lost in crude formulations of natural law ethics, which assume that the appraisal of particulars, their classification, and their subsumption under rules are not problematic. Thomas makes no such assumption. In the questions on law, he repeatedly refers to concrete circumstances of actions as "variable and uncertain." He does compare practical reasoning to the deductive character of speculative reason. He states, for instance, that human laws can be derived as conclusions from premises of the natural law; the prohibition against killing can be directly derived from the general precept against harming. The speculative and the practical orders include common and proper principles. There is a crucial difference, however, between common and proper principles in the two orders. In the speculative order, common principles are not limited to this or that science, whereas proper principles operate within a specific science. In the practical order, common and proper principles pertain to the one discipline of ethics—that is, to the entire arena of human action. Nowhere, moreover, does Thomas speak of proper, speculative principles as failing. Their applicability is limited to a particular science; because they never apply to particulars, but only to unvarying universals, they are not liable to exceptions in the way some practical principles are. Although the most common precepts in the practical order are immutable (*ST,* I-II, 94, 4), some proximate, detailed principles can be changed because they may fail in certain circumstances (*ST,* I-II, 94, 5).

Even where practical reason operates deductively, it remains at the level of proximate precepts, which is another disparity between the practical and the theoretical orders. Whereas the conclusions of demonstrative syllogisms reach necessary, universal truths, those of

---

[8] MacIntyre, *Three Rival Versions of Moral Enquiry,* 136.

practical reason issue in conclusions having to do with particulars, which are true always or for the most part *(ut in pluribus)*. The more we descend to particulars, the more defects we find (*ST*, I-II, 94, 4). In certain cases, following a precept—for example, that goods entrusted to another should be returned to their owner—may "be injurious." It might seem that we can solve the difficulty by adding a list of qualifications to the original precept, but the more conditions we add, the more ways there are for the principle to fail (*ST*, I-II, 94, 4).

Another difficulty for the deductive view of practical reasoning is that even at the level of principles, the relationship between common and proper is not always a matter of deduction. There is an alternative way of moving from one to the other: *determinatio*, which is more like an artist's realization of a general pattern in concrete reality than it is like deduction (*ST*, I-II, 95, 2). Although Thomas initially compares determination to artistic *techne*, his full account of this process indicates that determination is a matter for the virtue of prudence or for an operation of the mind that integrates elements from each. Furthermore, in both deduction and determination, we reach only a proximate precept, not the singular object of action. Thomas does not hold out the possibility that multiplying moral principles will ever get us to the particular, without which there is no action. Facility of moral reasoning, then, cannot occur apart from prudence. The restoration of prudence would also have the advantage of helping to specify the scope and limits of law.

A further advantage to shifting our focus to prudence is evident in situations where principles appear to conflict. Indeed, a crude natural law view must resort to preposterous measures in order to salvage the coherence of the system of precepts. Without some basic capacity of discerning what rules are relevant and in what respect, the problem of an infinite regress of rules seems unavoidable. One might respond that if there is an absolutely first principle of the natural law, then any regress would have to end at that principle. But this response ignores two difficulties. With respect to intermediate and proximate precepts, the first precept of the natural law has the same status that the principle of contradiction, the first principle of speculative reason, has in relationship to more determinate principles of the particular sciences. None of the latter is deduced from the former. Hence, it is unclear what chain of reasoning, based in principles alone, will get us from particular situations of deliberation back to the first principle. Also, the problem is not simply one of tracing particular precepts back to primary precepts or to the primary precept. Rather, the difficulty is that we shall have to multiply precepts endlessly to anticipate all the possible contingencies of action. It is not surprising, then, that Thomas, following Aristotle, appeals not to a multiplication of rules, but to the virtues of *synesis* and *gnome* as capacities for recognizing and applying universal and common principles to concrete circumstances, in ordinary situations and in cases where proximate principles fail (*ST*, II-II, 51, 3 and 4). Moreover, to state which principles apply and which do not presupposes an appraisal of the circumstances that rules themselves cannot provide. This is the realm of the *visio* of prudence that operates through a certain collation (*per quandam collationem agitur; ST*, II-II, 47, 1). Prudence requires experience, memory, and practice in perception (*experimentum prudentiae non acquiritur ex sola memoria sed ex exercitio recte percipiendi; ST*, II-II, 47, 16, ad 2).

Another benefit of the retrieval of prudence is that it restores the harmony of reason and inclination to its proper place in ethics. The *recta ratio agibilium* (reasoning rightly about things to be done) of prudence cannot operate without rectified appetite: "the things to which the moral virtues incline are as the principles of prudence" (*ST*, I-II, 65, 1 ad 4). To be well disposed with respect to ends depends on rightly ordered appetite (*ST*, I-II, 57, 4). Because the principles of moral reasoning are described as ends to be pursued, even the correct apprehension of moral precepts presupposes rectified appetite. Unlike other intellectual virtues, which are lost primarily through forgetfulness, prudence is destroyed through "vicious passions" (*ST*, II-II, 47, 16). Here, we can see a parallel to the precepts of the natural law, which can also be abolished through corrupt customs and bad habits. The proximate ground of the precepts of the natural law is the order of natural inclinations. Even though problems arise primarily at the level of particulars, problems at that level have a way of obstructing our apprehension of prior, more general precepts. The repetitious performance of vicious actions has consequences not only at the level of application but also at the level of proximate principles because vice can undermine principles as fundamental as the one against theft (*ST*, I-II, 94, 4 and 6). As Aristotle puts it, to apprehend the starting points in ethics, one must have been well brought up.

Thomas allows that individuals and communities have access to the most general precepts even in the midst of corrupt practices, which helps to explain how individuals and communities can understand and desire visions of the good that run counter to the vision of a corrupt, dominant culture. But it is unlikely that individuals or communities will make much progress in living a virtuous life without implementing practices to succor the virtues. Without some articulation of the common good to which human life is ordered and its embodiment in a communal way of life, the intelligibility and purpose of the precepts are likely to be lost. Practices inculcate habits that rectify the appetitive part of the soul with respect to appropriate ends, which supply principles of action. The correct ordering of inclination, its harmony with reason, is important not just as a prerequisite to the operation of prudence, but also as a mark of true virtue. To support the thesis that moral virtue cannot exist without passion, Thomas quotes Aristotle: no one is " 'just who does not rejoice in just deeds' " (*ST*, I-II, 59, 5).

The various qualifications on the role of principles or rules in the moral life illustrate that the theory of law is but a fragment of a larger whole. In the finest available study of natural law in Aquinas, Yves Simon underscores the link between natural law and prudence:

> If law is a premise rather than a conclusion, if, universally, law admits of no immediate contact with the world of action, the ideal of a social science which would, in each particular case, procure a rational solution and render governmental prudence unnecessary is thoroughly deceptive. Whatever the science of man and of society has to say remains at an indeterminate distance from the world of action, and this distance can be traversed only by the most obscure methods of prudence which involve . . . the power of sound inclinations. In a judgment marked by singularity and contingency we recognize features opposite to those of law. Between law and action there always is space to be filled by decisions which cannot be written into law.[9]

Even a perfunctory acquaintance with the Aristotelian virtue of prudence reveals the remedial role of prudence with respect to the defects inherent in a legalistic ethic. Prudence is at once an intellectual virtue that aids in the application of principles to circumstances and a virtue that presupposes rectitude of the appetite and so secures

---

[9] *The Tradition of Natural Law*, 85 and 83.

our knowledge of intermediate precepts and of how they apply to concrete circumstances. Without the formation of character through habit, practical reason is likely to be derailed at virtually any point. The connection between prudence and moral virtue ensures the vitality and efficacy of moral knowledge. The association, furthermore, of law with the practices that succor communal life evinces yet another link between law and virtue, for virtue secures, embodies, and displays an appreciation of such practices. A more detailed account of prudence and the moral virtues is now in order.

Aquinas borrows from Aristotle the definition of prudence as an intellectual virtue that reasons rightly about things to be done (*recta ratio agibilium*) and that arises from experience and memory (*ST*, II-II, 49, 1). Prudence mediates between principles and experience, between the general and the particular: "actions are in singulars; and thus it is necessary that the prudent man know both the universal principles of reason and singulars, with which actions are concerned" (*ST*, II-II, 47, 3). The virtue of prudence supplies what the laws cannot; it enables one to judge particular matters appropriately. An emphasis on concrete perception dominates the discussion of prudence. The inclusion of *ratio* and *intellectus* among the parts of prudence is surprising because these virtues are usually treated as perfections of the speculative intellect. But, in this context, they are skills of moral perception; they mark a trained attentiveness to the particular and the contingent.

The classification of *"intellectus vel intelligentia"* as a part of prudence provides evidence for viewing *intellectus* as having much broader scope than is usually thought. Thomas says of *intellectus,* "understanding . . . is certain right estimation of a particular end" (*ST*, II-II, 49, 2). The function of understanding is to grasp what is pertinent and to assess what ought to be done in complex circumstances. Prudence is a *visio* that provides for the future by collating past and present experience (*ST*, II-II, 47, 1). Whenever Thomas classifies *intellectus,* he places it in the category of intellectual virtues, and, as is the case with every virtue, its development requires training and experience. In disputes over the character and ranking of principles within a certain practice, Thomas appeals not to pristine and unadulterated intuitions, but to a correct education in the practices in question.

But prudence is not purely cognitive. It also has reference to the volitional and appetitive components in human nature. As Thomas writes, "prudence . . . requires that one be well disposed concerning ends, which occurs through rectified appetite. Thus, prudence presupposes moral virtue, which rectifies the appetite" (*ST*, I-II, 57, 4). Vagrant appetites are the chief impediments to the sound operation of practical reason. I have already noted the way bad education and inordinate passion can eradicate knowledge of the secondary precepts. Thomas speaks in a similar vein about the dissolution of prudence: "Prudence is not destroyed through forgetfulness alone, but much more is it corrupted through the passions" (*ST*, II-II, 47, 16). The parallel between the dissolution of prudence and the dissolution of knowledge of the natural law is instructive; highlighting the way moral education and rectified appetite mediate between primary precepts and circumstances indicates a disparity between the kinds of knowledge operative in speculative and practical reason.

Virtuous activity is not a matter of overcoming an opposition between reason and passion; to do so is but a preparation for virtue. Virtue involves the harmony of reason and appetite, the concourse of many good dispositions. This conclusion is evident from the discussion in *Ethics* II, already treated in detail, of that portion of the irrational soul that is amenable to rational persuasion. The account of these dispositions or habits is crucial to Thomas's account of moral knowledge. In his discussion of the relationship between virtue and passion, Thomas notes that inordinate sensitive passions are incompatible with virtue. This does not mean that virtue is a "kind of freedom from passion and disturbance." Such an assertion "must be qualified"; virtue requires freedom only from passions that are "not as they should be as to manner and time" (*ST*, I-II, 59, 2). Indeed, no virtue can be without passion. The virtues that directly concern the passions—for example, fortitude and temperance—do not "deprive the powers beneath reason of their proper activities," but assist them in "exercising their proper acts" (*ST*, I-II, 59, 4). The virtue of justice, however, concerns not the passions but operations; still, joy resides in the will as a result of the performance of just acts, and a sign of the perfection of the virtue is that joy overflows into the sensitive powers. Even moderate sorrow for what ought to make us sad is a "mark of virtue" (*ST*, I-II, 59, 3).

The doctrine of the "mean" might seem an anomaly in this context. Virtue is indeed a mean between excess and deficiency, but such a description remains at a certain level of generality. Thomas does at times speak of the "mean" as a proportion. But to take the mathematical element as anything more than a metaphor would do violence to the supple account of the virtues. Thomas himself associates the mean not with abstract proportionality, but with a sensitivity to "diverse circumstances" (*diversas circumstantias; ST*, I-II, 64, 1, ad 2). He writes, "In actions we must consider who acted, by what aids or instruments the act was done, what was done, where, why, how he acted, and when the act was performed" (*ST*, I-II, 7, 3). The mean operates as a sort of metaphor for action that is right not just in one way, but in every way. An action observes the mean when it is in accord with the rule of reason—that is, when the action is performed when and where it should be, for the right end, and so forth. Prudence is the capacity for finding the mean in moral virtues (*ST*, II-II, 47, 7). The centrality of prudence does not weaken obligations; instead, the standard of virtuous action is more rigorous, although less ascetic, than that of a narrow legalism.

To say simply that one has acted in accordance with a rule or a measure fails to capture the various perspectives from which we normally assess human action. In response to the objection that magnanimity or greatness of soul concerns great honors and hence does not observe a mean, Thomas distinguishes between the various circumstances of action: "in a certain virtue, nothing excludes there being an extreme according to one circumstance, which is nonetheless a mean according to other circumstances, by its conformity with reason." Virtues such as magnanimity tend to a "maximum according to the rule of reason—that is, where it is right, when it is right, and for an end that is right" (*ST*, I-II, 64, 1, ad 2). Any appraisal of human action must take into account the concrete context and contingent circumstances within which human acts are embedded. A purely legalistic appraisal of human actions presumes and fosters a view of human actions as discrete events, isolated from the character and history of the moral agent. But this appraisal abstracts actions both from the conditions that make them intelligible and from the capacities in the agent that enable him or her to discern what is salient in a particular situation. In his discussion of the reductionist "decision-procedures" of Kant and Mill, Joel Kupperman writes, "Ethics in this view is at work only at those discrete moments when an input is registered and the moral decision-procedure is applied." However, "before we can implement a decision-procedure," we must "notice that a situation is problematic and then reflect on it. Thus, priority must be given to the moral agent's sensitivity."[10]

Kupperman's emphasis on the need for the agent's sensitivity underscores the need for a complex moral pedagogy. Both Aristotle and Aquinas compare education in the moral life to a *techne*. In support of the view that we are born only with dispositions to the virtues, not with their actual possession, Aquinas writes, "by acting in accord with the virtues we come to possess the virtues, just as happens in the arts, in which men learn to make by making."[11] To become virtuous we must practice the acts of the virtues. Authoritative teachers are necessary if we are to profit from our practice. No mechanical notion of repetition will do; we shall have to identify contingently different actions as actions nonetheless falling under a certain type, say, the type of just actions. As Nancy Sherman puts it, "there is no external husk of all just actions that we can isolate and repeatedly practice. Any just action will be contextually defined and will vary considerably, in terms of judgement, emotion, and behavior, from other just actions." Moreover, repetition cannot mean simply "doing just what one did before" or we shall simple repeat our errors and fail to make progress.[12] Practice precedes perfect habitation; consequently, as beginners, we are likely to fall prey to all sorts of misunderstandings of the life of virtue. We might see the virtues as instrumental to the good life, as leading to a happiness that we will possess independently of the virtues. We may see the virtues as skills that we can possess and use at our discretion. In our early education, we will have to avoid all sorts of acts that are destructive of virtue, so we may think virtue involves merely following a list of prohibitions. We may see the virtues in isolation from one another and thus be deceived into supposing that we can perfect one virtue without perfecting the others. In gradually coming to be virtuous, we shall have to correct all of these misconceptions. We will do so by engaging with others in the practice of the virtues and in conversation about them. Just as is the case with crafts, progress in the virtues requires submission to a teacher. Our acquisition of the virtues as well as our understanding

---

[10] *Character,* 72.

[11] *In Libros* Ethicorum, II, lectio 1, note 250.

[12] *The Fabric of Character,* 178.

of the relationships among the various virtues—their integration into some unified way of life—is impossible apart from a communally acknowledged account of the goods to which human life is ordered and of the means to their acquisition.

In establishing that the mean is the focus of virtue, Aristotle adduces another comparison to crafts. A sign of the link between the mean and virtue is that the arts are said to be perfect when "nothing can be added or subtracted" *(nihil est addendum vel minuendum)*. Thomas grants the similarity but adds the contrast that "virtue is more certain than any art, and even better as is nature" *(virtus est certior omni arte, et etiam melior, sicut et natura)*. Moral virtue inclines to something determinate as does nature, while the operation of art is open to diverse ends. There is also a certain distance, not present in the moral virtues, between the possession and operation of the productive virtues: "virtue makes good not only the agent's work, but also the agent himself. . . . Art, however, ensures only the cognition of a good operation."[13] Another passage supports the assertion that the "cognition alone of good operation" perfects art: "someone is able to be a good artist, even if he never chooses to operate according to art or if he fails to persevere in his work."[14] These passages are problematic. They conflict not only with the general description of the practical virtues as ordered to doing or making, not merely to knowing, but also with certain passages from Aristotle's *Metaphysics* IX. In the latter passages, Aristotle argues that operative powers both arise from and are ordered to the practice of the appropriate operations: "We achieve some operative powers by previous actions and exercises. . . . These are acquired through custom or teaching . . . it seems impossible, for example, that someone should become a builder unless he has first built."[15] Practical capacities are possessed that they might be exercised: "men have the power of building that they might build" *(ad hoc homines potentiam habent aedificandi ut aedificent; Sententia super* Metaphysicam, IX, lectio 8, note 1859). What are we to make of the diverse descriptions of what constitutes an art? The disparity between crafts and moral virtues might be expressed in the following way. In the moral virtues, there is

---

[13] Aquinas, *In Libros* Ethicorum, II, lectio 2.
[14] *In Libros* Ethicorum, II, lectio 4, note 284.
[15] *Sententia super* Metaphysicam, IX, lectio 7, note 1850.

no gap between who we are, what we know, and what we do. This view is congruent with the statement that a willing error in the making of artifacts is less blameworthy than in the performance of moral actions. In the crafts, the gap between knowledge and performance makes it possible for one to possess the virtue of art without exercising it.

A sign that the primacy of rules in much of contemporary Kantian and utilitarian ethics tends toward an abstract view of action is that the virtues receive little attention; when they are addressed, they tend to be collapsed into one virtue, which is something like the virtue of self-control, the virtue that restrains the passions and thus removes impediments to doing what one ought. Thomas holds, on the contrary, that the "whole structure of good works originates from the four cardinal virtues" (ST, I-II, 61, 2). Among these virtues, he distinguishes virtues concerning the passions—temperance and fortitude—from the virtue concerning operations, justice (ST, I-II, 60, 2). Especially on the latter point does his view differ from the modern tendency to collapse the virtues. Although all the virtues about operations concur in the "general notion of justice," which concerns what is due to another, they differ in that "the thing due is not identical in all the virtues; for something is due to an equal in one way, to a superior, in another way, to an inferior, in yet another, and a debt varies as it arises from a contract, a promise, or a benefit received" (ST, I-II, 60, 3). The virtues thus differ in accord with their proper objects; for example, religion concerns our debt to God, piety our debt to country or parents, and gratitude our debt to benefactors.

Of course, the distinctions among the virtues do not entail the independence of one virtue from another. Following Aristotle, Cicero, and a number of Christian ethicists, Thomas holds that the virtues are connected; as Gregory puts it, a virtue cannot be perfect if it is isolated from the others (ST, I-II, 65, 1). The abstraction of one feature of action and character from the whole is inevitable not just in a legalistic ethic, but also in a fragmented account of virtue. Once again, there is a sharp contrast between the intellectual and technical virtues, on the one hand, and the moral virtues, on the other. The various arts and sciences are in many cases independent of one another; thus, the virtues appropriate to these disciplines are not inherently unified (ST, I-II, 65, 1, ad 3). Things made are not related to one another as are things done (ST, I-II, 65, 1, ad 4). The operations and passions, which are the concern of the moral virtues, can be seen to be connected in two ways.

First, if we take any purportedly virtuous act—say, an act of courage—and subtract from it other components of a virtuous action—say, moderation or discretion—then the act is no longer unequivocally to be commended. We can commend such an act only so long as we isolate one feature of the act from the remainder. The possibility of a selective attention to particular features of a person's character accounts for our appreciation of and even limited admiration for a character such as the "courageous" thief. Clearly, individuals often have a greater disposition toward one or another virtue. In the case of children and of adults undergoing a kind of conversion to the life of virtue, the nascent predilection for a particular virtue or set of virtues can be a means through which the other virtues come initially to be practiced. Thus, we might appeal to the former thief's sense of courage to inspire her to redouble her efforts toward justice, or we might appeal to an individual's sense of justice to encourage him to exercise greater temperance or courage, neither of which requires the presence of a complete and perfect virtue, but only the flawed or partial possession of virtue. Aristotle's moral pedagogy presupposes precisely such a moral psychology, for he does not depict the transition to the state of virtue as a magical, momentary transformation, but as a gradual appropriation of the virtues.

Second, all the moral virtues "fall under the one rule of prudence" and are thus unified. The impossibility of moral virtue without prudence and vice versa underscores the complex appraisal of human action required in an ethics of the virtues. An action is not completely good unless it is performed with due attention to all its circumstances, but due attention to all circumstances brings many, if not all, the virtues into play. Moreover, as will be discussed in more detail in the later consideration of the vices opposed to prudence, the failure to exercise certain virtues has a way of adversely affecting other virtues we are attempting to exercise. The subversion of one virtue by a vice is often subtle and indirect. For example, if we strive to restrain anger but neglect temperance, which restrains concupiscence, then the habit of restraining anger will remain imperfect, for, according to Thomas, concupiscence undermines prudence by derailing the process of deliberation, especially when in our attempt to do what we ought we are distracted by some object of pleasure.

The account of prudence provides a response to certain criticisms of virtue ethics. In his book *Character,* Joel Kupperman argues that virtue ethics is akin to "genre criticism" in literature, which allows for the classification and appraisal of actions in terms of the standards appropriate to particular virtues.[16] The deficiencies of virtue ethics, Kupperman insists, surface when an action "spills out" of a particular category or when "two or more categories arguably are involved in what we are attempting to judge." Character ethics, he claims, is superior to virtue ethics precisely because it focuses on "what people are like when decisions are called for that involve factors of more than one kind." In his consideration of the resources of virtue ethics in such cases, Kupperman looks at justice as the principal and unifying virtue. He fails, however, to consider the role of prudence, which is precisely to appraise all the germane circumstances and determine what ought be done. Once prudence is introduced, the difference between virtue theory and character ethics may well be only verbal. Indeed, the centrality of prudence entails an emphasis on character in moral education. Thomas embraces Aristotle's statement that as a man is, so does the good appear to him.

One of the most persistent and apparently damaging criticisms of virtue theory is that it lacks the resources for social critique; according to Jurgen Habermas, it is susceptible to the "dogmatism of life-practices."[17] Thomas's coupling of natural law with prudence makes his position less vulnerable to such an objection, but it is important to see that prudence, understood Thomistically, can itself be the basis of social criticism. Indeed, the parts of prudence and the list of vices opposed to prudence suggest a powerful critique of certain kinds of practice. In his marvelous little book on prudence, Josef Pieper laments the contemporary misconstrual of prudence as "timorous, small-minded self-preservation." A prudent person is a "clever tactician," striving to "escape personal commitment."[18] At least in part responsible for the currently debased appreciation of prudence is the tendency among Kantians to segregate prudence from moral reasoning and to relegate it to the realm of the calculation of means to personal happiness, understood in terms of the personal preference

---

[16] 106–8.
[17] "A Review of Gadamer's *Truth and Method,*" 357.
[18] *Prudence,* 11.

of a life plan. By contrast, Thomas locates prudence at the very center of the moral life and provides a sufficiently determinant understanding of it to put into question various kinds of corrupt social order.

Thomas begins his discussion of the parts of prudence by discussing memory, from which prudence arises. As Pieper notes, memory means more than a capacity for recalling facts. Instead, he calls it "true to being" memory, which can be succored only by "a rectitude of the whole human being."[19] How does Thomas understand such rectitude?

Prudence cannot operate successfully unless virtue informs all the stages of practical reasoning—deliberation, judgment, and command. The vices that derail these stages are *praecipitatio, inconsideratio,* and *inconstantia.* Neglect of taking counsel or *praecipitatio* arises from a lack of docility "through the force of will or passion"; in its extreme form, it is a kind of pride that opposes submission to the authority of another (*ST,* II-II, 53, 3). Inconsideration condemns or neglects those things from which right judgment proceeds (*ST,* II-II, 53, 4). Inconstancy, finally, signifies an incapacity to hold oneself firmly to a course of action that one judges to be good (*ST,* II-II, 53, 5). Not just pleasure but also fear can result in inconstancy. Often the failure to follow through on what has been judged a right action evinces a lack of courage. A defect of reason, which shrinks from commanding what it ought to command, is also present in inconstancy. Thomas traces these vices of omission to *luxuria,* which fosters division of the soul and duplicity of consciousness. Luxury is evident in the avoidance of making decisions or, more violently, in the frenetic process of making, unmaking, and remaking decisions (*ST,* II-II, 53, 6).

The previously mentioned vices disrupt the operation of reason in obvious ways, but a second set of vices is less easily detected because its opposition to prudence is more subtle. In fact, these vices, allied to prudence by similitude, are the ones we often substitute for prudence. The first vice, prudence of the flesh *(prudentia carnis),* consists in taking bodily goods as the ultimate end of human life (*ST,* II-II, 55). Two things are odd about *prudentia carnis.* First, as one objection has it, none of the other virtues, to which prudence is superior, retain their names and become vices. Thomas's response to this

---

[19] *Prudence,* 27.

objection distinguishes between the other virtues, which in their very meaning (in sui ratione) contain the essence of virtue, and prudence, which is taken a providendo and which "is able to be extended to evil" (ST, II-II, 55, 1, ad 1). But this distinction raises a second difficulty to which Thomas does not directly respond—namely, how can prudence, which orders means to ends, become a vice by reference solely to the end pursued (ST, II-II, 55, 1, obj. 1)? The teaching on the unity of the virtues, that a person cannot have one virtue without having all of them, suggests a response; there cannot be true prudence unless the means are ordered to a true good by the moral virtues. In prudentia carnis, the capacity of prudence is put at the service of a false end and is thereby corrupted. In this way, the end enters into the very description of prudence, which provides further support for a point I made earlier about the means-end relationship. In a technical understanding of the means-end connection, the means is merely instrumental and is productive of a state extrinsic to the process of its engendering. In the prudential understanding, by contrast, the means is to varying degrees constitutive of the end. In the present passage, Thomas insists that prudence is not some capacity that can be isolated from the ends it helps to realize, as if one were considering merely its efficiency in marshalling raw material to arbitrary ends.

Unlike the vices that directly disrupt the stages of action, the vices that simulate prudence do not result from luxury. Instead, they are rooted in avarice, the vice most damaging to justice. The difference between the sorts of vices has to do with the function of reason in each. The set that arises from luxury totally suppresses the power of reason, but the other set retains a likeness to true prudence precisely in the continued functioning of reason (ST, II-II, 55, 8). The latter erode the moral virtue of justice, which resides in the rational appetite. The same sorts of vices, then, are capable of undermining both prudence and justice. The daughters of avarice include not only fraud and illiberality, but also restlessness of soul (inquietudo), for the affections of the grasping are anxious about superfluous matters. Thomas speaks of luxury as absorbing the soul (ST, II-II, 45, 6). Both vices incite restlessness of soul and thus impede the contemplative moment that is the necessary prelude to prudent action, a moment involving both self-possession and an apprehension of the way things are in a concrete setting.

Thomas's moral writings are replete with richly detailed and amply illustrated descriptions of the way the presence of one vice either directly or indirectly renders tenuous our possession of a host of virtues. It is on this concrete level that he makes his strongest case for the unity of the virtues. Another important implication of the subtle links between the virtues is that very general depictions of the virtues invite serious misconstruals of them. How is this so? Some commentators have supposed that any account of the virtues, indeed any social embodiment of them, must basically overlap with any other. So long as the descriptions remain at a general level, the thesis retains a certain plausibility. Once the details of the accounts have been worked out, however, it is inevitable that striking differences will emerge. The more we descend to detailed descriptions, the more specific, and hence the more exclusive, is the articulation of the goods that the virtues embody. There is an important lesson here about how Aquinas's moral teaching must be read. I have suggested above that the so-called treatise on law should not be read in isolation from the examination of the virtues or from the subsequent and more detailed analysis of the application of particular precepts. A similar point holds concerning the initial and general discussion of the virtues in relationship to the later and more ample treatment of them.

From Prudence Back to Law

The emphasis on the indispensable need for experience and training in the moral life has led some recent commentators to shift entirely the balance from natural law to virtue. In a book entitled *The Priority of Prudence,* Daniel Mark Nelson goes further than any recent author in repudiating the view that Thomas is a proponent of natural law ethics. From a reading of various sections of the second part of the *Summa Theologiae,* Nelson makes a cogent case for seeing virtue rather than law as the fundamental moral category. But his position cuts deeper by relegating natural law to a negligible status in moral deliberation. What does Nelson have to say about the articles on natural law? "Such knowledge serves the explanatory function of accounting for how it happens that we come to reason practically and for the origin of the virtues. Thomas's general point is that we have a created, natural ability to act for the good appropriate to our nature and to develop the habits that perfect that capacity."[20] Clearly, he is right to think that the function of natural law is explanatory; the question is, however, whether it does not have other evaluative and normative functions. On his view, it is difficult to see what, if anything, natural law adds to Aristotle's comment that virtue is natural in the sense that we have the capacity to acquire it. But why call that "natural law"? The notion of "law" in "natural law" would be eliminated. The problem with Nelson's account is that he has allowed polemics against his opponents, especially against those who see natural law as a sufficient guide for the determination of action, to set the terms of the debate. He is right to note that in concrete circumstances, natural law cannot "guide action" or "provide a formula" for correct choice.[21] But to deny these simplistic renderings of natural law does not entail the repudiation of natural law as an important part of moral reasoning.

Most contemporary retrievals of prudence, as I have noted, resist aligning prudence with any strong conception of the role of moral precepts; universal rules are seen as impediments to the agent's spontaneity and to the particularity of experience. Such resistance is often accompanied by a tendency to depict the virtues in quite general terms so as to render them applicable to any social and political setting. The resistance to rules and to a thick conception of the virtues is sometimes of a piece with an attempt to fuse certain features of Aristotle's ethics with democratic pluralism. The alignment of prudence with liberalism and pluralism is problematic. In a pluralistic society, the pedagogical dominance of notions such as tolerance and equal regard tends to flatten the contours of our moral experience. Moreover, the result of individualism—of the severing of ties to tradition, history, and local communities—is not a society of Nietzschean supermen or even of Aristotelian prudent men. Instead, individuals become absorbed in the pursuit of petty pleasure and the endless accumulation of external goods, precisely the vices that undermine prudence. In such a social context, the memory that nourishes prudence would be eviscerated, and the vices opposed to prudence would be fostered.

Prudence presupposes moral education in specific practices as well

---

[20] *The Priority of Prudence*, 103.
[21] *The Priority of Prudence*, 114 and 119.

as in a fairly determinate conception of the human good. An impediment to the liberal appropriation of prudence is Aristotle's emphasis on the role of law in inculcating prudence. As Thomas puts it in his comment on the germane passage from the end of the *Ethics* (X, 9),

> It is difficult for someone to be led to virtue from youth by healthy customs, unless he be raised under good laws, through which we are led to the good by a certain necessity. . . . It is important, then, that the raising of youth be ordained by good laws, from which by a kind of force we are compelled to become accustomed to the good. When we have attained the habit, we will not find virtue sorrowful but delightful. . . . To this end, we need laws and not only at the outset when one has just become an adult but also for the entirety of human life. (*In Libros* Ethicorum, X, lectio 14, notes 1248–51)

The passage provides yet another reason for rejecting the thesis that the virtues must be roughly the same in meaning wherever they appear. The passage does not shift the emphasis from virtue to law, for law is pedagogically ordered to the inculcation of virtue. Law itself is a "logos" proceeding "from prudence and understanding" (*Ethics,* X, ix, 1180a22). But it proceeds from an understanding of the principles that inform the nature of the political regime one inhabits, principles that embody rival conceptions of the human good. The failure to see that any lived conception of the virtues is likely to differ dramatically from any other is the result of an error I mentioned at the outset of the book, the error of treating ethics in isolation from politics.

Martha Nussbaum has made the most notable contemporary attempt to align Aristotle with liberal political practice. Although conceding the importance of "ongoing commitments and values," she insists that this "general background" of action is "not immune to revision even at the highest level."[22] Nussbaum's thesis runs counter to Aristotle's regular practice of adverting to a natural and universally valid hierarchy of ends. Often cited in discussions of the law's need for prudential application is Aristotle's insistence on equitable application of law. Laws must be tailored to the customs of a people, ought not to be onerous, and should lead from the imperfect to the perfect.[23] This Aristotelian claim needs to be balanced by passages where Aristotle argues that changes in laws are for the most part

---

[22] *Fragility of Goodness,* 306.
[23] Dunne, *Back to the Rough Ground,* 273.

imprudent because they erode customs that give rise to the habits that make virtue possible. Aristotle's insistence on the necessity of equity in the application of law to particular cases seems to support the view that laws provide nothing more than rules of thumb. It is not clear, however, that there is a simple correspondence between the application of civil law and that of moral principles. If we do not adopt the model of equity, how then are we to construe the application of moral principles to concrete circumstances? Aquinas would certainly concur that experience and education enable us to understand better the import and scope of general principles; he would even embrace the statement that "excellent choice cannot be captured in universal rules."[24] Much more is required of us than mere conformity to the rule. But, according to Thomas, conformity to certain rules is also required of us. At issue here is the relationship of principles to circumstances and the mediating role of prudence. As I have already noted, Thomas holds that principles are known through experience and that even basic principles apply only for the most part. Some commentators want to reason from this position that Thomas supposes the basic principles to be revisable. Does he?

Thomas begins with a set of distinctions—distinctions not usually made by those who see only the mutually exclusive alternatives of reducing ethics to legalism or of regarding laws as mere guidelines that are revisable from top to bottom. He distinguishes between positive and negative precepts as well as between those that hold universally and those that hold only for the most part. Universal, positive precepts such as "do good" or "perform the acts of the virtues" are indeed inviolable, but they are so broad as to issue in no particular codes of conduct. Negative, universal precepts, on the other hand, may well issue in inviolable codes of conduct. Thomas regularly mentions precepts whose violation undermines the common good of a community, which does not mean, however, that there are not problematic cases—that is, cases that appear to be justified exceptions to a precept. For example, in the discussion of the prohibition against theft, Thomas argues that in cases of necessity it is not a sin to take what one needs. An objection to the thesis is taken from Aristotle's statement in *Ethics,* II, 6, that certain names denote acts that are inherently evil *(secundum se malum)* and that theft is among these

---

[24] Nussbaum, *Fragility of Goodness,* 303.

acts. Thomas responds that in the case of extreme necessity taking what one needs does not have the *rationem furti,* properly speaking (*ST,* II-II, 66, 7, ad 2). In a case of evident and urgent need *(evidens et urgens necessitas)*, all things are common. This response is not an ad hoc adjustment; he is not engaging in "verbal gymnastics" or using some covert "consequentialist calculus."[25] For Thomas, the existence of a political regime and of its understanding of the common good is antecedent to the institution of private property, whose practice is thereby limited. The act of theft in cases of need is not an exception to the prohibition; rather, the conditions constitutive of the prohibition are no longer present. A similar strategy is operative in Thomas's discussion of whether it is permissible to kill sinners. The just and the innocent may never be killed, but those who sin gravely against the community may be slain: "by sinning, someone withdraws from the order of reason; and thus he lapses from human dignity" (*ST,* II-II, 64, 2 ad 3).

Thomas does not view the relationship between all general precepts and apparent exceptions to them in this way. The key distinction here is not between positive and negative, but between precepts that hold always and those that hold only for the most part. For example, the principle that borrowed goods should be returned is one that should not be followed when doing so would be "injurious." The principle is itself a specific rule following from more general principles of justice. In the case in question, the ultimate purpose of the rule would be undermined by following it. Thomas's remarks about the necessity of keeping promises is germane. The evil involved in not fulfilling a promise has to do with altering one's explicitly stated intentions *(animum mutat)*. But there are cases in which promises need not be kept—for instance, when what one has promised is something evil. One is also excused from keeping the promise if the "conditions of persons are changed" *(sunt mutatae conditiones personarum)*. The stability of relevant circumstances is inherent within the practice of promising: "He promises what he has in mind, assuming appropriate conditions" (*ST,* II-II, 110, 3, ad 5).

---

[25] Bernard Hoose, *Proportionalism: The American Debate and Its European Roots,* 99, note 97, and 119. For a corrective, see McInerny, *Ethica Thomistica,* 59–62; Simon, *The Tradition of Natural Law,* 146–58; and Jean Porter, *The Recovery of Virtue,* 124–54. I address the debate between proportionalists and absolutists in "Interpretations of Aquinas's Ethics Since Vatican II."

In the problematic cases concerning the returning of borrowed goods and stealing, no recourse is had to any sort of proportionalist weighing of goods against one another. Instead, recourse is had to prior and more fundamental principles, which secure the intelligibility of the precepts concerning borrowing and theft. In light of the more fundamental precepts, prudence judges that in certain cases what might seem to require an application of the proximate precept does not. The discussion of *synesis* and *gnome*, virtues adjoined to prudence, indicates that the negotiation of circumstances by reference to principles pertains to prudence. *Synesis* is the virtue of rightly judging; it ensures that an agent "apprehends a thing as it is in itself" (*apprehendet rem secundum quod in se est; ST*, II-II, 51, 3, ad 1). It appraises experience by reference to common principles. In instances where common principles fail to provide adequate guidance, there is need of another virtue—namely, *gnome*—that recurs to "higher principles" (*altiora principia; ST*, II-II, 51, 4). Although the reciprocity of precepts and prudence could not be more explicit, it is also significant that Thomas provides no list of rules whereby the virtue of *gnome* might trace a path from a particular circumstance or common precept to the higher principles in light of which it judges. If the virtue judges with respect to the higher precepts, how it mediates between the particular and the universal is not itself a rule-governed activity.

The casuistic analysis of cases in light of natural law often seems a rather thin approach to ethics. Thomas's deceptively quick handling of the cases of theft and borrowed goods conceals the rich background understanding that constitutes the horizon of moral reasoning about singular cases. Often, this sort of knowledge, both customary and institutional, will be only tacit, but it can be—and in times of crisis, confusion, or debate needs to be—made explicit. In judging particulars, we may need to advert not only to proximate precepts, but also to the way the common good is distinctively embodied in our regime. The regime can in turn be appraised in light of the natural hierarchy of goods appropriate to human nature. This appraisal provides no ready-made set of remedies for regimes. Aquinas's confident settling of apparently difficult cases would appear to contravene Aristotle's prudential restraint, but there is a difference between the resolution of moral cases and the advocacy of determinate political action. Thomas would concur with the claim that the guidance

supplied by the natural order of goods makes possible both "devotion
to and critical distance from the local political context."[26] Still, we
should be careful not to be too conservative in our willingness to use
the guidance afforded by natural law reasoning in our criticism of
extant customs and regimes; otherwise, a slavish cowardice will replace imaginative and prudential courage. The dispute here is not
about law, but about the nature of the human good.

The argument on behalf of the inviolability of certain precepts
does not minimize the role of prudence. It does mean that prudence
cannot operate in a vacuum or without a background in light of which
it judges. In cases of uncertainty about the applicability of a principle,
prudence must intervene. In the appraisal of circumstances, prudence is at work. Thomas is careful, moreover, to distinguish prudence from art and theoretical knowledge. His initial discussion of
prudence sets it apart from the other intellectual virtues. In contrast
to wisdom, understanding, and knowledge, which concern necessary
matters, prudence concerns the contingent conditions of action. In
contrast to art, which has to do with things made in exterior matter,
prudence has to do with actions and reaches its perfection in operation itself (*ST,* II-II, 47, 5). As we have already seen, neither the
matters about which there are intellectual virtues nor those concerning art are connected in the way that the objects of the moral virtues
are. Because art is "ordained to a certain particular end" and reaches
the end through determinate means (*ST,* II-II, 47, 4, ad 2), it has no
need of counsel, which is a part of prudence. The chief act of prudence, the act of commanding, terminates in an action, whereas the
perfection of art occurs in the act of judging (*ST,* II-II, 47, 8). There
is a gap between the possession and the exercise of the knowledge of
art as well as of the intellectual virtues. Both of these sorts of virtues
confer the "aptness" to act well but not the right use of that aptness.
A grammarian may commit a barbarism, and a craftsman may make
a bad pair of shoes. No such gap is present in prudence, which influences what someone is, not just what someone knows. An affective
dimension, absent in art and in the intellectual virtues, is intrinsic to
prudence. As Thomas puts it, "As long as the geometer demonstrates
the truth, how his appetitive part may be affected is of no concern,
whether he be joyful or angry, even as this is irrelevant to the artisan"

---

[26] Salkever, *Finding the Mean,* 135.

(*ST*, I-II, 57, 3). Persons who are morally vicious or virtuous can equally well appraise a geometrical proof or an article of clothing. Art and the intellectual virtues can thus be lost through forgetfulness, but prudence is uprooted through the corruption of the passions. In these ways, then, the practical virtue of art has more in common with the speculative, intellectual virtues than it does with the practical moral virtues or with prudence. On the basis of these distinctions, Thomas holds that only the moral virtues are virtues absolutely because virtue is a habit by which we work well (*ST*, I-II, 56, 3). The other "virtues" are called virtues in a relative and imperfect sense. If someone possesses not merely an aptness to do well but the capacity that confers the good use of that aptness, he or she does well actually. But to do well actually is under the control of the will; hence, virtue in its proper sense belongs only to those whose wills have been perfected by the relevant practical moral virtues.

The subordination of art and of the intellectual virtues to the moral virtues insofar as they are virtues raises the possibility of a more encompassing sort of subordination. As Thomas puts it, the use of knowledge pertains to the will, which confers the good use of the speculative habit and of the habit of art (*ST*, I-II, 57, 1). The latter habits share in common a focus on the "quality of the object," not on the appetite of the agent. Of course, there is no question of the moral virtues judging the proper objects of art or of a particular speculative science, neither of which falls under the scope of prudence (*ST*, I-II, 66, 5, ad 1). On the basis of the objects of the various virtues, the intellectual virtues are better than the moral virtues (*ST*, I-II, 66, 3). This comparison is not, however, the only sort possible: "If we consider virtue in relation to act, then moral virtue, which perfects the appetite, whose function is to move the other powers to act, . . . is more excellent. And virtue is so called from its principle of action. Because it is the perfection of a power, the nature of virtue agrees more with moral than with intellectual virtue, although the intellectual virtues are more excellent habits absolutely speaking" (*ST*, I-II, 66, 3). From the perspective of the appraisal of human life as well lived, the possession of the intellectual virtues is not an autonomous and overriding consideration. One must appraise not only the possession but also the use of these virtues, and the latter consideration locates the activities of the intellectual virtues within the whole of one's life—that is, within an encompassing practical context. Thomas goes well beyond Aristotle in his development of this larger context for the appraisal of the acts of all the virtues.

In spite of Thomas's emphasis on the distinctiveness of prudence, there is recurring doubt about the prospects for uniting a flourishing theory of virtue with a theory of natural law. Some think that the presence of any nongainsayable principles reduces ethics to *techne* and makes the contingent features of action irrelevant. As Joseph Dunne puts it, "The 'universal' ideas that make up one's habitual practical-moral knowledge—such as justice, bravery, truthfulness—cannot be 'stamped' on each act or situation, nor do they provide the kind of specification for action that a craftsman's working out of the *eidos* of his product provides."[27] Although Thomas does compare the determination of the general precepts of the natural law precepts to the realization of the artist's notion in the artifact, he also underscores the disparity between *techne* and moral knowledge. Even where the analogy to *techne* applies, it does not extend to the application of principles to concrete circumstances, only to the derivation of intermediate from common precepts. The treatment of the precepts of the natural law in no way violates what Thomas states about prudence in the commentary on the *Ethics:* "Discourse on moral matters even in their universal aspects is uncertain and variable, so the uncertainty only increases when one descends to a teaching bearing directly on singulars, for this falls under neither art nor narration, because the conditions of singular deeds vary indefinitely" (*In Libros Ethicorum*, II, lectio 2, note 258). The multiplication of rules engenders an infinite regress, broken only by the authoritative judgment of prudence. Nonetheless, the use of the language of irreducible particulars trades on an ambiguity.[28] Particulars, admittedly, are not universals, and the sensation of a particular can never be reduced to a knowledge of universals. But the merely particular is not intelligible to us; there must be something about the particulars that makes them more than mere particulars.

Thomas states that the *intellectus* of prudence, which involves the apprehension of a particular, does not reside in a power of the external senses, but in the interior sense, which operates through a certain collation and judges of particulars (*ST*, II-II, 47, 1, and 47, 3, ad 3).

---

[27] *Back to the Rough Ground*, 272.
[28] See *Back to the Rough Ground*, 295–314.

There is a role for universal or general knowledge in the apprehension of particulars, but its origin is the reverse of that ascribed to universals in artistic production. In the latter, the forms are abstract and are imposed on matter; in the former, the forms emerge from the particular. Commenting on Aristotle's discussion of prudence's apprehension of particulars, Thomas states, "Prudence . . . is of an extreme, namely, of a singular action, which stands as the principle in actions." He adds that Aristotle is not referring to the external sensation of proper sensibles—of colors, for example—but of the "interior sense by which we perceive imaginable things." He then turns to Aristotle's example of recognizing that what we are imagining is a particular triangle *(cognoscimus extremum triangulum idest singularem triangulum imaginatum)*. The passage recalls the mediating role of the imagined phantasm, its dual role as both a "this" and a "such," as an individual and as intelligible object of knowledge (*In Libros* Ethicorum, VI, lectio 7, notes 1214–16).

Any assumed dichotomy between universal knowledge and the particularity of sense perception obfuscates the intrinsic link between sense and human understanding. Given the emphasis on the indefeasible role of the phantasm in human knowledge, the fusion of sense and understanding in prudential knowledge is no anomaly. Prudential reasoning is properly rational. As Thomas says, "The conclusions of syllogisms are not only universals, but also particulars, because the intellect [*intellectus*] extends itself to matter by a certain reflection" (*ST,* II-II, 47, 3, ad 1). There is a certain universality present in sense experience itself *(universale in particulari),* without which there would be no knowledge of the universal and no intelligibility to action. The clearest statement of this idea occurs in the *Commentary on the* Posterior Analytics: "It is clear that the singular is sensed properly and essentially, but sense is also in a certain way of the universal. It knows Callias, not only as Callias, but also as this man" (*Sententia super* Posteriora Analytica, II, lectio 20, note 595). *Intellectus* is rightly listed as a part of prudence because it involves the "right estimation of a particular end" *(recta aestimatio de fine particulari),* not just the sensation of a particular (*ST,* II-II, 49, 2, ad 3).

Given that a virtue cannot be undermined by a particular vicious act, it might seem that Thomas's emphasis on rules is misplaced, unwarranted. It is not the case that the rules are absolute, if one means by "absolute" equally applicable always and everywhere.

Thomas does not hold that an individual can never act against any of the precepts, for, in some cases, lower precepts give way to higher ones, and they do so in two ways: either by a limitation in their scope, as is the case with the prohibition against theft, or by a failure in the principle itself, as is the case with the precept concerning returning borrowed goods. What a person ought never to do is act against a relevant precept—that is, against the command of prudence. To do so would be to court imprudence and other vices. The account of the principles that cannot be abrogated is not grounded in a view of others' rights, nor is it grounded exclusively in the goods of others. For Thomas, who we are and what we become as moral agents are equally involved in fundamental prohibitions. Without adherence to the basic precepts of the natural law, we cannot be virtuous persons. Of course, one vicious act here or there need not erode a virtuous character, but it seems a consideration more appropriate to a person who lacks virtue, not to a person who possesses or longs for virtue and understands with what cost and care virtues are cultivated. In this sense, the contemporary insistence that inordinate emphasis on rules distorts human life and ethical reflection is surely correct. The virtue-based account of moral precepts—of acts that, as Aristotle states, do not admit of a mean—captures the insight that there are certain kinds of actions that never or nearly never enter into a virtuous person's deliberation. Thomas's account of prudence, then, does not countenance a merely provisional view of all moral precepts. On the contrary, it brings out what was missing in the neoscholastic and Kantian emphasis on rules—namely, how these rules are inextricably bound up with the moral agent's view of his or her good, a good shared with others. As MacIntyre puts it,

> To understand the application of rules as part of the exercise of the virtues is to understand the point of rule-following, just because one cannot understand the exercise of the virtues except in terms of their constituting the type of life in which alone the human telos is to be achieved. The rules which are the negative precepts of the natural law thus do no more than set limits to that type of life and in so doing only partially define the kind of goodness to be aimed at. Detach them from their place in defining and constituting a whole way of life and they become nothing but a set of arbitrary prohibitions.[29]

---

[29] *Three Rival Versions of Moral Enquiry,* 139.

All sorts of things put prudence and the other virtues at risk. One of them is a failure to understand what binds one human being to another. For Thomas, we need not start with complete agreement about the highest good, but we should at least begin with the view of human life as a quest for the good. In his discussion of the prohibition of lying, Thomas states that "one man owes to another that without which human society is not able to be preserved" (*ST*, II-II, 109, 3, ad 1). Clearly, human society can survive without uniform adherence to the precepts of the natural law; indeed, in advanced capitalist societies, we are tempted to think that natural law flourishes in contexts where moral rules are subordinate to Machiavellian *virtù* or prudence. What Aquinas helps us to see is that it is not the mere survival of a group or its material pulchritude that is at issue, but rather the fragile existence of a community committed to a view of human life as a quest for the good. Insofar as this is how we understand ourselves and our relationship to others, we will find that the cultivation of certain virtues presupposes and can never do without conformity to certain precepts. Precepts are constitutive and enabling with respect to the goods that sustain communal inquiry and practice. Nothing in this account of the ideals of communal life dictates precisely how and to what extent the precepts of the natural law should be embodied in this or that community. Thomas nowhere demands of existing regimes that they immediately, or ever for that matter, enact laws in complete correspondence with the exalted goals of the natural law.

JUSTICE: ITS SCOPE AND LIMITS

A fully elaborated Thomistic account of natural law and virtue would depict a rather exalted vision of the good life for human beings, a life achievable by only a few individuals or communities. From a political perspective, this account is problematic: it seems to leave us with a quixotic ideal. And yet, as we have already seen in his natural law teaching, Aquinas has a decidedly prudential reticence about precisely how and to what extent the ideals of law and virtue are to be realized in specific regimes or communities. The suppleness of his position comes especially to the fore in his treatment of the virtue of justice. Among contemporary virtue ethicists, the neglect of justice, which is the political virtue, seems an egregious omission. The absence of positive proposals on justice is a bit odd, especially given that so many of these ethicists profess allegiance to Aristotle, who had a thing or two to say about justice.[30]

Aquinas's treatment of justice puts him in a position to respond to some contemporary challenges to virtue ethics. What are these challenges? The first objection is that virtue theory is incomplete because it lacks the notion of perfect duties and thus cannot adequately address disputes in political settings where disagreement is a prominent and ineliminable feature of public life. The second objection concerns the agent orientation of virtue ethics, which seems to neglect the importance of singular acts, especially "intolerable acts," as Louden calls them.[31] The agent orientation of virtue ethics seems to collapse goodness and evil into the agent and to be oblivious of the benefit received by others or the harm done to them. Correlatively, it is claimed that virtue theory is actually less social, less other oriented than is modern legal theory, which might seem an odd objection, given that the recovery of virtue has been accompanied by a rehabilitation of friendship and community as essential to ethical life. But the objection is that virtue theory fails to extend its regard for others far enough, that it can function only in exclusive, romantic settings. Another way of putting this objection would be to say that virtue theory is trapped in an idealized vision of the self-sufficiency of the agent. Jerome Schneewind claims that modern legal theory, in contrast to virtue theory, reminds us of "the basic needs we share, and the difficulties, inherent in our nature, in overcoming them."[32] Legal theory is thus more realistic and more democratic. Finally— and this last objection might be said to sum up all the previous ones—it is alleged that virtue theory is intrinsically reactionary and that its inability to say much of interest about politics lies precisely here. If it were to articulate a political theory, its reactionary character would become embarrassingly obvious.

Schneewind argues that the modern decline of virtue ethics is a direct result of its inability to meet the needs of more complex, mod-

---

[30] Recent work on the strengths and weaknesses of virtue ethics suggests that whether virtue ethics ultimately succeeds or fails may well depend on its ability to "expand its recent moral horizons so as to take in larger questions of political morality." See Crisp and Slote's introduction to the anthology *Virtue Ethics,* 24.

[31] "On Some Vices of Virtue Ethics," 207.

[32] "The Misfortunes of Virtue," 187.

ern societies, wherein the "central difficulties of life" arise "from disagreement—disagreement involving nations, religious sects, parties
to legal disputes, and ordinary people trying to make a living in busy
commercial societies." On these issues, Schneewind contends, "classical virtue theory is of little or no use."[33] To fill in this gap on political
matters, modern thinkers such as Grotius and Pufendorf construe
justice as indifferent to the motive of the agent: "to be just is simply
to have the habit of following right reason with respect to the rights
of others."[34] Justice is the realm of perfect duties, which catalogs the
acts whose performance or avoidance is necessary for the very existence of society. These duties are highly specific and compulsory;
they must be performed regardless of our inclinations. Schneewind
would have us believe that on the question of political principles the
tradition of virtue must be either silent or aggressively oppressive.

In response to Schneewind, Aquinas would argue that his account
of justice already has built into it a codification of perfect duties. In
fact, Aquinas's doctrine of natural law is best read not as an anticipation of the modern split between the norms of right conduct and the
goodness of action, but rather as an articulation and specification of
the demands of the virtue of justice. All the precepts of the Decalogue, Aquinas insists, concern justice (*ST,* I-II, 122, 1). The treatise
on law is indeed separate both from the general consideration of
virtue, which precedes it, and from the detailed consideration of virtue, which follows it. But the determination of which acts count as
violations of the common precepts of the natural law (for example,
whether taking from another's surplus in time of dire need counts as
theft) occurs in the section on the virtue of justice (*ST,* II-II, 56, 7).
The precepts of justice especially concern those matters without
which human society cannot be preserved; thus, they prohibit hei-
nous acts against our fellow citizens—for example, murder and theft.
To this extent and in this respect, Aquinas can accommodate Schneewind's understanding of modern legal theory, with its insistence on
perfect duties, which must "be carried out if society is to exist at
all," which are susceptible to codification, and whose performance is
obligatory regardless of one's internal motivation.

Yet here we must pause to note an important disagreement be-

---

[33] "The Misfortunes of Virtue," 199–200.
[34] Schneewind, "The Misfortunes of Virtue," 183.

tween Aquinas and modern legal theory, at least as it is defended by
Schneewind, who claims that "the man who regularly carries out all
his perfect duties is a just man even if he dislikes acting justly."[35] This
assertion is problematic. On Schneewind's own terms, it seems to
collapse the distinction between act and character that Schneewind
commends modern legal theory for developing. Instead of doing
what he faults virtue ethics for doing—namely, subsuming goodness
within the agent—he makes the opposite error. He reduces the goodness of the agent to that of the act. Of course, Schneewind might
counter that it is the regularity of the conduct that allows us to call
the agent just, which does seem to be one of the criteria necessary
for the attribution of justice to an individual's character. The question
is whether more is not needed to call an individual a "just human
being." For Aquinas at least, to be just it is not sufficient, although it
is necessary, to fulfill the "due"—that is, to perform the appropriate
external act; to be called a just human being, one must rejoice in just
deeds—that is, perform them from a character that is just. Justice is
defined as a "perpetual and constant will" to give another what is his
or her due (*ST,* II-II, 58, 1). Human law, accordingly, is designed in
accord with this more complex account of justice; law concerns itself
directly with the external act but indirectly with virtue, without some
modicum of which the performance of the external acts of justice is
unlikely to endure.

Aquinas's account of justice turns back another objection to contemporary virtue ethics—namely, its failure to account for intolerable
acts. Robert Louden argues that all contemporary schools of normative ethics are "mononomic"; each is incomplete, providing only a
part of what is needed.[36] Virtue ethicists are fond of aiming this
charge at Kantian and utilitarian theories, so they may be surprised
to find Louden turning the objection against themselves. Nonetheless, he urges that the "strong agent orientation" of virtue ethics leads
to an exclusive focus on agents over acts. Louden contends that the
question fundamental to virtue ethics—"What sort of person ought I
to be?"—cannot be separated from the question "What ought I to
do?" Without some answer to the latter, we shall not know how to
become virtuous and be left with vague, hypothetical descriptions of

---

[35] "The Misfortunes of Virtue," 186.
[36] "On Some Vices of Virtue Ethics," 204.

exemplary characters. For Louden, the problem with the exaltation of agent over act is not just the threat of moral skepticism. The strongest objection concerns what Louden calls "intolerable acts . . . certain types of action which produce harms of such magnitude that they destroy the bonds of the community and render (at least temporarily) the achievement of moral goods impossible."[37] Attentive readers will hear in this passage echoes of MacIntyre's insistence in *After Virtue* that a list of virtues needs to be paired with a list of actions never admitting of a mean. But Louden fails to articulate the complementarity of virtues and rules in MacIntyre's Aristotelian language. In fact, MacIntyre describes rules, in Aristotelian and Thomistic terms, as specifications of the virtues. By contrast, Louden appeals to Frankena's thesis that "The Greeks held that being virtuous entails not just having good motives or intentions but also doing the right thing."[38] If we set aside Frankena's dubious imputation of a good/right split to Greek ethics, we might more accurately say that for Aristotle an act is good only if it is good in every respect. More broadly for Aristotle, being virtuous is a matter of having a certain kind of character, spelled out in terms of possessing a set of virtues. A virtue is a habit standing midway between potency and act, or more precisely a potency that is oriented in a determinate way. But such a habit exists in order that it may be actualized, which accords with Aristotle's doctrine of *energeia*, wherein capacities are ordered to activities (cf., *Metaphysics*, VII). Habits are defined by reference to their acts. Thus, Aristotle does not leave specific acts unappreciated. However, the accusation of reductionism can be reformulated: even if acts are given their due, they are valuable only insofar as they are signs or manifestations of virtue, of the excellence of the agent. Whatever may be the proper interpretation of Aristotle, it is clear that Aquinas does not completely collapse the goodness of acts, at least the acts of justice, into the goodness of the agent.

Aquinas's principal focus is on the virtues and their distinctive and proper matters. Some acts are intolerable because of the harm they do to others and because they thwart the fundamental goods of political life. It is not as if an extrinsic account of acts has to be added to that of the virtues; instead, once the virtues are differentiated, it be-

---

[37] "On Some Vices of Virtue Ethics," 207.
[38] "On Some Vices of Virtue Ethics," 213.

comes clear that some virtues require perfect duties. Justice is distinguished from the other virtues in the nature of the mean. In contrast to the other moral virtues, where the mean is directly relative to the character of the agent, the "due" or mean of justice does not reside in the subjective disposition of the agent or in the passions; it consists rather in the external act, in "operations or things," in the harm or good done to the other (*ST*, II-II, 58, 10).

Although Aquinas does not use the language of rights, he does refer to justice as the "good of another." Of all the virtues, only justice has built into its very definition an essential relation to others; its neglect in the contemporary recovery of virtue is perplexing, especially given the prominence that virtue ethicists accord to human beings as social and communal animals.

As I have already noted, both Aristotle and Aquinas subordinate their discussions of laws, rules, and procedures to the virtue of justice, which is the comprehensive virtue. Justice, Aquinas writes, is the human good. He cites Cicero's assertions that men are "chiefly called good from justice" and that "the splendor of virtue is greatest in justice" (*ST*, II-II, 53, 3). For Aquinas, the precepts of the natural law are but the rudimentary expressions of the constituents of virtue, focusing especially on the fulfillment of our duties to God and neighbor.

This exaltation of the virtue of justice undermines the objections that virtue theory is insufficiently social and that virtue theory is trapped in an idealized vision of self-sufficiency. These claims may not be different formulations of the same objection, but they are closely connected. Recall Schneewind's assertion that modern legal theories, in contrast to virtue theories, remind us of the "basic needs we share, and the difficulties, inherent in our nature, to overcoming them."[39] We have already seen that, according to the basic precepts of justice, certain kinds of harm to others must always be avoided. To the most fundamental prohibitions on murder, theft, and adultery, Aquinas adds prohibitions on lying because truthfulness is necessary for the preservation of society and is thus a precept of justice. To arrive at an adequate account of justice, we would also have to include a set of virtues—including gratitude, liberality, affability, and mercy—that in some cases specify and in others supplement justice.

---

[39] "The Misfortunes of Virtue," 200.

Affability, for example, is the virtue of "behaving toward all," even strangers, "in a fitting way" (*ST*, II-II, 114, 2, ad 3). Affability fulfills neither a legal debt nor a debt from a favor received, the latter of which is fulfilled by the virtue of gratitude. Moreover, affability falls short of perfect friendship; hence, it does not exhibit the intimacy appropriate to perfect friendship. Still, because of our common humanity, we are "every man's friend," even a stranger's friend (*ST*, II-II, 114, 1, ad 2).

If the virtue of justice renders Aquinas's ethical and political theory less vulnerable to contemporary assault, it also contains resources for criticizing corrupt social and political practices. Consider the virtue of liberality, a virtue for which there is little place in either right-wing libertarianism or left-wing social engineering. Liberality, a mean between prodigality and covetousness, has to do with the proper stewardship of excess riches (*ST*, II-II, 117, 1). Prodigality is not just wastefulness but the spending of money on the flesh that leads one to take no pleasure in virtue. In the treatment of covetousness, the inordinate love of possessing, Aquinas refers to its "daughters" or offspring: treachery, fraud, falsehood, perjury, violence, restlessness, and insensibility to mercy.

Nearly all the vices bred by covetousness assault justice. One of the "daughters," insensibility to mercy, erodes our ability to see and respond appropriately to others in need. The root of this vice is a hardening of the heart such that we are not moved to assist the needy. Aquinas's explication of mercy takes direct aim at a certain conception of self-sufficiency. Although conceding that a passion cannot be a virtue (*ST*, II-II, 30, 3), he insists that the feeling of sorrow, which is part of mercy, is not a vice or defect. He cites Aristotle: among the friendly qualities is a willingness "to grieve with a friend" (*amicibilia condolere amico; ST*, II-II, 30, 2). He contends further that "to repute oneself happy" and invulnerable to suffering is a result of the vice of pride, whose false sense of justice is actually a form of scorn (*ST*, II-II, 30, 2, ad 3). By contrast, the wise who have fallen into misery are more merciful. The proudly self-sufficient disown any connection between themselves and those who suffer; yet this lack of connection is an illusion, a failure to see themselves as at least always potentially in the very position of the needy and suffering other.

The nesting of justice within a host of other virtues evinces the precise scope and limits of justice. If Aquinas fails to reduce our needs to a short list, he does underscore our neediness in other, more pronounced ways. Moreover, the modern account described by Schneewind embodies its own conception of self-sufficiency because it tends to view individuals as isolated, lacking any common vision of their good and primarily needing others in an instrumental fashion. The contractual model of justice presupposes a clean slate, where debits and credits emerge only after we have entered into the contract. On Aquinas's view, by contrast, many of our debts are incurred prior to and without an individual's conscious consent, and some can never be fully repaid. Such is the case, for example, with the debts we owe to God, country, parents, and those who exercise offices of dignity in the community. At the heart of the Thomistic account of justice is the paradox of debts that cannot be fully repaid, the virtuous response to which is gratitude, liberality, and hospitality. Pieper writes, "The just man, who . . . realizes that his very being is a gift, and that he is heavily indebted before God and man, is also the man willing to give where there is no strict obligation. He will be willing to give another man something no one can compel him to give."[40]

Of course, however intriguing many contemporary political theorists may find this or that observation of Aquinas, they will in the end insist that someone who defended monarchy and a quasi-theocratic form of government cannot be taken seriously in contemporary debates, which brings us to the last objection to virtue ethics. In an article that provoked a quick response from the famous intellectual historian Brian Tierney, Samuel Beer argues against any assimilation of Aquinas's political theory, which is fundamentally hierarchical and celebrates the "rule of the wise and holy," to modern democratic politics. Not only does Thomas not anticipate modern developments, but the "whole thrust of Thomas's system . . . is in the opposite direction. It is the system that is impressive: not just the preference for the hierarchical form of government in state and church, but the derivation of that preference from a comprehensive and coherent

---

[40] *Four Cardinal Virtues,* 111. Pieper's analysis of justice underscores the limits to justice, and in this he anticipates many of the contentions of contemporary communitarians and feminists about the "need for more than justice." Nonetheless, because Pieper has access to a preliberal conception of justice, he can also defend a robust understanding of that virtue. The more deeply we probe the virtue of justice, the more we see that it is at odds with both the communitarian and the liberal points of view.

worldview."[41] Much, although certainly not all, of what Beer has to say about hierarchy and the rule of the virtuous is indisputable, but Beer is woefully ignorant of the Thomistic or, indeed, the broadly classical understanding of the distinction between theory and practice. To see that Aquinas's political thought is of more than antiquarian interest, we would have to examine the distinction not only between theory and practice, but also between the best and legitimate regimes.

On the surface at least, the commitment to political theory of any sort puts Aquinas at odds with a host of contemporary virtue ethicists, communitarians, and feminist proponents of care whose resistance to justice in its dominant modern conceptions is accompanied by a repudiation of the theoretical aspirations of Kantian and utilitarian moral and political writing. These contemporary writers and others resist the turn to theory because they think it requires abandoning the concrete, the contextual, and the particular (all of which virtue ethics celebrates) for the sake of the abstract, the impersonal, and the universal. Thus, they tend to deflate the pretensions of ethical theory itself.

But this conception of theory cedes too much ground to Kantians and utilitarians. The failure in contemporary virtue ethics to envision an alternative to theory as understood by its rivals is akin to the lack of imagination with regard to justice. A broadly Aristotelian conception of theory cannot be assimilated to either of the dominant, rival, modern conceptions of theory. How political theory is to inform the founding and guidance of regimes is a matter of art at the service of political prudence, a matter of constructing laws and fostering local and intermediate institutions conducive to the inculcation of virtue. What virtue politics needs, then, is a theory that is at once more ambitious than anything that has been mustered thus far in virtue ethics and more prudent than what counts as theory in Kantian and utilitarian circles. By "more prudent," I mean more attuned to the distinction between theory and practice, to the ways mistakes about

---

[41] "The Rule of the Wise and Holy: Hierarchy in the Thomistic System." Tierney responded not so much on behalf of Aquinas but on behalf of late-medieval political theory generally; see "Hierarchy, Consent, and the 'Western Tradition.'" A later and more able response on behalf of Aquinas, emphasizing the role of consent in Aquinas, was put forth by Mark Murphy in "Consent, Custom, and the Common Good in Aquinas's Account of Political Theory."

the nature of each and about their relationship can undermine the life and understanding of the virtues.

There is, of course, no easy way to deduce an appropriate way of life for individuals or communities from a hierarchy of natural ends. Consider, for example, the hierarchy of goods or inclinations toward goods that, according to Aquinas, supply the foundation for the precepts of the natural law (*ST*, I-II, 92, 4). Given the distinction between theory and practice, no deliverances of a theory of human nature can provide an immediately practical teaching. It falls to prudence to determine how any account of human nature is to inform a way of life. This is true in politics as well as in ethics. The dialectical movement back and forth between the ideals of human nature and the best regime, on the one hand, and the concrete and varied way in which human beings pursue the good, on the other, is evident in the very structure of the *Politics*. Beer's assertion that Thomas derives his politics from his cosmology is simply and dangerously false.

From the perspective of Aristotle's politics, the contemporary divide between communitarians and liberals or between particularists and universalists is the result of an artificial severing of the particular or singular and the universal. The danger is that we will be saddled with the equally unwelcome options of mere particularity or mere universality without any way of mediating between them.[42] The lack of mediation entails the demise of dialectic as Aristotle understands and deploys it. For him, dialectic is not just a method of sorting out and reconciling inherited opinions. It is also a method of engaging the particular—be it an individual or a community—in light of its aspiration for the good, not merely for the good as it appears to me or to my community. Concerning justice, Aristotle asserts that "all cling to justice of some kind, but not to the whole of it" (*Politics*, III, 8). The teleological structure of practical reasoning presupposes that there is no such thing as a mere particular.[43] The method of engaging individuals and communities is dialectical in that it appeals to the

[42] On the political implications of the classical intertwining of particular and universal and the modern severing of the two, see Pierre Manent, especially *The City of Man*.

[43] There are important metaphysical issues lurking here. Aristotle's understanding of the relationship between particularity and universality in ethics and politics is a correlate of his conception of substance as a this-such, a concrete singular that bears a universal nature, a real synthesis of singular and universal.

aspiration for the good universally operative in human action. This dialectic presupposes *(a)* a teleological conception of human action because agents and communities are engaged in light of ends they are already explicitly or implicitly pursuing, and *(b)* the possibility of mediating between particular and universal because, as I have just noted, the good, and not merely the apparent good, is that at which all persons aim.

Although this account of theory does not constrict or denigrate prudence, it does provide a corrective to the reactionary tendency that some critics of virtue impute to virtue theory—namely, the tendency to retreat to local communities severed from the wider world.[44] Local communities are unlikely to foster virtue for long if they ignore larger economic and political forces. If local communities provide a setting for the initial cultivation of virtue, they fail to meet another of Aristotle's criteria for a human community: self-sufficiency. Aristotle's conception of the particularist aspiration for the good thus moves in a direction opposite to that of a reactionary politics.

FRIENDSHIP, POLITICS, AND HUMAN EXCELLENCE

The particularist aspiration for the universal good is most dramatically evident in Aristotle's discussion of friendship, which encompasses a remarkably large percentage of the pages of the *Ethics*. A number of obstacles block our appreciation of Aristotle's view of friendship. Modern reflection on the moral life often supposes a dichotomy between selfishness and altruism.[45] Aristotle's assertion that friendship originates in self-love is apt to seem misguided, even pernicious. But self-love is not selfishness, nor does self-love exist prior to and independent of love of others, for we are at birth thrust into a position of dependence on and affection for others. An ineliminable reciprocity exists between love of self and love of others.[46] Aristotle's

---

[44] I'm not sure that this accusation touches any contemporary virtue theory. Indeed, the tendency may be a natural consequence of modern proceduralism with its centralizing and homogenizing tendencies. At least Tocqueville makes a convincing case for this tendency in his discussion of individualism.

[45] On this, see John Cooper, "Aristotle on Friendship."

[46] See Nancy Sherman's discussion of the "friend as another but separate self" in *The Fabric of Character*, 138–44.

account focuses on the movement from a narrow and private to a shared, public appreciation of the good.

Love of another does not entail self-abnegation. The key distinction is not between selfishness and altruism, but between different sorts of self-love and love of another. The virtuous man wishes "to live and to be preserved"; he desires especially the preservation of that "by which he thinks" (*In Libros* Ethicorum, IX, lectio 4, note 1806). He also loves another for his own sake and not as a means to his own good. The self-love of the good is more complete than that of the vicious. The latter are plagued by inconstancy and regret. The soul of the vicious person is divided against itself. Vicious people love only apparent goods and hence do not really love themselves; conversely, what they love in others is the utility or pleasure they afford. For the good person, "the true and apparent goods are the same thing" (*eadem enim sunt apud ipsum vera et apparentia bona*). Good human beings naturally take delight in the contemplation of goodness, both in themselves and in others. They are justifiably lovers of self. They thus assign to themselves what is "noblest and best" and "[indulge] the most authoritative element." As the seat of conscious and reflective awareness, the rational principle can be said to be the "man himself" (*Ethics*, IX, 4 and 8).

Although we may enter into friendships by many avenues, only friendship based on virtue is permanent and does not involve mutual exploitation. The friend who loves only for pleasure or utility does not love another for that person's own sake, but because of what he or she expects to receive from the other. The other is loved only accidentally. Friendships of utility or pleasure are counterfeits. In these associations, which are impermanent and full of complaints, the friend is loved only incidentally as an instrument to the attainment of some good. Persons who love for utility or pleasure have not fully entered into the realm of the human. Aristotle's depiction of these associations is reminiscent of his remarks about the self-indulgence of children and about the self-defeating behavior of the intemperate, who are "pained for their pleasure." Imperfect forms of friendship are characterized by undeveloped motives. True friendship is possible only among healthy and mature members of the human species. Far from involving the dissolution of the other in oneself, the notion that the friend is another self entails a union of affections wherein one is affected as one's friend is (*In Libros* Ethicorum, IX, lectio 4,

1811). Following Aristotle, Thomas compares the love of one friend for another with the love mothers bestow on their children.[47] This account of friendship reflects and provides a model for a particular view of moral education. Following Plato, Aristotle notes that the right education for children is to habituate them so that they are pleased and pained in appropriate ways. The passions are formed with respect to pleasure and pain by social practices of praise and blame; we gain an understanding of what is good and best for us by imitating the exemplars of human action embodied in the practices of our community.

In the discussion of friendship, the term *activity (operatio)* surfaces repeatedly. Happiness is itself an activity, not a state of subjective satisfaction. We are conscious of ourselves and of others by means of the mutual activities in which we engage. As Thomas observes, "the reflective act in which we perceive that we perceive and know that we know is a source of pleasure." But we "take delight only in that which we know, and we are better able to contemplate those near to us than ourselves" (*In Libros* Ethicorum, IX, lectio 10, note 1896). According to the Aristotelian view of self-knowledge, we have no direct access to the operations of the soul. The rational power is a potency that is made actual through its interaction with the world. It is easier to study and take delight in the virtuous actions of our neighbors than it is to contemplate our own actions. We gain self-knowledge through friendship. Shared participation in virtuous activities enhances and expands our experience and our happiness. There is no notion here of the modern understanding of friendship as an ecstatic union of wills in which the focus on the other is exclusive of the world and of the activities in which the friends engage.

Aristotle underscores the political dimension to friendship when he writes that friendship is a source of "unanimity," that it expels faction, and that it "holds cities together." Lawgivers "aim for it [friendship] more than for justice" (*Ethics*, VIII, 1, 1155a22–25; see also Aquinas, *In Libros* Ethicorum, VIII, lectio 1, note 1542). In these passages, Aristotle explicitly links friendship with the common good. Thomas comments: "Every friendship consists in communica-

---

[47] *"Amicus vult suum amicum esse, et vivere gratia ipsius amici et non propter seipsum, ut scilicet quaerat ex eo solum proprium commodum. Et hoc patiuntur matres ad filios"* (*In Libros* Ethicorum, IX, lectio 4, note 1799).

tion; every communication is reduced to the political" (*In Libros Ethicorum*, VIII, lectio 9, 1657). Friendship is not, however, merely a means that the legislator deploys to render the citizenry docile. As modern individualist and proceduralist politics attests, the lower forms of communication, rooted in pleasure and utility, are more sure means of control. Indeed, friendship, as Aristotle understands it, is both a substantive good and a training in a range of goods proper to human beings.

The connection between the excellences of human life depicted in the *Ethics* and the political order is evident in the very structure of the *Ethics*, which begins and ends by reminding the reader that moral inquiry is part of a larger investigation—namely, politics. Aristotle's *Politics* begins with a genetic account of the polis. A consideration of the way the polis emerges or grows from its elements renders it intelligible.[48] The analysis is not reductionist; it does not uncover autonomous, complete individuals, calculating their interests. In Aristotle's account, deliberative reason is posterior to the prerational inclinations of human nature. Male and female exhibit a natural propensity—a propensity that is "not from deliberate choice"—to join together for the propagation of the species (*Politics*, I, 2). The clearest expression of the primacy of the political over the private is the statement that "the polis is by nature prior to the home and to each of us; for whole is necessarily prior to part" (*Politics*, I, 2, 1253a19–21). Just as a part is insufficient and unintelligible in separation from the whole, so too the individual is insufficient apart from the community. The home (*oikia*), for example, is established according to nature to meet daily needs. The natural desire to satisfy human needs by means of concerted efforts motivates the transition from local forms of community to more complete communities. How far communities naturally tend in the direction of the best is questionable. An ambiguity in the term *natural* is operative here. *Nature* means that to which something tends in an organic process of development and which is achieved always or for the most part, but it also means a state of excellence to which the organic process points but which is

---

[48] *Politics*, I, 1. Aristotle underscores the naturalness of the polis, yet nature is not always deemed an appropriate standard for political matters. See Wayne H. Ambler, "Aristotle's Understanding of the Naturalness of the City."

realized rarely. Both the best regime and the good life for individuals are natural in the latter sense, but not in the first.[49]

The primacy of the political involves more than the observation that individuals are insufficient apart from the community. There is the danger here of an exclusively instrumentalist view of the political order. Subpolitical or prepolitical life, the life of families and villages, can satisfy many of the physical needs of human life. The chief sign that human beings are naturally political is that they are endowed with speech. Once again, the duality of the term *logos* is operative. In this context, Aristotle links quite closely the exercise of speech with the human capacity to perceive and reason about the beneficial and the harmful, the just and the unjust. Thomas comments that Aristotle "proves from the proper operation of man that he is a civil animal" (*In Libros* Politicorum, I, lectio 1, note 36). From the priority assigned to reason, some might suppose that speech and the social nature are afterthoughts for Aquinas, but what is more striking is the thesis that Aristotle's conception of reason entails human sociability. How different is that from the modern calculative, individualistic view of reason? The presence of logos is manifest in communal deliberation; the polis is the appropriate forum for the actualization of this capacity. Thomas adds, "The city is a perfect community. . . . Because every communication among men is ordered to some necessity of life, the perfect community will ensure that man possesses sufficiently whatever is necessary [*necessarium*] to life. Such a community is the city. It is of its very essence that all things necessary for human life are found in it" (*In Libros* Politicorum, I, lectio 1, note 31). Thomas's comments seem to support the instrumental view of the *civitas*. The term *necessarium* is, however, being used broadly to cover whatever contributes to the sufficiency of human life. Clearly, these necessities are not limited to the exigencies of the body; the goods of speech and virtue are higher than physical needs. Only the goods of speech and virtue are ends in themselves; they are integral to friendship and explain why friendship requires a political setting (*In Libros* Politicorum, I, lectio 1, notes 36–37). As I have noted, the perfect city is not natural in the sense that it is realized always or for

---

[49] On the complex relationships between friendship and the political order, see Tessitore, *Reading Aristotle's* Ethics, 73–95.

the most part. Rather, its naturalness is akin to that of the virtues, excellences to which nature points. As the virtues are acquired through exercise, so cities are instituted through human industry (*In Libros* Politicorum, I, lectio 1, note 40). The discussion of the polis moves from its universal utility to its nobility. The education and expansion of natural desires move beyond self-interest narrowly construed to the recognition of goods held in common.

The guiding notion of the legislator is the common good. Certain misconstruals usually attend modern attempts to describe the common good. The chief impediment to our understanding of the common good is our tendency to formulate the issue in terms of the mutually exclusive alternatives of totalitarian, bureaucratic regimes and the regimes of liberal individualism. Aristotle's comment that the individual is a part of the city evinces the incompatibility of liberal individualism with his understanding of the common good. The city is not, however, an organic unity; it is not a person writ large. It has what Aquinas calls a unity of order. Charles De Koninck writes, "The totalitarian solution is that the individual person is ordered and subjected to society. We are inclined, in rejecting this doctrine, to swing in the opposite extreme; but if we prescind from the common good of the persons which is the final, therefore first cause of society, we are left with a mere aggregate of individuals."[50]

To see that Aristotle's view of the common good does not entail totalitarianism, we need only consider his critique of the theses of Plato's *Republic*. In contrast to Plato's purported idealistic view of politics, Aristotle's account of the political order is said to be realistic or practical. It aims at the good realizable by human beings. In the *Politics,* Aristotle signals out two features of Plato's *Republic* as problematic: its monistic conception of community and its tendency to supplant indigenous practices in favor of artificially engineered social structures (*Politics,* II, 1–7). According to Aristotle, the community is a plurality. The various members and groups within the community

---

[50] "In Defense of St. Thomas: A Reply to Fr. Eschmann's Attack on the Primacy of the Common Good," 22. For a recent examination of the debate among Thomists over the common good, see Mary M. Keys, "Personal Dignity and the Common Good: A Twentieth-Century Thomistic Dialogue." For an argument that Thomas's political theory avoids the "shallow individualism of liberal theory and the social determinism of communitarian theory," see E. A. Goerner and W. J. Thompson's "Politics and Coercion."

are to be united through education and law. In order to understand his conception of law, it is necessary to turn to the conclusion of the *Ethics*, where he underscores the limits to moral argument. Passion responds more readily to force than to argument; a compulsive power is necessary if most people are to possess "some share of virtue" (*Ethics*, X, 9, 1179b19). But law is not simply an instrument of fear and compulsion, for it is a "rule proceeding from prudence and intellect" (*Ethics*, X, 9, 1180a22). Speech and instruction (*sermo et doctrina*) affect only the virtuous; others obey through violence (*violentia*) and necessity (*necessitas*). The point is to educate the passions: those who are not persuaded must be compelled by law to the good (*compellatur ad bonum; In Libros* Ethicorum, X, lectio 14, note 2147).

Law has a number of goals. It serves the ends of justice by rectifying wrongs and inequities; it seeks to curb acts rooted in excessive passion; and it hopes to foster the habits of virtue, to harmonize reason and passion. Obedience to law offers a vicarious participation in reason. In his discussion of ruler and ruled, Aristotle recurs to the relationship between soul and body, noting that the soul rules the body by a despotic rule, but the intellect rules the appetites with a constitutional rule. Certain human appetites are capable of sharing or participating in reason. One of the tasks of the moral life is to bring these appetites under the sway of reason and to "harmonize" passion and reason. The teaching concerning the participation in the reason of another pertains to all human beings. Aristotle writes that human beings are praised for knowing both how to rule and how to obey; the citizen does both. Participation in the reason of another is the necessary means by which one learns to exercise reason for oneself. As Aristotle puts it, "the ruler must learn by obeying" (*Politics*, II, 4, 1277b10). In the *Ethics*, too, he argues that lawgivers should study the soul, in particular the connection between its rational and irrational components. The goal of the legislator is to form citizens' habits, which gives the starting points or first principles of action (*Ethics*, I, 13).

In spite of the contrast with Plato, Aristotle's own view does not merely save the appearances of conventional political life. The standard to which Aristotle continually adverts is nature, even if the nature of political things is disclosed at least implicitly through the constitutions, laws, and customs of existing regimes. Just as in an individual life there is a natural aspiration to pursue the best life available to one, so too at the level of regimes there is an impetus toward the best. The good, we may recall, is that at which all things aim. We may in fact choose only apparent goods most of the time, but we do not choose them as apparent goods. Instead, we always choose what we take to be true goods. There is also an impetus toward a comprehensive account of the good life for individuals and communities. The need for theory arises from practice itself and even theoretical truth has a certain utility. If Aristotle's attempts in the *Ethics* and *Politics* to persuade the legislator of the relevance of the principles of political philosophy to the legislator's own task were successful, then the legislative art would operate in light of a theoretical account of politics. That the realization of the ends of political association requires the decisive intervention of human artifice is evident from the crucial role that laws and customs play. Politics is the highest art, and the political philosopher is the "master craftsman" (*architekton; Ethics*, VII, 11, 1152b1–2). Of course, the art of legislation would have to be inherently prudential, as it would mediate between philosophy and the contingent circumstances of existing regimes. Thus, the theoretical, the artistic, and the prudential complement one another in the ethical and political pursuit of the good life.[51]

The legislator's art does not eradicate natural motives and attachments, but moves the individual from the private and narrow bounds of self-interest to a gradual appreciation of the common good. The laws of the community are intimately connected with and must operate in conjunction with the inveterate customs of a society.[52] Aristotle states that customary laws have more weight and relate to more important matters than written laws (*Politics*, III, 16, 1287b5–7). The emphasis on custom is a sobering commentary on the limitations to law. The political relationship between law and custom reflects the connection in ethics between the rational and the appetitive parts of the soul. In each case, the goal is to harmonize the two elements, to enable custom and appetite to share in the rational principle. Pre-

---

[51] For an account of the relationship between theory and practice in Aristotle, see Salkever, *Finding the Mean*. See also the important reservations about Salkever's position in David O'Connor's review of this book in *Ancient Philosophy*.

[52] In the words of Aquinas, "custom has the force of law, abolishes law, and is the interpreter of law" (*ST*, I-II, 97, 3).

cisely this sort of strategy is operative in the defense of private property against the thesis of the *Republic*. Private property is not a first principle of the political order; nor is it a self-evident right. Instead, it is justified by reference to the common good. The attachment to the local and the particular enables the citizen to participate in the polis. Without private property, the practice of certain virtues, such as benevolence, would be impossible (*Politics*, II, 5–6). Private property aids in uniting the proper good with the common good. The art of legislation mediates between proper and common good through the inculcation of virtue.

As I have insisted throughout, Aquinas's focus on the common good and on the role of law as pedagogue does not provide any sort of prescription for particular regimes. It does, however, provide standards in light of which we might begin to think reflectively and critically about political life. The centrality of the political in Aristotle and Aquinas comports with Aristotle's observation that the sort of beings we are would be inconceivable apart from the polis. A being that exists apart from the polis would be either a "beast or a god." The statement has often been read as demarcating the proper realm of the human and distinguishing that realm from what stands both beneath and above it. But we should not be content with such a tidy division; indeed, human beings might be described as the only living beings who simultaneously touch both the animal and the divine. As is evident from our previous consideration of the place of human beings within the genus of animal, we cannot exalt the human at the expense of animal. Conversely, we cannot so diminish the human that its likeness to the divine is entirely obscured. The very fact of the human orientation to the whole and of its knowledge of higher beings evinces the kinship of humanity with the highest beings. To the divine element in human nature and to the relationship of that element to other human capacities we now turn.

3

Contemplation and Prudence; Philosophy and Politics

I HAVE ALREADY MENTIONED some of the peculiar features of ancient politics—the pedagogical conception of law, the focus on virtue and the common good, and the centrality of friendship. We have yet to come to terms with the most peculiar feature of ancient political theory, at least from the perspective of modern politics: the defense of the contemplative life as the best life. The advocacy of the contemplative life as the good life is sometimes thought to be an anomaly in Aristotle's texts. Some view its presence as an unfortunate remnant of Platonism.[1] Aristotle's preoccupation with contemplation is more pervasive than this reading allows. The confrontation between the active and the contemplative lives might be said to be the dramatic centerpiece of Aristotle's corpus. Certainly the introduction of the contemplative life into the debate over the good life raises difficulties for any attempt to harmonize the philosophical and the political. The disparity between the philosophic life and the life of political and ethical activity has been a source of much controversy.

Yet it is precisely in the *Politics,* in the most unlikely of texts, that we find a sustained, if indirect, defense of the life of contemplation. The route to the defense of contemplation is oblique and dialectical; it rests on a reversal of the common understanding of contemplation as inert and lifeless or as a covert form of power. Contemporary dismissals of contemplation often fail to move beyond the initial stage of the dialectic, a stage that mirrors the perspective of those Aristotle calls the "political men," who identify the life of conquest and honor

---

[1] See Nussbaum, *The Fragility of Goodness,* 373–77. She thinks it invites the appraisal of the various goods of human life in terms of a species-independent criterion.

as the best life. If Aristotle held that the godlike aspiration to contemplation were utterly foreign to our embodied and political nature, then not only would we have to excise key passages from the *De Anima, Ethics,* and *Metaphysics,* but we would also have to distort the culminating teaching of the *Politics.*

WISDOM AND/OR PRUDENCE

Aristotle's repeated reference in the *Ethics* and the *Politics* to the hierarchical structure of the powers of the soul raises the question of the perfection of the rational part itself. In *Ethics,* I, 12, Aristotle makes a division of the soul into rational and irrational parts, a division to which he frequently recurs in both the *Ethics* and the *Politics.* Thomas comments: "A certain part of virtue is rational through itself and is called intellectual; another part, which is in the appetitive part of the soul, is rational through participation and is called moral" (*In Libros* Ethicorum, I, lectio 20, note 243). The distinction serves various functions and thus is apt to be misconstrued. In the context of the early books of the *Ethics,* the division primarily helps to demarcate the sphere of moral virtue, which has to do with that part of the irrational soul that is able to participate in reason. Moral virtue is largely a matter of educating the passions so as to act in concert with reason. That one part of the soul, the appetitive, is able to share in reason belies the view that there is a strict division of the soul into rational and irrational, a division that would render Aristotle's notion of practical reason as reasoning desire or desiring reason otiose. There is, furthermore, a reciprocal relation of dependence between the moral virtues and the intellectual virtue of prudence. Even the intellectual virtues have at least an indirect relationship to the passions: there is a natural desire to know, and the philosopher is a lover of wisdom. Nonetheless, certain virtues such as courage and temperance are more immersed in the passions, in the feelings of fear and pleasure, and have a more immediate relationship to particulars, to the here and now. Of course, some moral virtues such as justice resist easy classification. Aristotle's consideration of justice immediately before the intellectual virtues is an acknowledgment of its intermediate status. Thomas locates justice not in the passions, but in the will.

The structure of the *Ethics* moves from the virtues, such as temperance and fortitude, through justice and the intellectual virtues to the contemplative life. Friendship occupies a pivotal location between the last two discussions. How is friendship, which has to do with our social and active life, an appropriate prelude to the contemplative life? In the discussion of friendship, Aristotle observes that it is not easy for an isolated person to be continuously active. Even those devoted to the philosophic life will find that communication with others assists their pursuits (*Ethics*, IX, 9, 1170a5–12). One of the commendable features of the contemplative life is its self-sufficiency; in contrast to the active life, the life of philosophy is not dependent for its very existence on the presence of others. Nonetheless, as Thomas says, "it is better for the wise to have cooperators in the consideration of truth, because one person sees what does not occur to another" (*In Libros* Ethicorum, X, lectio 10, note 2096). One is reminded of Aristotle's method of dialectical engagement, the offspring of the Platonic dialogue. Friendships offer training in the intellectual and moral virtues (*Ethics*, VIII, 1, 1155a16). The philosophic assistance offered by association with others mitigates, without eliminating, the tensions between contemplation and action, between the cultivation of the divine element in the soul and the pursuit of a life more in keeping with our embodied nature. In living together and by sharing in discussion, human beings are better able "to think and to act." A salient similarity between friendship and the intellectual life is that both are clearly ends in themselves, even as they contribute to all sorts of other goods.

In his discussion of the best regime in the *Politics*, Aristotle returns to the division of the soul into the rational and the irrational. He then lists a series of disjunctions: body and soul, action and contemplation, war and peace, and business and leisure. These pairs are not opposed simply; the former term in each pair is ordered to the latter. A society must tend to the needs of the body and to the pragmatic concerns of business and war. Leisure, however, is the first principle of all action, and it is this principle that statesmen have neglected. A political community, whose first principle is leisure, will not only embody the highest form of social life, but will also mitigate numerous social evils. The unpreparedness of the citizens for peace perpetuates a vicious cycle, beginning in bellicose ferocity, proceeding through victory and dominance, and ending in despotism and decline (*Politics*, VII, 14). Philosophy is not simply a luxury; it is a necessity.

The argument just given presupposes the discussion of the relationship between the best regime and the best way of life for human beings. Without that discussion, we are unlikely to be persuaded by the argument that philosophy is necessary because we will fail to understand why peace, leisure, and contemplation are superior to war, business, and action. The rhetorical difficulty is especially vexing for the intended audience of the *Ethics* and *Politics*, those "disposed to an active life of political involvement."[2] The seventh book of the *Politics* opens: "He who would duly inquire about the best form of state ought first to determine which is the most eligible life; while this remains uncertain the best form of the state must also be uncertain" (VII, 1, 1323a14–16). Having distinguished three sorts of goods—external goods, goods of the body, and goods of the soul—Aristotle subordinates the first two to the third. Against those who hold that happiness consists solely or principally in the first two goods, he states: "God is a witness . . . , for he is happy and blessed, not by reason of any external good, but in himself and by reason of his own nature" (*Politics*, VII, 1, 1323b21–25). In the subsequent chapter, Aristotle focuses on the two chief candidates of the best life: the life of the philosopher and the life of the statesman. For the most part, the latter sort of life is identified as a life of "arbitrary and tyrannical rule," a sign of which is that in most cities "if the laws aim at anything, they aim at the maintenance of power" (*Politics*, VII, 2, 1324b2–15). Aristotle notes that such a view exploits the independence of power from justice and makes a necessary means into a restless end. If the view were correct, it would not be possible for isolated cities, which are not ordered to conquest, to be happy and well governed.

Even if the view of happiness as the active pursuit of power over others is flawed, another objection to the superiority of contemplation remains. Some suppose that happiness consists in virtuous activity and that "he who does nothing cannot do well." They reason from this supposition that the philosopher is neither virtuous nor happy.

---

[2] Tessitore, *Reading Aristotle's Ethics*, 20. Tessitore's thesis concerning the audience is a modification of that of Bodéüs, who argues that the intended reader is a legislator. See *The Political Dimensions of Aristotle's Ethics*. Tessitore speaks, instead, of a dual audience of legislators and potential philosophers. For an appraisal of the strengths and weaknesses of Tessitore's reading of the *Ethics*, see my review in *Review of Politics*.

Aristotle concurs that we should not "place inactivity above action, for happiness is activity" (*Politics*, VII, 3, 1325a19–32), but he denies that the life of philosophy is inactive and impractical. He writes, "Not that a life of action must necessarily have relation to others, as some persons think, nor are those ideas only to be regarded as practical which are pursued for the sake of practical results, but much more the thoughts and contemplations which are independent and complete in themselves; since acting well and therefore a certain kind of action is an end. . . . If this were otherwise, God and the universe, who have no external actions apart from their own energies, would be far enough from perfection" (*Politics*, VII, 3, 1325b14–32). It is regrettable that Aquinas never finished his commentary on the *Politics* and hence did not directly address this passage. Elsewhere, however, in addressing the question whether intellectual habits are virtues, he poses the objection that they cannot be virtues because they are not operative. He responds to the objection by saying that it is false to circumscribe activity to the realm of the practical intellect. The virtues of the speculative intellect are operative; they are ordered to the "interior act of the intellect, which is to consider truth" (*ST*, I-II, 57, 1, ad 1).

The philosopher, whom Aristotle at one point likens to a god in comparison with the rest of humanity, might seem to be capable of existing apart from the social order. Thomas refers to certain holy men who have lived as hermits. In neither case does moving away from the polis constitute taking refuge in some idiosyncratic way of life. We are tempted to construe such transcendence of the political order as a state of lifelessness, as an absence of activity. Instead, it is a participation in the sort of actuality appropriate to the divine. Such an actuality is not beneath but rather eclipses every other form of actuality. It is thus a movement toward greater union with that which is intelligible to all in varying degrees. As I have noted, knowledge is a prime example of what Aquinas calls a common good, but this does not mean that all can share it in the same way or to the same degree.

If the discussion of the best regime in the *Politics* ascends to a consideration of the best life as the contemplative life, it does not remain at this exalted level. The suggestion that human beings are neither gods nor beasts but touch both finds support in the very structure of the *Politics*, which alternates between ascending and descending movements. After an introductory discussion, Aristotle offers a critique of the purportedly "idealistic" depiction of the political in Plato and proceeds to examine various actually existing regimes. From this quasi-historical examination, he ascends to an investigation of the best regime and the best life, then ends by descending to a consideration of the proper education of children. But even this descent contains the impetus for a subsequent ascent. How is this so?

Aristotle turns to poetry as a means of enabling citizens to participate in the life of leisure. Music and poetry inspire "enthusiasm which is an emotion of the ethical part of the soul" (*Politics*, VIII, 5, 1340a, 10–20). Poetry can, accordingly, contribute to the sort of initial and general education in the moral life that Aristotle recommends in the *Ethics:* an education of the passions. Because the irrational appetites are temporally prior to the development of the rational principle, the passions must be trained first. Poetry is especially suited to the task of educating children. Aristotle's defense of poetry contains a response to the Platonic objection that poetic artifice marks a retreat from reality. For Aristotle, poetry is not a falling away from reality, but a path leading to a greater appreciation of it. Our response to representations is "not far removed from the same feeling about realities" (*Politics*, VIII, 5, 1340a20–1340b20). The imitation reveals rather than conceals the reality. Elsewhere, Aristotle suggests that poetry and philosophy have a common source— wonder, which is the primordial source of leisure. Both poetry and philosophy appeal to those human passions that are open to the moral and intellectual aspirations proper to us. Wonder is proper to us precisely because we occupy an intermediate place in the hierarchy of beings. We are middle creatures, the offspring of poverty and plenty. The desire for leisure is rooted in the natural and even prerational appetite for the good, an appetite exhibited in human openness to the cosmos, to what is intrinsically desirable, and to higher things. In the political project of raising citizens to some degree of participation in the good life, philosophy finds an ally in poetry.

The alliance is made possible by the silent domestication of poetry, which presupposes rather than reverses the Platonic critique. Nowhere does Aristotle treat tragic poetry as a serious rival to philosophy. Of course, Aristotle's political standards are not as radical as those put forth in the *Republic*, but then neither is the tragic poetry considered by Aristotle an independent threat to the political order. Notably absent from the *Poetics* is any sustained attention to the function of the gods or of necessity in the tragic plot. Aristotle's type of tragic poetry is utterly devoid of the Dionysian element that Nietzsche would later identify as its dynamic source. Thus, Aristotle's accommodation of philosophy to poetry presupposes that it has already been purged of most of the elements Plato found destabilizing of the commonwealth.

The prominence of poetry in Aristotle's discussion of the best regime is, nonetheless, striking and instructive. It calls to mind his brief but suggestive remarks concerning poetry, history, and philosophy in the *Poetics*. Poetry is more philosophic than history because it extends beyond what is merely factually given to a consideration of the possible. Hence, it has what history lacks, a sense of the range of human possibilities and aspirations (*Poetics*, 1451a36–1451b10). Poetry's ability to uncover more than what is factually given in historical documentation is the basis of its claim to speak about the good. Aristotle's acceptance of this claim marks the distance that separates him from the founders of modern political thought. Hobbes, for instance, associates philosophy not with poetry, but with history, which he calls a knowledge of facts.[3] The elevation of history over poetry is already complete in Machiavelli's repudiation of "imagined republics."[4] In their eschewal of poetry, both thinkers are likely to miss the range and depth of human possibility. Those who reject contemplation also repudiate the view of the polis as the arena for the pursuit of human excellence.

Although the *Politics* culminates with a discussion of leisure and of the education of the body and the passions, it is silent about the education of the intellect. Poetry appeals to our appreciation of beauty and goodness; thus, according to Aristotle, there is no incompatibility between the education of the passions and that of the intellect. Where the *Politics* leaves off, speculative philosophy begins. As Aristotle puts it in the *Ethics*, politics would be the highest science only if human beings were the highest of existing beings. Speculative philosophy studies the world of nature and its causes. The official hierarchy of the sciences in Aristotle is the tripartite one of physics, mathematics, and metaphysics (*Metaphysics*, VI, 1). Although Aristotle devotes independent treatises to the first and last of these sci-

---

[3] *Leviathan*, I, 9.
[4] *The Prince*, chapter15.

ences, he offers no such consideration of mathematics, in which he departs from Plato, who aligns mathematics with the soul's search for self-knowledge. The disciplines that fall most neatly between physics and metaphysics are psychology, ethics, and politics.[5] Aristotle treats the *De Anima* as a continuation of natural philosophy, whereas the inquiries into ethics and politics build on and extend the inquiry into the nature of the soul. In what sense are these disciplines propaedeutic to metaphysics? The soul is a potency that is made actual through its interaction with the external world. The perfection of the soul consists in engaging in those activities appropriate to the human being's rational nature. The *Ethics*, which offers a delineation of those activities, ends by pointing to politics, the architectonic art of the human good. But the final book of the *Ethics* does not point solely to politics. The final chapters of the work evince a tension between the demands of the contemplative and the active lives. Book X has two trajectories. The most obvious one points toward politics, the other toward metaphysics. "First philosophy," as Aristotle often refers to metaphysics, is thoroughly grounded in anthropology, in the observation that all human beings naturally reach out for knowledge.

Another sign that metaphysics marks the completion not just of physics but of psychology and ethics as well is the difference between the descriptions of the prime mover in the *Physics* VII and of God in the *Metaphysics* XII, 7. In both texts, Aristotle argues the existence of a prime mover as the cause of motion in the world; yet in the former work he offers no information concerning the nature of the life of the unmoved mover. In the *Metaphysics,* on the other hand, he offers an effusive description of the internal and exclusively intellectual life of God. His description of the perfections of the divine life is similar to the account of rational thought in the *De Anima*. In his commentary on the *De Anima*, Thomas argues that "we are not able to reach an understanding of divine and highest causes, except through the knowledge we acquire from the power of the possible intellect. If the nature of the possible intellect were unknown to us, we would not know the order of separate substances" (*In Aristotelis De Anima*, I, lectio 1, note 7). The passage also recalls the arguments in the *Ethics* for the desirability of the contemplative life and espe-

---

[5] I prescind here from questions of chronology and from the question whether Aristotle had the connections worked out in advance.

cially the considerations of *Politics* VII, where Aristotle defends contemplation against the criticism that it is inert and lifeless. Aristotle and Thomas realize that human beings share much in common with other animals. The philosophic examination of human nature begins from and remains anchored in the perception that we are animals. A careful and inclusive account, however, of the phenomena of human experience would include those parts of human nature that resemble the divine and that make human beings peculiar members of the animal kingdom.

Metaphysics answers to the natural, human desire to know; it culminates in a depiction of the excellence of the contemplative life: "Delight follows the connatural operation of the one understanding or desiring, as is clear from Book X of the *Ethics*" (*Sententia super Metaphysicam*, XII, lectio 8, note 2537). Thomas supplies here a principle for interpreting the structure of Aristotle's *Ethics*. Far from being an afterthought, the introduction of contemplation in the final book follows naturally the consideration of the role of pleasure in the good life. The praise of contemplation does not introduce some otherworldly criterion of excellence. According to Aristotle and Thomas, the good is desirable and pleasant precisely because it is congruent to human nature (*In Libros* Ethicorum, X, lectio 11, note 2109). Instead of seeing the discussion of contemplation as an anomaly, Thomas ties it into the central issue of the *Ethics*, happiness. He returns to Aristotle's definition of happiness in the first book: "it is of the very meaning of happiness that it be self-sufficient and lacking in nothing" (*In Libros* Ethicorum, X, lectio 9, note 2069). He adds, "happiness is maximally continuous and permanent" (*felicitas est maxime continua et permanens; In Libros* Ethicorum, X, lectio 9). The account of the active or moral life, which constitutes the bulk of the *Ethics*, partially fulfills the definition of happiness, but the speculative life is its more perfect realization. Although both the inquisition and the contemplation of truth are delightful, the latter is more perfect (*perfectius*), for it is the goal of the former (*In Libros* Ethicorum, X, lectio 10).

The reason that human beings can appreciate and aspire to the divine life is that such aspiration is a fitting part of what it means to be human. Thomas's comments on the discussion of contemplation in *Ethics* X exhibit a balanced assessment of the similarity between human and divine: "The intellect is not simply something divine, but it is the most divine thing in us on account of its greater affinity with the separate substances, insofar as its operation is without a corporeal organ. . . . What is highest in man and found perfectly in superior substances is in man imperfectly and by participation" (*In Libros Ethicorum*, X, 10 and 11). The embodied intellect cannot fully achieve the contemplative life; we are capable of only a dim and discontinuous participation in the life proper to God. The proper response to the limits of human contemplation is not to close ourselves off from our aspiration toward higher things, but to enliven our sense of wonder.

Although most contemporary interpreters neglect what Aristotle calls the divine element in human nature, some see it as the centerpiece of his teaching.[6] Their view is the ethical correlate of Averroës's psychological doctrine of the unity of the agent intellect. The intellect is itself divine and not just a likeness of the divine. Accordingly, the contemplative life constitutes the complete and perfect life and fulfills Aristotle's criteria for the end of human life. The departure from Aquinas is clear. For the Averroists, Aquinas's depiction of the human intellect as similar to the divine does not go far enough. As evidence of his misinterpretation, they would appeal to passages such as the one from *Ethics* X, where Aristotle urges us to make (*facere* in the Latin translation Thomas used) ourselves divine. In his commentary, Aquinas counsels us only to strive or reach out toward (*intendere*) the divine (*In Libros* Ethicorum, X, lectio 11, note 2107). They would also contend that Aquinas fails to consider the following Aristotelian line of reasoning: in its act of knowing, the intellect becomes its objects, and its ultimate objects are eternal; thus, the intellect itself must be eternal in its act of knowing the highest things. How would Thomas respond?

One response is that the activity of contemplation is but one activity among many, an activity in which we can engage only intermittently. The appraisal of the happiness of a human life applies to the whole of one's life, not just to its peak moments, which seems to be an implication of Aristotle's statements that happiness must be attributed to a "complete life" and that we should call no man happy until he is dead (*Ethics*, I, 7, 1098a18–19, and I, 10, 1100a10–30). The context of the latter remark is an investigation primarily of the

---

[6] See Jaffa's critique of Thomas in *Thomism and Aristotelianism*, 142–66.

way luck or fortune can strip blessedness from those devoted to the
active life, but it indicates a temporal dimension to our appraisal of
human life, one that Aristotle introduces in his assertion that our
composite nature makes impossible a continuous participation in the
life of contemplation. The Averroist may recur here to a twofold
definition of human nature, as composite and as pure intellect. But
this definition returns us to an unwelcome dualism, which Aristotle
explicitly rejects in the *De Anima*. The philosophic dictum to live in
accord with reason can of course inform the entirety of the philosopher's life, just as she can organize all of her activities so as to maxi-
mize the quantity and quality of the time spent in contemplation.
The activity of contemplation must, nonetheless, be set within the
whole of human life, as are all other activities.

Another response to the Averroists' claims is that the nature of our
contemplative activity is not identical to that of God. Critics of Aquinas might concede that certain passages from the *Ethics* maintain an
ambiguity concerning whether the intellect is actually divine or only
akin to it. The reason for the lack of clarity is the political context
of the book and its intended, nonphilosophical audience. Of course,
Thomas's explication of contemplative life is not limited to the *Ethics,*
but extends to the *Metaphysics*, which has a strictly philosophical
audience. His reading of the study of the divine in that text runs thus.
The study of the divine enters into first philosophy (metaphysics) as
the cause of and the intelligible ground for sensible entities. The
contemplation of the divine marks a kind of completion of what is
most natural to human beings. The completion does not, however,
exhaust the intelligible. Metaphysics culminates or fails to culminate
in an avowal of its own ignorance, an acknowledgment that it knows
that it does not know. Metaphysics begins and ends in wonder. Aristotle's description of the divine life is germane: "The act of contemplation is what is most pleasant and best [*to hediston kai ariston*]. If,
then, God is always in that state in which we sometimes are, this
compels our wonder [*thaumaston*]; and if his is better, this life in a
better way, then this compels it yet more [*thaumasioteron*]"
(1072b23–27).[7] The accent on wonder at the end of the inquiry of

---

[7] The Latin text, which provides an unobjectionable translation of the Greek, is:
"*Si igitur sic bene habet, ut nos quandoque, Deus semper, mirabile. Si autem magis,
adhuc mirabilis, habet autem sic.*" Thomas comments, "*Cum igitur delectatio, quam
nos habemus intelligendo, sit optima, quamvis eam non possimus habere nisi modico*

first philosophy is striking. An initial part of the passage ("if God is always in that state in which we sometimes are") does support the reading Thomas opposes. The second part (if his is better) suggests, however, that our intellect and the divine do not coincide. Although we can know eternal truths, such as those of mathematics, we never know the intelligible without knowing it through a phantasm. We know separate substances only indirectly, by analogy to sensible things. Because we take our bearings from sensible things, even in metaphysical inquiry, we can reach only to the existence of God and not to a knowledge of what God is. There is a gap between our aspiration to and our achievement of contemplative wisdom. Thomas thus underscores the erotic element in the life of the philosopher, and in so doing he might be said to have reintroduced a Platonic feature that Aristotle had downplayed. The philosopher is never more than a "lover of wisdom" (*amator sapientiae; Sentencia super* Metaphysicam, I, lectio 3, note 56).

As I have noted, most contemporary critics of Aquinas's interpretation caution against taking seriously passages concerning the worthiness of the contemplative life. Thomas's reading rightly focuses on Aristotle's definition of happiness as more completely realized in the contemplative life than in the active life. The definition of happiness is not the only feature of the *Ethics* that should prepare the reader for the consideration of contemplation. I have also commented on the structural movement from the virtues having to do primarily with the passions to those that are more properly intellectual. When Aristotle turns to the intellectual virtues in the sixth book of the *Ethics*, he does so primarily to treat of prudence, the intellectual virtue that is crucial for the practical life. The preceding discussion of the virtues in the first five books is incomplete, as is clear from the initial consideration of the mean in Aquinas's commentary: "That someone should give something to one to whom it ought to be given and how much ought to be given and when it should be given and for the right reason and in the right way is neither for anyone nor is it easy. On account of its difficulty it is rare, difficult, praiseworthy, and virtuous" (*In Libros* Ethicorum, II, lectio 11, note 370). Aristotle's description

---

tempore, si Deus semper eam habet, sicut nos quandoque, mirabilis est eius felicitas. Sed adhuc mirabilior, si eam habet potiorem semper, quam nos modico tempore" (*Sentencia super* Metaphysicam, XII, lectio 8, note 2543).

of the virtues thus far in the *Ethics* has remained at a certain level of abstraction from the concrete conditions of human action; the judgment of the virtues, according to Aquinas's commentary, "consists in sense, not the exterior but the interior sense, through which someone rightly appraises singulars and to which pertains the judgment of prudence" (*In Libros* Ethicorum, II, lectio 11, note 381).

We have already considered prudence; some further indication of its relationship to the other intellectual virtues is now in order. Two of the intellectual virtues, prudence and art, are practical, whereas three of the intellectual virtues—understanding, science, and wisdom—are speculative. Among the practical virtues, prudence is in one important respect more akin to the intellectual virtues than is art. In his commentary, Thomas refers to the distinction in *Metaphysics* IX, 8, between immanent and transitive activities: "For the action remaining in the agent himself is called an operation, as to see, to understand, and to will. But making is an operation passing into exterior matter to form something of it, as to build and to cut" (*In Libros* Ethicorum, VI, lectio 3, note 1151). The immanent perfection involved in the operations of the speculative virtues and of prudence distinguishes both from the productive virtues of the mechanical arts. The good life is not a life of production, even if it requires that we engage in practices characterized by determinate modes of proceeding from means to ends. The goods pursued in the practice of the intellectual and moral virtues are not extrinsic to those very activities in the way the goods realized in crafts are. Instead, the goods are internal to practices. Given the anti-instrumental understanding of what constitutes human excellence, the uselessness of metaphysics is a sign of its intrinsic desirability. In the commentary on the *Metaphysics*, Thomas puts it thus: "When through the action of a power some work is constituted, that action perfects the work, not the agent of the work. . . . But when there is no other work beyond the operation of the power, then the action exists in the agent as its perfection and does not pass into some exterior thing. . . . Happiness clearly consists in such an operation . . . because it is the good of the one who is happy and is his perfection" (*Sententia super* Metaphysicam, IX, lectio 8, notes 1864–65). Thomas makes a related argument in the opening of his commentary on the *Ethics*, where he distinguishes four sorts of order with respect to human reason. First, there is the order that "reason does not make but only considers, as is true of the order of natural things" (*ratio non facit, sed solum considerat, sicut est ordo naturalium*). Second, there is the order that reason introduces "in its proper act" (*in proprio actu*), which concerns the ordering of its concepts and words to one another. Third, there is the order that reason makes in the will. Fourth, there is the order that reason makes in exterior things (*In Libros* Ethicorum, I, lectio 1). Only the last, Thomas explains, is properly a making or generating order.

Although both the speculative and the moral virtues are immanent operations and are not properly productive or constructive, the former are distinct from and superior to the latter. Thomas addresses the question whether politics, which *Ethics* I asserts to be the architectonic science, is superior to speculative wisdom. He notes that one science rules over another in two respects, concerning its use or practice and concerning the determination "of its work" (*sui operis; In Libros* Ethicorum, I, lectio 2, note 27). Politics commands the use of speculative philosophy but does not determine the content of the sciences because they depend not on human will but on the nature of things. There is thus no question here of human control over the objects of speculative philosophy; as Thomas puts it, we can only know, but not make, the natures of natural things. These passages and similar ones, which I have adduced above, entail a denial of the modern, Baconian identification of knowledge and technological power, and implicitly eschew the project of commanding nature in practice. In his attempt to supplant the authority of the ancients, Bacon argues that because ancient philosophy is barren of works, it must not contain knowledge. He proposes the following hypothetical syllogism: If the ancients had knowledge of causes, they would have been able to produce the germane effects. But they did not produce the effects. Therefore they had no knowledge. Aristotle's account of speculative knowledge involves a resolute denial of Bacon's first premise. Knowledge is not productive power, although it is a power of a different and, according to Aristotle, higher sort. It is the immanent actualization of the highest capacities of the human soul.

Following Aristotle's lead in *Ethics* VI, Thomas argues that, absolutely considered, wisdom is superior to prudence or politics. Prudence and politics regard the various practical activities of human life and seek to order them to the good, respectively, of the individual and of the community. Indeed, our first appreciation of wisdom arises from observing masters in particular arts and sciences. Particular sci-

ences are like practices in that they achieve determinate ends
through habitual ways of proceeding. Only through these particular
sciences can we be habituated in the intellectual virtues requisite for
the life of wisdom: "because the consideration of reason is perfected
through habit, there are diverse sciences corresponding to the diverse orders that reason considers" (*In Libros* Ethicorum, I, lectio 1,
note 2). The sciences are not primarily found in books or in a set of
propositions; they are embodied in the intellectual virtues of their
masters. Unlike the moral virtues, the intellectual virtues are not necessarily bound up with one another; they are "about different matters
having no relation to one another" (*ST*, I-II, 65, 1, ad 3). One can be
a geometer without being a physicist and vice versa. The ability to
reason demonstratively *(scientia)* in a particular science depends,
however, on the apprehension of the principles *(intellectus)* appropriate to that science. With respect to its foundation, no specific science is comprehensive, for no science proves its starting points.
Comprehensive knowledge requires wisdom. Both *scientia* and *intellectus,* then, depend on wisdom *(sapientia),* "which judges of them
all, not only with respect to conclusions, but also with respect to
principles" (*ST*, I-II, 57, 2, ad 2). The comprehensive and fundamental science of metaphysics studies not only the starting points of the
other sciences, but also the highest objects to which all knowledge is
ultimately ordered. The relationship of metaphysics to the particular
sciences allows the latter a limited autonomy even as it corrects the
dangers of specialization. Short of first philosophy, every inquiry must
be understood as limited and partial; otherwise, the natural operation
of the intellect would be truncated and its telos frustrated.

In contrast to the circumscribed scope of particular arts and sciences, wisdom concerns the whole of being: "wisdom is a certain
virtue of all the sciences" *(sapientia est virtus quaedam omnium sci-
entiarum; In Libros* Ethicorum, VI, lectio 5, note 1183). For that
reason, it most deserves the name of wisdom: "we judge those to be
completely wise, that is, in respect of every genus of beings and not
according to a part" (*In Libros* Ethicorum, VI, lectio 5, note 1181).
The unity of wisdom also bespeaks its excellence. Because "prudence
is said according to a proportion and relationship to something" *(prudentia dicitur secundum proportionem et habitudinem ad aliquid; In
Libros* Ethicorum, VI, lectio 6, note 1187), it is not possible for it
to be absolutely one. It must adapt itself to particular, contingent

circumstances. But wisdom, which concerns the first and highest causes of the whole of being, is unchanging. As Aristotle puts it, prudence would be best only if humans were the highest beings. Given that contemplative activity most fulfills the definition of happiness, prudence does not judge this end. Given the necessity of the objects of the speculative sciences, there is no need for counsel "concerning the objects that it investigates" (*quantum ad ea de quibus sunt; In Libros* Ethicorum, VI, lectio 6, note 1187). As Thomas notes elsewhere, the superiority of the speculative to the moral virtues arises from the greater nobility of the objects studied in the former. What Aristotle and Thomas provide, then, is a theoretical, not a practical, teaching concerning the superiority of contemplation. As Walter Jay Thompson puts it, "If . . . practice is concerned with ultimate particulars, then a theoretical teaching on human nature and the human good cannot be determinative of action; it cannot simply be enacted."[8] If one appraises contemplation and action not in terms of their objects, but "in relation to act," which is more of the nature of virtue, then the rightly ordered movement of the powers to action is superior to the intellectual virtues. There is, moreover, need for counsel with respect to the use of the intellectual virtues, to determine "how and in what order we must proceed in them" (*sed quantum ad usum earum, utputa quomodo vel quo ordine sit in eis procedendum; In Libros* Ethicorum, III, lectio 7). The moral virtues in concert with prudence are ultimately determinative of the good life, which consists in living and acting well.

In subordinating prudence to wisdom, Thomas states that prudence "commands for its sake, prescribing how we are able to reach wisdom. Just as health is more powerful than the art of medicine because it is its end, so wisdom is more eminent than prudence" (*In Libros* Ethicorum, VI, lectio 11, note 1290). Lest Thomas's subordination of prudence to wisdom seem too facile a resolution of the apparent tensions between the practical and the speculative life, it is important to note two respects in which prudence rules contemplation. First, teaching is a practical activity, and hence the pedagogy of the sciences is subject to the rule of prudence. Second, and more importantly, prudence or politics commands the use or practice of the sciences—that is, it determines precisely what role they have in

---

[8] "Aristotle: Philosophy and Politics, Theory and Practice," 115.

the whole of human life. Clearly the pervasive, if understated, emphasis on the philosophic life in both the *Ethics* and the *Politics* indicates that teaching ought to influence practice. Yet there is no evidence that the theoretical life provides a model for the active life or that one can deduce guidelines for how to live from a theoretical conclusion about the superiority of contemplation. We must revert to the domain of prudence, informed by the knowledge of the desirability of contemplation. This way of arguing for the inseparability of contemplation and prudence is different from the typical approach that depicts the moral virtues as preparatory to the life of contemplation. Some degree of temperance, fortitude, justice, and prudence are indeed propaedeutic to the life of philosophy, but on Thomas's view they are more than merely instrumental. Because those individuals most equipped for philosophy can engage in the contemplative life only sporadically, that activity cannot constitute a life simply in its entirety. Even the individual who successfully exercises the intellectual virtues can be said not to live well, for the latter appraisal applies to the whole of an individual's life, not just to his or her exercise of this or that virtue.

Contemporary scholars rightly see Aristotle's treatment of the practical life as a break from the Platonic alignment of contemplation and practice. Aristotle's repudiation in *Ethics* I of the Platonic idea of the Good signals the departure. Thomas is careful to circumscribe the scope of the critique: "Aristotle does not intend to disprove Plato's opinion that there is one good separate from the whole universe, on which all goods depend" (*In Libros* Ethicorum, I, lectio 6, note 79). Instead, what Aristotle finds objectionable is that Plato "posits a separate good as a common idea of all goods" (*In Libros* Ethicorum, I, lectio 6, note 79). Thomas refers us to the *Metaphysics* for Aristotle's affirmation of God as a good existing separately from the whole universe. After showing that the first mover is "intelligent and intelligible" (*intelligens et intelligibile*), Aristotle proceeds to show "how the first mover is good and desirable" (*qualiter primum movens sit bonum et appetibile; Sent8 super* Metaphysicam, XII, lectio 12, notes 2627–2663). Because the first mover moves the whole as an object of desire and because the good is defined as that which all desire, God is the supreme good. The ordination of philosophy to the highest good explains why in antiquity philosophy presupposes a kind of conversion, a reordering of one's whole life to the good, and why the introductory genre is called a *protreptic,* a turning, an exhortation or persuasion. Although contemplation perfects reason and not the passions, the affections of the philosopher are not indifferent. The philosopher has a natural human longing for contemplation, for the delight accruing to this activity; the philosophic way of life informs his or her whole being.

NEGATIVE PHILOSOPHY: THE LIMITS OF METAPHYSICS

Aquinas's interpretation and appropriation of Aristotle's conception of the philosophical life and metaphysics is a mean between the tendency of most contemporary commentators to dismiss the importance of the divine in Aristotle's thought and the tendency of others to exaggerate the similarity between human and divine intelligence. To see more clearly how Aquinas understands the scope and nature of philosophical inquiry, we need to attend to his Aristotelian teaching on the speculative sciences, the inquiries in which the intellectual virtues are practiced and perfected. In his brief discussions of the order of the speculative sciences, Aristotle defends the notion of a hierarchically ordered and irreducibly plural set of discourses, con · sisting of physics, mathematics, and metaphysics. In the second book of the *Physics,* he distinguishes mathematics from natural philosophy, and in the opening books of the *Metaphysics* he seeks a science distinct from all others. In the first lectio of his commentary on the *Physics,* Thomas appeals to Aristotle's teaching that the intellect in act is the intelligible in act; thus, "every science is in the intellect" and is "abstract from matter" (*In Libros* Physicorum, I, lectio 1, note 2). Every science abstracts a whole or universal from its particular instantiations; otherwise, we could not have the definitions from which science begins or the universal conclusions in which it terminates. Definitions regard what is essential and common to many individuals and thus disregard the merely accidental features of the things defined. Although human beings cannot exist without having particular shapes, sizes, and colors, the definition of human nature does not refer to these attributes. The truth of the Pythagorean theorem, similarly, applies to all right-angle triangles, not just to the particular triangle we find before us. The common note of abstraction might seem to render the sciences essentially the same or to base their distinctions primarily on psychological grounds. Neither is so. Habitual modes of proceeding constitute the sciences. The speculative sciences are distinguished in accordance with their habitual modes of defining and proceeding: "it is necessary to distinguish the sciences according to their diverse modes of defining" (*In Libros* Physicorum, I, lectio 1, note 2).

The differences in the manner of defining arise from a twofold relationship of the objects defined to matter. The object can exist in sensible matter, and it can depend on sensible matter in its definition. The division engenders four possibilities: an object can depend on matter both to be and to be understood; it can depend on matter to be, but not to be understood; it can depend on matter neither to be nor to be understood; and it can depend on matter to be understood, but not to be. Because the last possibility is absurd, three possibilities remain. As examples of the first two, Thomas refers to "curve and snub" (*curvum et simum*). He writes, "For snub is in sensible matter, and it is necessary that its definition include sensible matter: snub is a curved nose, and all natural things—for example, man and stone—are defined similarly. Curve, on the contrary does not include sensible matter in its definition, nor do any mathematical things—for example, number, magnitude, and figure—even though they cannot exist apart from sensible matter" (*In Libros* Physicorum, I, lectio 1, note 3). Different modes of defining distinguish physics and mathematics. Although the objects of both exist in matter, only the objects of physics include sensible matter in their definitions (*In Libros* Physicorum, I, lectio 1). So, the definition of any species of animal will include flesh and bones, whereas the definition of a circle contains no reference to sensible matter.

Thomas's introductory remarks presume the teaching of the *Physics* itself, especially of II, 2, where Aristotle attempts to distinguish physics from mathematics. Because mathematics and physics consider points, lines, surfaces, and bodies, it seems that they are not distinct sciences or that one is a part of the other. Thomas concedes that they consider the same things, but not in the same way (*sed non eodem modo*). He notes that "many things, of which one is not necessarily included in the understanding of another, may be conjoined in one thing, as, for example, white and musical are conjoined in some subject, even though one need not understand one to understand the other" (*In Libros* Physicorum, II, lectio 3, note 331). Given that there is no dependence of white on musical or vice versa, they can be understood separately *(separatim intelligi)*. In other cases, where there is a dependency of one thing on another, the prior can be understood apart from the posterior, but not the reverse. Thomas gives the example of the priority of animal to human. We reach the notion of human by adding something to animal; we cannot understand human without understanding animal, but we can understand animal without understanding human. How is the example relevant to the distinction between mathematics and physics?

Just as animal is prior to human, so too there is an order among the accidents accruing to substance, wherein quantity is first and is followed by the sensible qualities. There cannot be color where there is no magnitude or extension. The priority of quantity to the sensible qualities allows for a consideration of substance subject to quantity, a consideration that prescinds without falsity from sensible matter. The definitions of geometrical objects make no reference to color or to other sensible qualities. The ability of the mind to consider separately what does not exist separately is called abstraction. Plato's doctrine of separate ideas is a direct result of the failure to note this ability: "Because he [Plato] did not see how the intellect is truly able to abstract those things which are not abstract according to the existence of the thing, he supposed that all things that are abstract according to understanding were abstract in their being" (*In Libros Physicorum*, II, lectio 3, note 334). He thus posits separately existing ideas as the direct objects of understanding.

From what has been said thus far about the constitution of physics and mathematics by means of abstraction from matter, one might expect that metaphysics would arise from a further abstraction. Indeed, early modern commentators spoke of three degrees of abstraction. Thomas does not refer to "degrees" but to kinds or types of abstraction. As Charles De Koninck comments,

> They who define metaphysics by nothing more than generality would find this generality superseded by a far greater one; for what could prevent us from saying "let A stand for the subject of every such science including that of metaphysics," or "let B stand for what is impossible as well as for its opposite." The art that does not name anything . . . would be queen. But to the true nature of science and its true mode of definition all this kind of thinking is totally irrelevant. A degree of generality is not more actually intelligible in the measure that

it is more general, but in proportion as it is removed from matter. . . .
That a degree of generality does not carry with it more actual intelligibility can be seen from that fact that, in knowing man only as an animal, we do not know him distinctly as man, for the elephant too is an
animal. The general, here, is more potential and confused, whereas
the perfection of knowledge lies not in the direction of the more general but rather in the direction of something less general which must
include nonetheless the more general, in the way man includes animal.[9]

What distinguishes metaphysics is not a peculiar kind of abstraction,
operating at a higher level of generality. Returning to the previous
division of the possible relationships of a science to matter, we can
see that metaphysics depends "on matter neither according to being
nor according to reason" (*a materia nec secundum esse nec secundum
rationem*). There are two ways in which objects can be said to be
independent of matter in their being: "either because they never are
in matter, as is true of God and the other separate substances, or
because they are not in matter universally, as is true of substance,
potency, and act and being itself" (*In Libros* Physicorum, I, lectio 1,
note 3). If there were no objects capable of existing apart from matter, there would be no science of being distinct from physics. Both
the *Physics* and the *De Anima,* which are part of natural philosophy,
reach the immaterial as principles, in the first work as the unmoved
mover of natural motions and in the second as the immaterial principle of knowing in the human composite. But these works do not
study as their proper objects what transcends the order of forms in
matter. The difficulty of segregating metaphysics from the other sciences is not like the difficulty of separating mathematics from physics, which treat the same objects in modally different ways. The task
is not to show that what does not exist separately can legitimately be
considered separately, but that there are things that exist separately
from matter. Our access to metaphysics is much less direct than is our
access to the other sciences, as is clear from the lengthy dialectical
introduction to the *Metaphysics,* where Aristotle repeatedly speaks
of "the science we are seeking."

The mode of defining appropriate to metaphysics includes neither
sensible nor intelligible matter, which does not mean, however, that

---

[9] "Abstraction from Matter II," 60–61.

metaphysics is more abstract than mathematics.[10] Thomas contrasts natural philosophy's proximate foundation in the order of being with the remote foundation of mathematics. Metaphysics does not involve a further retreat from the real, but a movement toward a more adequate grasp of it. In defining the subject matter of first philosophy as *ens inquantum ens*, Thomas deploys the concrete participle *ens*, not the abstract infinitive *esse*. The phrase *ens inquantum ens* nicely captures the concrete yet common consideration proper to first philosophy.[11]

The contrast between mathematics and metaphysics can be seen in the statement that the latter studies what exists apart from matter and motion. Accordingly, metaphysics arises not from a peculiar abstraction but from *separatio,* the negative judgment that nonmaterial beings exist. The objects of metaphysics include beings such as God and angels, whose very being is immaterial, as well as those attributes of being—such as potency, act, and unity—that exist in but are not confined to matter. Metaphysics is

> about those things separate from matter and motion in their being, but this occurs in different ways. Something is able to be separate from matter and motion in its being in two ways. First, the very nature of the thing is completely incapable of existing in matter or motion; God and the angels are, accordingly, said to be separate from matter and motion. Second, although the very nature of something does not preclude its existence in matter and motion, it is nonetheless possible for it to exist without matter and motion, as being, substance, potency, and act are separate from matter and motion, not depending on matter and motion for their being. (Aquinas, *Expositio* De Trinitate, 5, 4)

The collage of objects included in the study of metaphysics has led some commentators to suppose that Aristotle was confused, or at least that his various statements about first philosophy mark different stages in his thinking. The upshot seems to be that one must choose between metaphysics as ontology, or as concerned with common being, and metaphysics as theology, or as concerned with the imma-

---

[10] If one were to ask which discipline is more abstract than mathematics, the answer would have to be logic. Logic studies second intentions such as genus and species that have absolutely no existence independent of the mind and that are parasitic on things as known.

[11] God is not the proper subject matter of metaphysics; God enters into metaphysics not as the proper subject matter of the science but as a cause or principle of *ens*.

terial and divine. If one chooses the former, then it is difficult to see how the consideration of God could be part of metaphysics. If one chooses the latter, then metaphysics has a particular subject genus and seems to be a special and not a universal science. Yet Thomas insists that both are parts of the study of metaphysics—not, however, in the same way. The things that can be but are not always found separate from matter and motion are the proper subject of the study, whereas the things that are never found in matter enter into the study as principles of its proper subject. How are we to understand the distinction?

Like physics and mathematics, metaphysics abstracts from determinate matter. Yet Thomas uses the term *separatio,* not *abstractio,* to describe the constitution of the objects of metaphysics. *Separatio* signifies the negative judgment that certain things are either not material in their very being or not necessarily limited to the order of material being. We cannot know that some things are able to be apart from matter and motion unless we are sure that there is at least one immaterial and atemporal being. Without a knowledge that there is some other substance beyond the order of composite natural beings, physics would be the first science (*Sententia super* Metaphysicam, VI, lectio I, note 1170). Aquinas notes that Aristotle disproves in the eighth book of the *Physics* the possibility that every being is material, where he reaches "an immobile being" (*Sententia super* Metaphysicam, IV, lectio 5, note 593). Given the existence of at least one immobile and immaterial being, it is possible to establish a science that studies being and what follows upon being, not insofar as being is material or immaterial, but simply insofar as it is being. Ralph McInerny explains,

> In the study of natural things we are compelled to appeal to causes which are not themselves natural and we come thereby to see that not everything which is is material. This serves as the basis for seeking yet another science which will have as its subject, not being of a particular kind, but being as such. Proceeding horizontally, so to speak, this science will seek knowledge of what belongs per se to being after the fashion of properties of its subject. In what may be described as a vertical procedure, it will seek the cause of its subject, the efficient and, preeminently, the final cause of whatever is, of being as being.[12]

---

[12] "Ontology and Theology in Aristotle's *Metaphysics,*" in *Being and Predication,* 66. McInerny's article is a response to Werner Jaeger's thesis that the *Metaphysics* contains disparate and incompatible notions of the subject matter of first philosophy.

Thomas states that "common being alone" *(ipsum solum ens commune)* is the subject of first philosophy. Nonetheless, every science aims at a "cognition of the causes of its genus." In this way, the first causes and the separate substances enter into the study of metaphysics *(Sententia super* Metaphysicam, VII, lectio 17, note 1660).

Given that the objects of metaphysics depend on matter neither for their being nor for their being known, metaphysics can be said to proceed intellectually *(intellectualiter)* and to terminate in the intellect *(Expositio* De Trinitate, VI, 1). Because images are indispensable for human thinking, the question arises how we can study the objects of metaphysics, which exist apart from matter and motion *(Expositio* De Trinitate, VI, 2). The objects of metaphysics are "eminently hidden" *(maxime mysticae)*. First philosophy terminates neither in sense nor in imagination, but in the intellect. The explanation of how we are to transcend the imagination is instructive. Thomas begins with the Aristotelian refrain that all knowledge arises from sensation. The common source of all ways of knowing does not preclude multiple points of termination. First philosophy culminates in judgments concerning things "entirely independent of matter both with respect to their being and their being known" *(Expositio* De Trinitate, V, 5, 4). Yet we have no direct access to what transcends matter and motion. We understand separate substances as causes of sensible things, as transcending them, or by negations of them. Metaphysics thus terminates in the intellect in two ways: first, negatively, in that it terminates neither in sense nor in imagination; and, second, positively, in that the intellect apprehends the relations of causality, negation, and transcendence.

Thomas denies that it is possible in this life to behold the divine form *(ipsam formam divinam inspicere; Expositio* De Trinitate, VI, 3). How, then, can we know God at all? The initial, vague apprehension of what a thing is typically occurs through locating the thing within a remote or proximate genus. In coming to know God, however, this strategy is not available because "God is in no genus." We can know only that God is, not what God is. Causality, transcendence, and negation are the only routes available. There is no unmediated access to the divine. As Dionysius teaches, even as we transfer the likenesses of sensible things to immaterial substances *(similitudines rerum sensibilium ad substantias immateriales translatas),* we must acknowledge that all sensible things are "unlike likenesses" of the divine *(dissimiles similitudines)*. Taken in isolation, the claim that metaphysics terminates at all is likely to be somewhat misleading. As Wilhelmsen puts it, "every conceptualization of 'to be' is indirect"; we have no "direct 'vision' of esse whatsoever."[13] Thomas's discussion underscores the disparity between natural science and mathematics, on the one hand, and metaphysics, on the other. Whereas the former conceptualize their objects by apprehending the proper natures of their subject matters, metaphysics cannot finally conceptualize *esse* as a what or as a determinate nature. Thomas thus accentuates the darkness of metaphysics, its restless incompleteness. First philosophy is ultimately a *philosophia negativa*. The contemplative life stands between the vicious and stultifying modern alternatives of presumption and despair: "To wonder is not merely not to know; it means . . . that one understands oneself in not knowing. And yet it is not the ignorance of resignation. On the contrary, to wonder is to be on the way, *in via.* . . . Out of wonder, says Aristotle, comes joy. In this he was followed by the Middle Ages: *omnia admirabilia sunt delectabilia.*"[14]

---

[13] "Existence and Esse," in *Being and Knowing*, 117.
[14] Pieper, *Leisure*, 136.

4

Contemplation, Action, and Divine Artistry

IN OUR ATTEMPT to recover Aquinas's teaching on human nature,
we have repeatedly come up against the texts not just of Aquinas, but
also of Aristotle, to whom Aquinas regularly appeals in his discussion
of nature, human nature, the human good, virtue, politics, and contemplation. Yet Aquinas's reading of Aristotle differs from that offered by many of Aristotle's commentators. Many classical and
contemporary commentators find in Aristotle a defense of the utter
self-sufficiency of the philosophical life and its conclusions regarding
crucial issues of the soul, knowledge, and the nature and achievement
of human happiness. By contrast, Aquinas sees Aristotle as quietly
underscoring the limitations to philosophical inquiry and to philosophy as a way of life. Indeed, Thomas sees philosophy at its highest
moments as engendering a series of "dialectical problems," about
which plausible arguments can be adduced on both sides and which
natural reason is unable to resolve. This view does not commit
Thomas to philosophical skepticism because the limitations to philosophy are evident only after one has appreciated its remarkable
achievements.

On the key issue, the question of the ultimate end of human life
and of who teaches authoritatively concerning that life, Aquinas argues that the ultimate end consists in the supernatural vision of the
divine essence, a vision available only through a divine gift. In a crucial sequence of arguments, he deploys Aristotle's definition of happiness—what is desired for its own sake and what is self-sufficient and
lacking in nothing—as the basis of a conclusion unknown to pagan
antiquity. Aristotle's conception of happiness transcends the view of
happiness as pleasure or honor, presenting it also as moral virtue
and philosophical contemplation. The gap between aspiration and
achievement leaves open the possibility of a dialogue between philosophy and theology. The possibility of a dialectical engagement of na-

ture by grace is also evident in the consideration of the Decalogue, which reveals precepts concerning our duties to God and neighbor that can be reached by the investigation of natural reason. Our need for a revelation of truths accessible to natural reason is a sign of the degree to which sin has derailed our natural inclinations and clouded our reason. In both the speculative and the practical orders, then, we naturally aspire to goods that exceed our natural capacity. Yet this aspiration raises the following difficulty. The apparently straightforward movement from the natural to the supernatural, from finite goods to their infinite ground, seems to invite an oblivion of nature and a forgetfulness of the manifold goods constitutive of human life. How should we respond?

If revelation bridges the gap between the aspiration for and the achievement of ultimate happiness, it does so through an unexpected reversal of our expectations. The theological path to the good life involves a complicated pattern, not just an ascent from this world to the next, but an ascent that paradoxically entails a descent. Two teachings help us to see the more complicated structure of Christian moral pedagogy: the integration of contemplation and action as well as the distinctive teaching on the virtues. In the previous chapter's discussion of Aristotle, I provided an argument for the integration of prudence and the practice of contemplation. Nonetheless, prudence and the moral virtues that accompany it do not enter directly into the practice of the intellectual virtues. For the Christian, by contrast, rightly ordered desire is a necessary means to contemplation; conversely, contemplation naturally overflows into the active life of teaching. Charity, which is the form of the virtues, eclipses in importance the moral and the intellectual virtues. Through love, the whole of human life is ordered to the ultimate end of union with God; in fact, contemplative wisdom arises from love. Unlike philosophic wisdom, which judges only of those objects of speculative philosophy, theological wisdom judges "all things." The Christian view of the good life resolves the ancient *aporia* concerning the relationship between action and contemplation. In spite of the disparity between philosophical and theological pedagogy, we should not construe the latter in terms of submission to an inscrutable lawgiver. Indeed, charity, which is both a law and a virtue, functions in ways remarkably akin to the ways prudence does. Charity discerns what ought to be done in concrete circumstances and orders all the other virtues.

There is no possibility here of a separation between what one is or knows and how one acts. In contrast, moreover, to the modern tendency to construe charity in terms of abstract principles such as equal regard, Thomas argues that there is an order to love, which corresponds to the various bonds we have to other human beings.

The emphasis, evident in the virtue of charity, on the discernment of particulars and on the integration of affective and cognitive elements is also present in the connection between the good and the beautiful. Thomas invites us to consider beauty as the way goodness manifests itself to rational creatures. The link between the two admits no notion of an autonomous aesthetics and thus precludes the possibility of construing human life in terms of artistic *techne* or self-creation. The beautiful, defined as that which pleases when seen, involves a mutuality of perception and feeling. The chief mark of beauty, its *claritas* or radiant splendor, always accompanies our experience of goodness. The appreciation of the good as beautiful is not so much a matter of abstracting from concrete singulars, but rather of attending to them. The peculiarly Christian features of the account of beauty have to do with Christ as a manifestation of the radiant splendor of the goodness of God. The incarnate Word mediates universal and particular, infinite and finite, eternal and temporal.

The motif of beauty is also present in Thomas's account of creation, which is an artifact of the divine artist. The artistry of God's creation and providence can be understood in narrative terms. Creation itself has a narrative structure with a beginning, middle, and end. God does not remain aloof from that which God has created; God can and does intervene in that artifact after giving it its first form. The metaphysics of creation, providence, and miracles undergirds a conception of God as present and active in history. The central act in the narrative of creation is the dramatic interaction between God and us in the Incarnation. According to Thomas, the most important feature of the Old Law is that it figuratively signifies the coming of the redeemer, in whom time and eternity are united. The Incarnation is the event upon which the significance of Scripture pivots. Christ is the concrete embodiment of the goal, both sign and signified, which has important consequences. The end of time does not eliminate the order of the world, but initiates its transfiguration. We are not the authors of the narrative of creation and redemption. Our participation in it is the result of an unmerited gift, bestowed by a divine artist. We are, however, free participants in that narrative; thus, we may cooperate with God in the re-creation and glorification of our fallen nature. Our participation in the divine artistry entails a transformed understanding of the relationship among contemplation, action, and art.

THE ULTIMATE END: REVELATION'S DIALECTICAL ENGAGEMENT OF NATURE

In chapter 3, we traced the trajectory of philosophy, its orientation toward contemplation of the highest things, and the limitations inherent in that aspiration. Aquinas's most sustained discussion of these issues occurs in explicitly theological contexts, especially in his examination of the ultimate end of human life in the *Summa Theologiae*. This inquiry is a prelude to his moral theory, an appreciation of which presupposes familiarity with his conception of the relationship between faith and reason. Central to his view of faith and reason are the "preambles of the faith" (*praeambula fidei*), which comprise those truths, such as "God exists" and "God is one," that are at once demonstrable by reason and yet part of the content of revelation.[1] The compatibility of faith and reason is the shibboleth of Thomism. The opening chapters of Thomas's two greatest works aim at rebutting the charge that faith is incoherent or irrational. Because the preambles display the truth of a segment of revelation, they offer limited confirmation of the reasonableness of faith. One must be careful not to overstate the case: only a very circumscribed portion of revelation can be known in this life; in fact, none of the articles of faith are susceptible to proof. The paucity of this knowledge does not, however, vitiate the achievement of philosophy. Reason is in some way ancillary to faith. If no knowledge whatsoever could be had of God, if revelation began where natural reason was suspended in ignorance, then Thomas's case for the harmony of faith and reason would be weaker. He could show only that there is no inherent contradiction

---

[1] Thomas's claims have received cogent articulation; concerns over the apparent threat of such claims to the supernatural character of the Christian faith have been assuaged. See Étienne Gilson, *The Christian Philosophy of Thomas Aquinas*, 7–25, 339–50; and Ralph McInerny, "On Behalf of Natural Theology," in *Being and Predication*, 247–58.

between faith and reason, which in itself would be rendered a more onerous task.

Often the preambles are envisioned as placing arguments and strategies at the disposal of the Christian apologist. In the opening of the *Contra Gentiles,* Thomas contrasts the religion of Christ with that of Mohammed, the latter of whom promises to satiate carnal desires and promotes the tyrannical rule of arms. These laconic remarks may appear crude. The principle behind them, however, is clear and, in this context, unimpeachable. Such a celebration and inflammation of concupiscence would indicate that the religion of Mohammed is not of divine origin. But, we might ask, how can we be sure? Thomas's rejoinder runs thus: Because the preambles inform us that God is transcendent and immaterial, any revelation proffering doctrines about God or the nature of the spiritual life that contradict these truths is thereby undermined. The preambles supply, consequently, a limited criterion for discrimination among the various claimants to divine revelation. They afford the believer some leverage in his or her encounters with those outside the pale of Christianity. The attempt to begin theological inquiry with what is in principle common to all inquirers is evident in each of the "five ways," where Thomas concludes that each way reaches that being "whom all call God" (*ST*, I, 2, 2, ad 1).

The *praeambula fidei,* then, exercise a certain influence on theological discourse. The existence of God and the unity of God's nature are the fundamental truths of philosophical theology. Any further descriptions of God must be compatible with these truths. Lest we infer from this conclusion that revelation can be reduced to reason, Thomas notes that the claims of natural theology are also revelatory concerning the limits of philosophy, which reaches only the existence of God, but cannot grasp the divine essence.[2] The affirmations of the preambles engender a negative theology. In his discussion of the names of God, Thomas distinguishes between the thing signified (*res significativa*) and its mode of signifying (*modus significandi*). Two words may signify the same thing but have different modes of signifying; for example, the words *running (currens)* and *to run (currere)*

---

[2] See the discussion of the divine names in *ST*, I, 13, and in *Summa contra Gentiles*, I, 30–36. On the grammar of theological language, see David B. Burrell, *Aquinas: God and Action,* and Mark D. Jordan, "The Names of God and the Being of Names."

signify the same thing, but they do so in modally different ways. The participle signifies that activity in a concrete way, whereas the infinitive signifies in an abstract mode. Our mode of signifying is inextricably tethered to the sensible world of composite entities; when we say that something is "good" or "wise," we mean that goodness or wisdom is an attribute of a substance, an accident. We would never say, except metaphorically, that "Socrates is goodness." Because in God there is no composition, we say not only that "God is good," but more accurately, if more awkwardly, that "God is goodness." We are able to make meaningful statements about God because, as transcendent cause of all things, God must possess in a simple and unified way the perfections creatures possess in varied and imperfect ways. As Thomas puts it, "Because it is possible to find in God every perfection of creatures, but through a more eminent mode, whatever names designate a perfection absolutely and without defect are predicated of God and of other things, such as goodness, wisdom, being. . . . Names that express perfections in the mode of supereminence . . . are said of God alone, such as the highest good, the first being, and so forth" (*Summa contra Gentiles* [hereafter *SCG*], I, 30). Although we can speak of God by using names originally crafted to refer to sensible, composite entities, we cannot escape our mode of signifying. Thus, negation always attends affirmation.

Consider, for example, Thomas's preferred name for God: "subsistent being" *(ipsum esse subsistens)*. In speaking about finite things, we habitually refer to perfections in the abstract mode—for example, goodness and wisdom—and to existing things in the concrete. God is neither merely one being among many nor an abstract perfection or set of perfections: God's perfection is inseparable from God's concretely existing being. In order to avoid conceptual confusion and idolatry, we must deploy both modes simultaneously in speaking of God. The name of God thus combines abstract *(esse)* and concrete *(subsistens)* modes of signifying. The jarring combination of these opposed modes of signifying evinces the conceptual limitations to any philosophic inquiry into the nature of God.

In many passages, Thomas labors to undermine precisely the sort of endeavor in which many modern Thomistic apologists have so enthusiastically engaged. He does not highlight the apodictic certitude and pellucid rationality of the preambles. The proofs for the existence of God, he notes, will be grasped only by the few after much labor, and even then with an admixture of error (*SCG*, I, 4). The brevity of the "five ways" in the *Summa Theologiae* conceals the labor required to gain an adequate grasp of any argument for the existence of God. The first way, the way from motion, is but a condensed version of an argument to which the *Contra Gentiles* devotes a lengthy chapter and to which several books of Aristotle's *Physics* and *Metaphysics* are devoted. The proofs, then, undermine the supposition that rational inquiry encompasses and exhausts the realm of the intelligible. The convergence of reason and faith, which the *praeambula fidei* exhibit, is a cause for wonder and an inducement to further theological exploration. In the *Contra Gentiles*, Thomas argues that it is not foolish to assent to those doctrines of the faith that transcend reason (*SCG*, I, 6). Although he mentions certain signs of the divine source of the Christian religion, he does not argue that these signs are sufficient grounds for belief, that they can be construed apart from submission to the whole of revelation, or that believers have some burden of proof before a neutral court of reason. His emphasis is twofold, on the natural human longing to behold the highest causes and on the limitations to human reason. As we saw in the introductory chapter, metaphysics begins in wonder and seeks to move beyond it to a knowledge of the first cause, but ends by avowing its own ignorance of the highest things.

Thomas's circumspection indicates that the *praeambula* are but part of a more comprehensive theological pedagogy. In considering their function, the rhetorical context should not be overlooked. The so-called proofs are not mathematical deductions intended for the inspection of disembodied creatures, indifferent to the outcome of such inquiry. Rather, the arguments answer to a concrete desire in human beings: the natural desire for knowledge of the causes of sensible things. The existence of God, Thomas argues, is not self-evident; nevertheless, God is known vaguely and naturally by all insofar as they implicitly seek God as their happiness (*ST*, I, 2, 1, ad 1). God is not simply the first truth and end of all speculative inquiry but also the supreme Good, the contemplation of which provides the only complete satisfaction of our natural eros. At its pinnacle, the theoretical pursuit of the highest causes coincides with the practical pursuit of the good to which our natures are ordered. As I noted in the discussion of the order of the precepts of the natural law, one of the ends to which human beings are naturally inclined is "to know the truth about God." What is the relationship between speculative thought and the ends of human life discussed in ethics?

Thomas considers the ultimate end of human life in the opening articles of the second part of the *Summa Theologiae*, the structure of which quite closely mirrors Aristotle's *Ethics* I. Thomas determines that we act for an end, that there is one end for which we do all that we do, that this end is happiness, and that happiness does not consist in wealth, honor, or pleasure (*ST*, I-II, 1 and 2). After establishing that there must be an end of human life, Thomas considers in the second question a list of potential candidates for that end. He dismisses goods of the soul as well as those of the body and concludes that no created good constitutes human happiness. In the course of these articles, he reiterates Aristotle's teaching that the good must be "self-sufficient."

In the third article, for example, Thomas determines that happiness is an operation of the intellect in relation to the most intelligible object—namely, the divine essence. In support of this position, he cites passages from Aristotle, particularly from *Metaphysics* I, where the Philosopher speaks of the natural desire to understand the causes of sensible things. The fifth article, moreover, argues that happiness is an exercise of the speculative, rather than the practical, intellect. Although the *sed contra* is from Augustine, the arguments in the body of the article are garnered from Aristotle's definition of happiness. The third argument is that in contemplation we share in the sort of life appropriate to higher beings. Even though Thomas does not cite the text, the argument might have been borrowed from *Ethics* X.

The origin of speculative philosophy is the desire to understand the "why" of sensible things, a desire at once mundane and sublime. Its inception is the human need to overcome ignorance and to understand the surrounding world (*Sententia super* Metaphysicam, I, lectio 1). Even at this level there exist the seeds of a more noble aspiration to knowledge for its own sake. The anthropological basis of this teaching has to do with human beings as creatures of open-ended wonder. A fundamental tenet of Aristotelian psychology concerns the commensurability of the intellect to all intelligible things (see *De Anima,* III, 4–5). The intellect is "capable of becoming all things" (*potens omnia facere et fieri*). For Aristotle, the intellectual virtues, which are acquired by engaging in the speculative sciences, perfect the natural inclination to know. For Thomas, speculative science is not the ultimate end; it does not extend beyond the knowledge gained from sensibles and fails to satisfy fully the contemplative yearning for knowledge of the highest things.

In the subordination of Aristotelian contemplation to the transcendent vision of the divine essence, some detect in Aquinas a shift away from Aristotle's mode of inquiry and a movement beyond his tentative claims about the end (*ST*, I-II, 3). As noted above, there are some structural similarities between *Ethics* I and Aquinas's treatise on the ultimate end; the structural differences are equally striking. Whereas Aristotle approaches the excellence of the contemplative life indirectly in the *Ethics* and the *Politics*, and praises it at length only in the *Metaphysics*, Thomas explicitly underscores its preeminence at the outset of his ethical writings and brings together the considerations of the *Metaphysics* and the *Ethics*. The presence of non-Aristotelian sources reinforces the structural differences; Augustine and Boethius are prominent in the arguments for the transcendent nature of the end. Thomas embraces the Augustinian doctrine that all limited goods are good by participation in the ultimate Good.[3] How is this doctrine compatible with Aristotle's repudiation of Plato's idea of the highest Good? Thomas avoids directly contravening Aristotle in two ways. First, he limits the scope of Aristotle's critique of Plato's assertions about the transcendent Good by arguing that Aristotle intends to reject not the existence of highest good, on which the whole world depends, but only the notion that ultimate good is an abstract idea.[4] In fact, Aristotle shows in *Metaphysics* XII that there is an ultimate Good, which all things in the universe desire—namely, the unmoved mover, who moves as an object of desire. Even if there is no direct contradiction of Aristotle, there is, once again, a unification of what Aristotle left segregated. Second, Thomas deploys the strategy of hierarchical subordination. Speculative science is desirable in that it is a likeness of perfect hap-

---

[3] ST, I-II, 2, 6. The language of Augustine is present in the response to the second objection, where Thomas says that the knowledge afforded by the speculative sciences is desirable insofar as it is a *similitudo* or *participatio* of perfect beatitude.

[4] See *Ethica Nichomachea*, I, 6, and X, 7–8. In his commentary on the former passage, Thomas is careful to limit the scope of Aristotle's critique of the Platonic notion of the Good. See *In Libros* Ethicorum, I, lectio 6.

piness and affords a participation in that happiness; Aristotle himself leaves open this possibility, giving in the *Ethics* an account only of imperfect happiness. The language of participation is instructive.[5] It enables Thomas to speak of different orders or degrees of happiness, just as Aristotle does. Conversely, Aristotle's postulation of an order of goods that are simultaneously desirable for their own sake and for contributing to other goods corrects the Neoplatonic tendency to negate all limited goods in our aspiration for the highest Good.

The strategy of hierarchical subordination does not merely involve placing one position on top of another. Instead, it involves a dialectical clarification, reformulation, and resolution of various positions and problems. Although philosophy achieves a certain completion that is proper to the order of natural reason, it is not an exhaustive, Hegelian system. The pinnacle of philosophic discourse raises questions—concerning the nature of God, the supreme Good, and life after death—that transcend the scope of reason. Seen from within the confines of the Aristotelian corpus, the question of the ultimate end remains an *aporia*. Even the philosophic life does not fully satisfy Aristotle's own definition of happiness. As McInerny puts it, Aristotle acknowledges the "gap between what we aspire to and what we can attain in the matter of happiness."[6] Thus, what allows Thomas to go beyond Aristotle is Aristotle. The view that Christian theology resolves an *aporia* in Aristotle's account of the good life is incompatible with an understanding of Aristotle's thought as peremptory.[7] Thomas praises Aristotle both for his account of what happiness properly consists in and for his acknowledgment of the limitations to what human nature could achieve. As Jan Aertsen comments, there is a "dialectic within the natural desire to know."[8]

Even if Aristotle leaves room for something more and if his own thought points beyond anything that he knew as a candidate for the

---

[5] The subordinate status of Aristotle can also be seen in Thomas's complicated response to the role of the body in happiness (*ST*, I-II, 4, 5) and in the treatment of Aristotelian epistemology as applicable only in this life (*ST*, I-II, 5, 1, ad 2).

[6] *The Question of Christian Ethics*, 38. McInerny is responding to Gauthier's claim that Aquinas's ethics is fundamentally at variance with that of Aristotle.

[7] Leo Strauss writes, "Aristotle did not leave room, intentionally or unintentionally, for a revealed teaching which could be added to his rational teaching." "Review of Anton C. Pegis, ed. *Basic Writing of Saint Thomas Aquinas,*" in *What Is Political Philosophy?* (285).

[8] *Nature and Creature: St. Thomas Aquinas's Way of Thought,* 217.

ultimate end, Thomas's accentuation of the stability, impregnability, and transcendence of the good appears to subordinate Aristotle to the tradition of Christian Neoplatonists. Most of the evidence for a transcendent end is negative: no temporal good fulfills the stringent requirements of beatitude. The typical mode of argument in these passages is *via negativa,* a procedure for which Thomas is indebted to Neoplatonism.[9] One is also reminded of the crucial role of eros in Platonic pedagogy. An erotic pedagogy appeals to the ordered incompleteness of human nature, a sign of which is a longing for the good and the beautiful. The partial satisfaction of our longing gives rise to an even greater desire. Accordingly, any stage in the pedagogy of the good life must underscore the gaps in our understanding of the good and the absence in our possession of it. Understood within this framework, Aristotle's definition of happiness discloses the inadequacy of all temporal goods. Thomas's rhetoric takes us beyond the conclusions of Aristotle's *Ethics.* It sounds more like Aristotle's effusive oration in *Metaphysics* XII on the contemplative life enjoyed by God, a life in which we participate only discontinuously and imperfectly.

Thomas's commitment to the integrity of our composite nature means that his position must be significantly more subtle than its Neoplatonic antecedents. The Neoplatonic view often leads to a denigration of limited, finite goods and to flirtations with dualism. Thomas's position is a mean between presumption and despair—presumption of the natural attainability of a transcendent end and despair over the impossibility of such an end. Some commentators have found the notion of a natural, transcendent end contradictory. The danger with their view is that it risks closing nature in on itself. Were human nature in no way naturally open to the vision of God, grace would involve not the perfection and elevation of nature but rather the destruction of one nature and the reconstitution of another, which would render grace inimical to human nature. But human nature is not as simple as other natures. As Anton Pegis comments, "Natures qua natures are closed only in the sense that they are not subject to more or less. There are, to be sure, closed natures,

---

[9] The most famous use of the *via remotionis* occurs, of course, in the discussion of the divine names. On the sources and nature of this mode of argument in Thomas, see Jordan, "The Names of God and the Being of Names."

but they are closed, not because they are natures, but because they are material. If there are creatures with spiritual natures, then they are open because they are spiritual."[10]

Thomas's insistence that our perfection involves openness to a knowledge of higher things does not introduce a standard of excellence independent of human nature, a standard that would be appropriate to angels or to God. The pure life of contemplation is indeed more appropriate to the angelic intellect. A life of practical activity that admits an element of contemplation—what Thomas calls imperfect happiness—is in keeping with our composite nature (*ST*, I-II, 3, 5). This is only part of the account, however. Although one may rank different activities based on the degree to which they participate in perfect happiness, *beatitudo* itself does not admit of various definitions. Imperfect happiness does not fulfill the definition of *beatitudo*, which satiates all desire. Imperfect happiness warrants the name only analogically, insofar as it is a partial realization of a life wherein all goods are possessed without diminution and without the possibility of loss.[11] Perfect happiness, *beatitudo* properly speaking, is naturally desired by the rational creature in every one of its acts.[12] Thomas does not, then, countenance the "aspiration to leave behind altogether the constituting conditions of our humanity, and to seek for a life that is really the life of another sort of being—as if it were a higher and better life for us."[13] The philosophic irresolvability of the question of the ultimate end reflects the failure of any human activity to fulfill the aspiration for happiness. It is important to note that Thomas embraces the dialectical conclusion of philosophy, its articulation of an end that escapes its grasp. Philosophy leaves open the possibility of a dialogue between itself and revelation. Because reason cannot show that there is a transcendent end or in what precisely it would consist, it cannot be expected to anticipate the teaching of revelation. Indeed, the prominence accorded to contemplation in Thomas's writings on the good life makes sense only in a context of revelation, where the gift of transcendent beatitude is offered to all.

The analogical account of happiness opposes both the reduction of happiness to what is attainable in this life and the repudiation of

---

[10] "Nature and Spirit: Some Reflections on the Problem of the End of Man," 69.

[11] See Kevin M. Staley, "Happiness: The Natural End of Man?"

[12] *ST*, I-II, 3, 6, ad 2, and I-II, 3, 8.

[13] Martha Nussbaum, "Transcending Humanity," in *Love's Knowledge*, 379.

imperfect happiness simply because it does not completely fulfill the definition of happiness. If Thomas presses certain Aristotelian principles to conclusions that philosopher never fully embraced, it is also evident that he deploys Aristotelian principles to foreclose the possibility of direct vision of the end in this life. Metaphysics, the highest of the Aristotelian sciences, does not extend beyond the knowledge gained from sensibles.[14] Aristotle thus operates as a restraint upon philosophic optimism. From another vantage point, the Christian tradition and human experience support Aristotelian pessimism concerning the human achievement of a transcendent end. In an article that asks "whether man can attain happiness," Thomas notes that the intellect as a receptive power is potentially infinite and that the will is able to desire the "universal and perfect good" (ST, I-II, 5, 1). In subsequent articles, he shows that such happiness cannot be had in this life. The impediments to happiness in this life are manifold and ineradicable: ignorance, disordered affection, and physical infirmities. Temporal goods are transient, and even the most secure forms of happiness are made tenuous by the fear of death (ST, I-II, 5, 3). The list is more Augustinian than Aristotelian; Thomas cites Augustine's City of God. But Thomas's acknowledgment of the fragility of human participation in happiness also follows from Aristotle's sense of the contingency of human happiness.

As if these pervasive ills were not enough, Thomas proceeds to argue that the vision of God surpasses the nature of every creature.[15] We are not completely bereft of resources, however, for "nature has given" us free choice by which we "can turn to God" (ST, I-II, 5, 5, ad 1). Is this just another way of saying that human beings cannot attain the end on their own? Thomas responds, the "rational creature, which can attain the perfect good of beatitude only with divine assistance, is more perfect than the irrational creature, which is incapable of such a good, but attains some imperfect good by the power of its own nature" (creatura rationalis quae potest consequi per-

---

[14] As we have already seen, this is the doctrine of the secunda pars. Interestingly, Thomas posits the same teaching in his commentary on a typically Neoplatonic passage in Boethius's De Trinitate. See Expositio super Librum Boethii De Trinitate, VI, 3–4.

[15] Even prior to the Fall, human beings did not know God directly. In this state, they possessed happiness only in a certain measure because they did not yet behold the divine essence, an end to which they were, nevertheless, destined (ST, 1, 94, 1, ad 1).

fectum beatitudinis bonum, indigens ad hoc divino auxilio, est per-
fectior quam creatura irrationalis, quae huiusmodi boni non est
capax, sed quoddam bonum imperfectum consequitur virtute suae
naturae; ST, I-II, 5, 5, ad 2). This state is what Jorge Laporta refers
to as the "disequilibrium of the intellectual creature," which is a
"mark of grandeur."[16] We achieve the transcendent good, not by
alienating ourselves from our proper location in the whole, but precisely by maintaining our openness to the whole and to the transcendent source of the whole, whose image we are. In Thomas's elegantly
paradoxical formulation, we are capable of a transcendent good because we are receptive of a gift. Something like this point underlies
the discussion, of whether any teaching besides philosophy is necessary, with which the entire *Summa Theologiae* begins. Another teaching is needed precisely because divine providence has ordered us to
a good that transcends the fragility of our nature. There is, then, a
certain fittingness and a magnificent beneficence in God's revelation;
otherwise, the highest truths would be known only by the few, after
enormous effort, and even then with an admixture of some error.

Aquinas's treatise on the ultimate end seems to complete the inquiry begun by Aristotle in the opening of the *Ethics*. The archers
now have their object clearly demarcated. Aristotle's questions have
generated the conclusion that the good is transcendent and escapes
categorization in human terms. But this returns us to a crucial dilemma in the Platonic tradition, for the relation between the transcendent, timeless Good and the temporal world is problematic. And,
as is clear from Aristotle's *Ethics* X, the conundrum is not peculiarly
Platonic. What is striking about the treatise on the ultimate end is
not just the doctrine itself, but also the way it influences the structure
of the *secunda pars* of the *Summa*. The prologue to the second part
states that what follows the treatise on the ultimate end concerns
those things "through which man is able to reach his end or by which
he might deviate from the end," for we must take from the end the

---

[16] *La destinée de la nature humaine selon Thomas d'Aquin,* 127. It was Henri de
Lubac's *Surnaturel,* of course, that rekindled the debate over the ultimate end. For
a discussion of the various responses that *Surnaturel* elicited, see Philip J. Donnelly,
"Discussions on the Supernatural Order." More recently, Staley has argued that
although de Lubac deploys a univocal conception of happiness and finality, Thomas
himself treats these notions analogically. See Staley, "Happiness: The Natural End
of Man?" Staley might well have added that the early modern scholastics, whom de
Lubac opposes, were equally given to univocity in their reading of Thomas.

reasons of those things ordained to the end. There is one end unifying the whole of human life and that end is contemplative union with
God. The danger with this formulation is that the entirety of life
will now be seen as merely instrumental to the achievement of a
transcendent end. The characterization of the end as contemplative
seems radically to subordinate action to contemplation and thus to
invite forgetfulness of the distinctive features of the life of prudence
and the moral virtues. How are we to construe the relation of the
single, ultimate end to the diverse practices that are the fabric of
human life? And how do we avoid eviscerating the multiplicity of
human goods?

The depiction of the relationship of means to end in the preface
to the second part is so brief as to be misleading. A number of initial
clarifications are in order. First, as noted in the discussion of Aristotle, the teaching on the superiority of contemplation is a theoretical
teaching, from which it is not clear precisely how contemplation is to
fit into the whole of our lives. Thomas holds, moreover, that perfect,
contemplative happiness is not possible in this life, but it is not at all
evident from this teaching alone how we are to order our lives here
and now to such a transcendent end, an end that exceeds our natural
capacities. Second, the Christian account of the end as union with
God is not nearly as "intellectualist" as has usually been thought. The
affections and the will have a pronounced role in Christian contemplation. The moral virtues and especially the theological virtue of
charity, which resides in the will, are essential to the achievement
of an end that is contemplative and transcendent. The Christian gift of
wisdom and hence the Christian practice of contemplation presuppose charity. The infused virtue of charity is not just a means; through
it, we are already united to the end. Third, the ordering of means to
end does not necessarily instrumentalize the whole of life. Thomas,
following Plato and Aristotle, countenances three sorts of goods:
goods that are solely means, goods that are ends alone, and goods that
are both desired for themselves and as conducive to other goods.
Crucial to the last category is the notion of a hierarchy of goods. It is
simply a misunderstanding of Thomas's conception of hierarchy to
view that hierarchy as instrumentalizing all lower goods or as inviting
the practice of weighing goods against one another in consequentialist fashion. Instead, lower goods participate in the higher goods, on

which they depend; the lower goods are images, actual manifestations, and imperfect realizations of the ultimate Good.

Finally, even as the Christian conception of the good life embraces the ancient aspiration for an ascent to the highest things, it corrects it by coupling the ascent with a descent. The Incarnation, on which the good life is modeled, embraces temporality, embodiment, and contingency so as to manifest their beauty and goodness. The way up is the way down. More so than the ancients, Thomas depicts the good life in narrative terms, in terms derived from the historical discourse of Scripture. Of course, the whole of time is ordered to a transcendent end; this involves not annihilation but elevation and transfiguration. There will then be a "new heaven and a new earth." In a reversal of the ancient understanding of contemplation as terminating in an individual's transcendence of the public realm of speech, the Christian conception of God is inherently communal. The God to whom we are to be united at the end of time is a community of persons in whom there is the most intimate communication of knowledge and love. God's being is indistinguishable from God's knowing, and both are inseparable from God's speaking and loving. Christ is the Word (Verbum), and we are images of God precisely in the procession of the inner word, an articulation of our knowing and a basis of our loving. How do these claims inform Thomas's ethical teaching?

To answer this question, it will help to have an overview of the structure of Thomas's moral teaching before us. An instructive way to read the *secunda pars* of the *Summa* is in terms of the hierarchies of law and virtue. At the outset, Thomas states that virtue is an intrinsic and law an extrinsic principle by means of which we are led to our end. The hierarchies provide a progressive education in the practices and virtues necessary for the attainment of the end. Thomas grounds the notion of hierarchical participation in the doctrine of creation, the avenue by which God instills the natural law into our souls: "The soul has a share of the eternal reason, by which it has a natural inclination to its due act and end; and this participation of the eternal law in the rational creature is the natural law" (*ST,* I-II, 91, 2.). The natural law, then, is the proximate ground of the hierarchy, but it is already a participation in the eternal law, which is the ultimate ground.

In the treatise on law, Thomas distinguishes between the types of laws on the basis of three principles: the end or goal to which the law is directed, the rigor and scope of its precepts, and the type of sanctions or inducements it employs (*ST*, I-II, 91, 5). The natural law, which is identical to our natural inclinations, provides initial clues to or intimations of our end. The precepts of the natural law are general and inchoate. Thomas highlights the indeterminacy of the natural law and observes that passion and bad education can erode all but the primary precepts (*ST*, I-II, 94, 6). It is difficult, furthermore, to discern what inducements or sanctions accrue to the natural law.

Human law is an articulation of the natural law, an unfolding of basic moral precepts with an eye to practical application. An increase in clarity and specificity accompanies the transition from natural to human law (*ST*, I-II, 91, 3). Explicit promulgation is an essential element in the definition of human law (*ST*, I-II, 90, 4). The binding force of the human law can also be seen in its palpable punitive responses to infractions (*ST*, I-II, 95, 1).

The ultimate end, however, transcends the scope of natural and human law. For an unambiguous affirmation of the possibility and existence of such an end, a revealed law is necessary. So that we "may know without any doubt" what we ought to do, we need a sure guide to the end (*ST*, I-II, 91, 4). Divine law is concerned not only with external obedience, but also with the interior movements of the soul. The human law is composed mainly of negative precepts, whereas divine law is replete with positive injunctions.

The articulation of a hierarchy of moral discourses seems to replicate the ascent passage from Plato's *Symposium*, where desire, aroused at one level, is satisfied at the next. The crucial and problematic difference, of course, is that certain levels in Thomas's hierarchy are unknown to natural reason. To clarify his understanding of the hierarchy of moral discourses and the role of the natural and the supernatural in it, we must return to the relationships between reason and faith in the *praeambula fidei*. What have the preambles to do with the moral life?

When we turn from the theoretical to the practical, the preambles resurface in the ascent from reason to faith. In the course of the discussion in the *Contra Gentiles* of the "twofold mode of truth" concerning divine things, Thomas observes that the Old Law promised temporal goods as suasions to the pursuit of virtue. The Old Law, accordingly, "proposed few things which exceeded the investigation of human reason" (*SCG*, I, 5). It falls into the category of those truths about divine things that can be known by rational inquiry, but it is also revealed. Its precepts are *preambula fidei*. What does the treatment of the preambles in the practical sphere add to the consideration of them in the speculative realm?

Thomas offers a protracted treatment of the convergence of the natural law and the Decalogue in the *secunda pars* of the *Summa*. In his analysis of the constituent parts of the Old Law, he articulates the relation between the natural law and the Decalogue. He divides the precepts of the Old Law into three sets: the ceremonial, the judicial, and the moral (*ST*, I-II, 99, 3–5). The force of the first two derives from institution alone; they are peculiar to the Jews. The moral precepts, central to which are the commandments of the Decalogue, are founded on natural reason itself. When Thomas refers to the fundamental, incorrigible precepts of the natural law, he usually has in mind those precepts against murder, adultery, theft, and so forth that are immediately derivable from the first precept, "do good, avoid evil" (*ST*, I-II, 96, 2). This group of precepts constitutes the second table of the Decalogue, which consists in precepts concerning behavior toward our neighbor. It may seem odd for him to consider the commandments of the first table, which concern duties to God, as part of the natural law. Religion is not, however, an infused virtue; rather, it is a natural virtue, falling under the species of justice.[17] Justice is the focus of the entire Decalogue, in that it concerns duties to God and to others.[18] But how are we to arrive at the notion of a duty to God? In what do the duties of natural religion consist?

In order to know that there is a God to whom we are indebted, we need not have a proof. Reason is naturally inclined to posit some ultimate principle as cause of the whole. But what attitude ought we to have toward such a being? It seems that we can know precious little about this attitude without the assistance of revelation. Thomas poses the objection that among the commandments of the Decalogue, the precept about observance of the Sabbath is ceremonial,

---

[17] See *ST*, II-II, 81, 1; and II-II, 121, 1, ad 2.

[18] The natural law does not exhaust the Old Law. As Thomas puts it, "The Old Law manifested the precepts of the natural law, and added certain precepts of its own" (*lex vetus manifestabat praecepta legis naturae, et superaddebat quaedam propria praecepta; ST*, I-II, 98, 5). The ceremonial and the judicial precepts apply to Jewish religious and political practice. Beyond the moral precepts of the Decalogue, which are evident to all, the Old Law is replete with other moral precepts that only the wise immediately know (*ST*, I-II, 100, 11).

not moral (ST, I-II, 100, 3, obj. 2). The response is that the precept is in part moral, in that it commands us to "give some time to God," and in part ceremonial, in that it "fixes the time" (ST, I-II, 100, 3, ad 2). Not only the time, but also the content of Sabbath observance is ceremonial: "to worship God . . . belongs to a moral precept; but the determination of the precept—namely, that he is to be worshipped by these sacrifices and those honors—belongs to the ceremonial precepts" (ST, I-II, 99, 3, ad 2). Indeed, the attempt, apart from revelation, to determine the content of worship seems to lead inevitably to idolatry. We need divine instruction to know the commandments that proscribe making graven images and taking the name of the Lord in vain (ST, I-II, 100, 1). With respect to the first table of the Decalogue, the natural law proves a less than adequate guide to the practice of worship.

Despite these limitations, the pedagogy of divine law presumes and builds on the content of the natural law: "Just as grace presupposes nature, so the divine law presupposes the natural law" (ST, I-II, 99, 2, ad 1). As was the case with the theoretical *praeambula*, the practical *praeambula* offer rational verification of a part of revelation and invite the reader to further inquiry. This verification provides further warrant for something Thomas had urged at the outset of both the *Summa Theologiae* and the *Summa contra Gentiles*—namely, that submission to revealed truth is not foolish. The strategy of the practical *praeambula* replicates that of the speculative. Although there are obvious similarities between the two treatments of the preambles, the relation between natural and divine law is more complicated than we have allowed thus far. Divine law enables us to understand the content and implications of what would otherwise be seen naturally. As for the content of the natural law, Thomas argues that the fundamental precepts are incorrigible. The precise sense in which these precepts are ubiquitously operative is unclear. Bad education can erode principles as basic as the one prohibiting theft (ST, I-II, 94, 6). At this juncture, Thomas advances the paradoxical suggestion that attention to divine law might help elucidate the content of the natural law. It is indeed curious that the divine law should play such a pivotal role in the cognition of a law that is purportedly natural. Thomas thinks that submission to divine law is likely to play an integral part in this education precisely because sin has derailed the natural impulses. Unlike the discussion in the *prima pars*, this treatment of the preambles countenances a more severe critique of the efficacy of reason. The shift in emphasis is congruent with Thomas's observation that the effects of original sin have had a more deleterious impact on moral inquiry than on speculative inquiry (*ST,* I-II, 109, 2, ad 3). In both the speculative and the practical orders, the revelation of the preambles "removes the manifold errors to which reason is liable" (*ST,* I-II, 99, 2, ad 2).

In the articulation and clarification of the precepts of the natural law, human and divine law can be of service (*ST,* I-II, 91, 3–4). Revelation, then, is needed not only that we may grasp supernatural truths, but also that we might re-cognize those natural truths that the effects of sin have hidden from us. Divine law confirms and clarifies what reason grasped inchoately. The first stage in divine pedagogy is strikingly reminiscent of Socratic recollection; it involves a repossession of what is already known implicitly.[19] This connection points up an important distinction between the theoretical preambles and those of practice: whereas the existence of God must be demonstrated by arguments that move from what is immediately given in sense perception in search of the ground of this experience, the precepts of the natural law are "known through themselves" (*per se nota; ST,* I-II, 94, 2). The practical preambles are not conclusions of arguments. The first moment in the pedagogy of divine law is self-reflexive; it involves a dialectical reduplication of the content of the natural law.

The law is an instrument of instruction, but it does not supply the sort of smooth, straightforward, didactic help one might expect. Our moral predicament, the symptom of which is estrangement from both God and ourselves, demands a more radical cure. The first stage in inquiry about the good is oblique and self-reflective rather than direct and "objective." The Old Law aids only by accusing. After the instruction of the law, human pride is exposed because we are unable to fulfill even what we know we ought to do (*ST,* I-II, 98, 6). Divine pedagogy is thus analogous to Socratic dialectic. And, as is clear from the Platonic dialogues, the ironic beginning is an unexpected circuit in philosophic discourse—unexpected, that is, from the point of view of the inquirer. The accusation of the law is an abrupt interruption of

---

[19] On Socratic recollection and dialectic, see Jacob Klein, *A Commentary on Plato's Meno,* 3–31 and throughout.

an individual's inquiry into the good. Why is such a point of departure necessary?

Human nature is incapacitated even with respect to natural things. The ravages of sin have left the intellect darkened, the will disordered, and the passions vagrant, and have inflicted manifold punishments on the human race. Human beings are often incapable of conforming to the standards of the law or to the ideals embodied in the virtues. The clues to the inability of human nature to act naturally, when coupled with the doctrine of original sin, form an explanatory nexus. Revelation offers an account of human nature's alienation from the natural.

Without the initial acknowledgment that one is presently indisposed to the inquiry, one is apt to misconstrue the character of the inquiry, particularly its application to one's present condition. Two benefits accrue to this apparently negative moment in moral discourse. First, one gains self-knowledge because one is now in a better position to gauge the character of the inquiry and its relation to one's capacities and needs. Second, one gains respect for the instrument— namely, the divine law—that provides the occasion for the knowledge and that offers grace as a cure. It is not accidental that the treatise on law in the *Summa* is comfortably ensconced between the treatises on sin and grace. Thomas highlights the dialectical role of law in relation to grace. The dialectic culminates in the depiction of the law as an occasion of sin. The law commands without empowering. We must look beyond the law for some sort of divine assistance. As Thomas puts it, God intended "to give such a law that by our own powers we could not fulfill, so that, while relying on ourselves, we might discover ourselves to be sinners and being humbled might have recourse to the help of grace" (*ST*, I-II, 98, 2, ad 3). The full import of the pedagogy of the laws can be had only from the perspective of salvation history. God sent the law as a help *(auxilium)* when the "natural law began to be obscured by an excess of sins." The Old Law was "given between the natural law and the law of grace" so that human beings might be led "gradually from the imperfect to the perfect." The Old Law was suitably given at the time of Moses because "the written law was necessary as a remedy for human ignorance" (*ST*, I-II, 98, 6, ad 1). Human ignorance is dual: ignorance of the good and ignorance of one's own ignorance. Both forms of ignorance are the effects of sin, original and actual.

The comparison of theological to philosophic pedagogy, either So-cratic recollection or Aristotelian dialectic, can take us only so far, however. The revealed law is more than a Socratic midwife that en-ables the inquirer to actualize his or her natural capacities. Indeed, errors rendering us unfit for inquiry and action are not merely vices to which we are alerted by a virtuous teacher; they are sins and rebel-lions against the one by whom we are being instructed. Put slightly differently, the certitude arising from the encounter with God is "founded not on having grasped but on having been grasped."[20] We are informed not only about our nature and its telos but also about things that wholly transcend our natural grasp. Thomas denies that we can infer the nature of or even the need for revelation simply by inspecting the data of nature. The dialectical pedagogy of Scripture is rooted in our experience of sin. To understand our experience of moral failure in terms of the doctrine of original sin, in terms of our alienation from a personal God, requires divine instruction. The overarching context of any particular revelation is the covenant be-tween God and his people. The philosopher's reflection on nature provides no direct access to the contingent, historical event that is the source of our alienation. The historical fact of original sin escapes the knowledge of the philosopher, who is ignorant of both the cause and the cure of our condition. Christianity locates our self-under-standing within a historical and dramatic narrative unknown to the gentiles.

The speculative preambles enable us to adjudicate between claim-ants to divine revelation; they also exercise a certain control over theological discourse. Can the same be said for the precepts of the natural law? Given the impotence of the law and of natural impulses as guides in the moral life, we have to wonder what positive function the natural law plays in Thomas's ethics. We must be careful not to overstate Thomas's view of the effects of sin on human nature, for he holds that "human nature is not altogether corrupted by sin." There is a limited sphere in which natural reason, acting in accordance with the dictates of the natural law, succored by the cardinal virtues, can operate adequately. The operation of practical reason is useful not only in the political arena, but also in the realm of philosophical the-ology. We have already seen him eschew the morality of Mohammed

---

[20] Hans urs von Balthasar, *Seeing the Form,* 134.

for its antipathy to spiritual goods. The impact of this critique would be made more immediate and more forceful by showing the incompatibility of Mohammed's morality with the dictates of the natural law. In fact, the latter route seems to be presupposed in the original argument.

Theology sustains a dialectical engagement of the natural order. If we were to claim that human nature is entirely bereft of the capacity for good, then we would be left with no means, except by way of negative critique, to link up the Christian life with human experience or reason, which would uproot the moral life from a framework within which the passage from one way of life to another might be spoken of intelligibly. A repudiation of the intelligibility of human life undermines any positive attempt to construct a coherent vision of human life. Thomas averts the difficulty by building on certain analogies between the natural and the supernatural, between the content and aims of pagan and Christian ethics. The motive for engaging philosophy is not primarily apologetic—that is, it is not a project extrinsic to Thomas's Christian vocation. He does not begin, as Karl Barth supposes those who engage in natural theology must, by bracketing faith and adopting the standpoint of "unbelief."[21] The project has a properly theological motivation. In order for the assertions of revelation to be intelligible to us, we must have some prior understanding of nature and the human condition. Revelation requires that we reappropriate our experience of the natural world and set that understanding in the comprehensive context of Scripture. For Thomas, an important part of that reappropriation involves attention to philosophy.

The engagement of the natural by the supernatural provides further evidence against the view that Christianity involves alienation from the natural order. Although the teaching of Christianity cannot be deduced from our natural experience of the world, its vision of human life is not utterly extrinsic to the life that we are presently living. Instead, it provides an intelligibility to that life, which it would otherwise lack. We must be careful how we characterize the relationship between philosophy and theology. As previously noted, Thomas does not abandon the perspective of belief in an attempt to accommodate philosophy, nor does he adapt one to the other in an attempt

---

[21] *Church Dogmatics*, 2: 1.

at synthesis, which would only dilute the content and sap the vitality
of each. The aspiration for contemplation is not alien to the Judeo-
Christian tradition; it permeates the Wisdom literature of the Old
Testament as well as the Gospel of John, whose recurring theme is
the beholding of the Father in the Son. By directing the contemplative aspiration toward a concrete, particular revelation, Christianity
corrects the philosophic tendency, evident in post-Aristotelian pagan
thought, to fulfill itself by abstracting from the concrete and abandoning itself to universal being. The contemplative aspiration of philosophy can be satisfied only by being transformed. Because in the
Christian religion "form does not stand in opposition to infinite
light," Christianity might be called "the aesthetic religion par excellence."[22]

Such a transformation presupposes faith, which Aquinas defines as
thinking with assent, the acceptance on the basis of divine authority
of truths not evident to the intellect. If, as I have just argued, there
is a danger in insisting too strongly on the analogy between philosophical and theological pedagogy, there is also a danger in depicting
the movement from philosophy to theology solely in terms of submission to authority. In such a depiction, the emphasis would shift from
an intrinsic conception of the good life, wherein we are already inclined to the goods proposed, to an entirely extrinsic conception that
relies primarily on the notion of a divine lawgiver. There are two
reasons why this depiction does not work. First, for Aquinas, faith is
a kind of knowing through an experience of the divine. We would not
be moved to assent to the doctrines of the faith without "an interior
instinct and attraction of teaching" *(interior instinctus et attractus
doctrinae)*, which is an "internal inspiration" *(inspiratio interna)* and
"experience" *(experimentum)*.[23] Second, the focus of moral theology
is not law but virtue, which, as he notes in the prologue to the *secunda pars*, is an intrinsic principle whereby human beings are led
to the ultimate end. By contrast, law is an external principle. If law
educates, virtue enables. Accordingly, Thomas devotes most of his
attention to the virtues. A hierarchy of virtues, to which I now turn,
parallels and completes that of the laws.

The practice of virtue educates our inclinations. Instruction occurs

---

[22] Urs von Balthasar, *Seeing the Form*, 216.
[23] Aquinas, *Lectura super Johannem*, c614n7, c1515n5.

in a number of stages. The structure of the virtues is isomorphic to that of the laws. The virtues, for example, exhibit an ontological dependency on God: "The exemplar of human virtue preexists in God, just as in Him preexist the types [*rationes*] of all things" (*ST*, I-II, 61, 5). God implants in us dispositions to virtue, and union with God is the end at which virtue aims. The ground and summit of the hierarchy are, once again, identical. Thomas makes his own the Neoplatonic hierarchy of the virtues: the political virtues, the cleansing virtues, the virtues of the cleansed soul, and the exemplary virtues. The political virtues are natural; they enable human beings to conduct themselves well in human affairs. The cleansing virtues and the virtues of the cleansed mediate between the natural, political virtues and the exemplary virtues. "Because it pertains to man to draw himself onward to divine things, as even the Philosopher declares in the *Ethics*, and as is commended to us many times in sacred Scripture . . . it is necessary to place some mediating virtues between the political, which are the human virtues, and the exemplary, which are divine" (*ST*, I-II, 61, 5). This is perhaps the clearest statement in the *Summa* of the way a hierarchy of moral discourses is designed to bridge the gap between human beings' present condition and their ultimate end. The cardinal virtues perfect the natural inclinations (*ST*, I-II, 61, 1). They are the virtues that the laws of the city hope to inculcate.

The cardinal virtues do not, however, suffice to lead to the ultimate end. For this, divine assistance is necessary. Imperfect virtue can exist without charity, as, for instance, when one is ordered to a particular good. But true virtue, which orders all things to our principal and ultimate good, is inseparable from charity (*ST*, II-II, 23, 7). The object of the theological virtues distinguishes them from the other virtues: "The object of the theological virtues is God Himself, who is the ultimate end of things, as exceeding the knowledge of our reason" (*ST*, I-II, 62, 2). The intellect grasps supernatural principles through faith, whereas the will tends to an attainable end through hope. Charity, "by which the will is transformed into the end," marks the culmination of the moral life in time (*ST*, I-II, 62, 3).

The disparities between the theological virtues and the natural virtues are striking. Although Thomas does not discount the importance of habit in the theological virtues, their source is an utterly unmerited gift. In their source, they are stronger and more efficacious than are the natural virtues. In us, however, the natural virtues may be more secure. Because the infused virtues do not entirely transform our natural dispositions, there remains the difficulty of acting well, especially for those individuals who retain contrary dispositions from previous vicious acts (*ST*, I-II, 65, 3, ad 2). The theological virtues escape classification in terms of the division between intellectual and moral virtue. They are ordered not to some practical activity but to union with God, which is made possible by the ordering of all our desires to the love of God. There is, moreover, no mean for the virtue of charity, for God is an infinite good, who cannot be loved excessively (*ST*, I-II, 64, 1). Thomas goes so far as to state that the acquired virtues differ in species from the infused. The mean with respect to pleasures, for example, is seen "under a different aspect" in the infused virtues than it is in the acquired virtues. In the taking of food, for example, "the mean established by human reason is that food should not harm the health of the body or obstruct the act of reason; but according to the rule of divine law, man is required to chastise his body and bring it into subjection (I Cor. 9. 27) by abstaining from food, drink" (*ST*, I-II, 63, 4). Thomas proceeds to differentiate the two kinds of virtues in accordance with the ends or forms of government to which they are directed, for, as Aristotle states, the virtues of citizens vary in accordance with their regime. On the basis of this principle, the two sorts of virtues differ, as do the human city and the heavenly city.

There is an inescapable reciprocity between understanding and loving in the Christian conception of the good life. Although the virtue of faith resides in the intellect, the object of faith is simultaneously the first truth and the good that is "the end of all our desires and actions" (*ST*, II-II, 4, 2, ad 3). Thus, while charity presupposes faith, as love presupposes knowledge, there cannot be faith without charity, which is the form and proper end of faith (*ST*, II-II, 4, 3). The reciprocity of contemplation and action is also evident in the connection between the theological virtues and the gifts of the Holy Spirit. As the treatment of the theological virtues indicates, the end is not a detached, intellectualist vision of the supreme separate substance. Rather, the goal is union with a personal God. The gifts render human beings docile to the promptings of God (*ST*, I-II, 68, 1), and an intimate union with the will of God perfects all the powers of the soul (*ST*, I-II, 68, 5). The gifts do not depose charity as the key to the moral life, for they originate and culminate in charity (*ST*, I-II, 68, 5). The intimate connection between charity and the gift of wisdom is instructive. The gift of wisdom is the fruit of charity. In contrast to the intellectual virtue of wisdom, the gift has reference both to speculation and practice. It empowers us to conduct human affairs in light of divine truth (*ST*, II-II, 45, 3). The mode of knowing appropriate to the gift operates by connaturality or sympathy (*ST*, II-II, 45, 2). It is the result, not of speculation, but of a different, higher mode of knowing, one that is analogous to the vision of the redeemed. The intellectual life is thus described in language reminiscent of that used to describe prudence: it is rooted in rectified appetite and knows not through abstract principles but through the mode of inclination.

Thomas's brief consideration of the hierarchy of the virtues clarifies his initial contrast between law and virtue as a difference between an extrinsic and an intrinsic principle. The gap between extrinsic and intrinsic principles is not so strict as it might have first appeared. Natural law, for example, is hardly extrinsic to nature. As noted earlier, natural law is instilled through creation; in human beings, law is simply identical to the "impression of an inward active principle" (*impressio activi principii intrinseci; ST*, I-II, 93, 5, obj. 1 and ad 1). Whatever sanctions, moreover, accrue to the violation of the natural law are not extrinsic to the performance of an undue act, but inhere in the agent, rendering her or him unfit to pursue the good life. The most explicit gap between extrinsic and intrinsic principles appears to exist in the relationship between human law and the life of virtue. The sanctions here are indeed extrinsic to the vicious act, but punishment, which is primarily ordered to the restoration of justice, has the additional intent of educating the agent concerning his or her natural good. Where there might seem to be the greatest gap between extrinsic and intrinsic principles—namely, in divine law—there is actually a remarkable union. Although the gap between the Old Law and the life of virtue was at times quite large, the New Law inclines us to fulfill our duties easily and joyfully. That grace restores and perfects the affinity between human nature and the transcendent end is clear from the fact that the New Law supersedes the Old Law in its mode of legislation: "the New Law is primarily a law impressed in our hearts, and secondarily it is a written law" (*ST*, I-II, 106, 1). The law of charity is more like an internal than an external principle and is, consequently, nearly indistinguishable from the theological virtue of charity.

The hierarchy of moral discourses, then, is the Christian answer to problems posed at the limits of pagan philosophy. The penchant of ancient philosophers for constructing a plurality of philosophic discourses, arranged hierarchically, enables Thomas to correct without eviscerating the moral discourse of those ancients. He resolves the question of the good and the means to its attainment only through the decisive subordination of philosophy to theology, reason to faith, and the rational understanding of nature to the revealed narrative of Scripture. The engagement of the natural by the supernatural demands and allows for the reappropriation of our natural teleology. There is no dichotomy or tension between the eternal law and the order of nature: We have a "natural inclination to that which is consonant with the eternal law, for we are innately capable of possessing the virtues" (*ST*, I-II, 93, 6). At this level, we are already participants in and subject to the eternal law. The emphasis on participation and subjection evinces the distance that separates Thomas's teaching on human perfection from various modern conceptions of autonomy. The more virtuous an individual is, the more he or she is subject to the eternal law; increased freedom coincides with increased participation in the supreme Good.

The dialectical status of the precepts of the natural law is a reminder that the transition from philosophy to theology, from reason to revelation, and from nature to grace involves more than the admission of a different set of authorities into an ongoing discussion about divine things. The impasse at which philosophic discourse about the good inevitably arrives is the result not just of the limitations to natural reason, but also of a breach, irreparable by human effort and knowable only through revelation.[24] The attainment of the good requires God's gratuitous assistance, a gift that we can never predict. The instrument—namely, the revealed law—that offers self-knowledge also promises a cure in the form of an incarnate God. The promise of a redeemer accompanies the initial, dialectical moment in moral pedagogy. From this vantage point, the recovery of our natural

---

[24] Even prior to sin, human nature was not adequate to the achievement of the beatific vision, but, Thomas argues, had we not sinned, we would have eventually been granted this vision (*ST*, I, 94, ad 1).

potentiality is but a minor and subordinate part of the pedagogy of revelation.

The depiction of the hierarchy of the virtues once again gives the impression of a straightforward ascent from time to eternity, from the sensible to the intellectual or spiritual, and from creation to the creator. That this ascent is not so straightforward is clear from the teaching on law itself, in which the moral instruction of the Decalogue is its least significant part. The distinction between ceremonial and moral components of the first table of the Decalogue distinguishes what revelation gives together. The ceremonial precepts provide "determinations of the moral precepts by which we are directed to God" (*ST,* I-II, 101, 1). What is striking in the ceremonial portion of the law is that it mirrors the descent of God to us and the manifestation of the eternal in time, of the spiritual in the sensible. It renders the divine truth proportionate to our embodied, temporal condition and enables the "ray of divine light to shine on us under the form of certain sensible figures" (*ST,* I-II, 101, 2). Through divine worship, the likenesses of divine things are "expressed in words" and "proffered to the senses" (*ST,* I-II, 99, 3, ad 3). The ceremonial precepts are a synecdoche for revelation itself; they evince the capacity of Scripture to encompass, divide, and order the whole of time. As Thomas puts it, "the external worship of the Old Law is figurative not only of the future truth to be manifested in the fatherland, but also of Christ, who is the way leading to the truth of the fatherland" (*ST,* I-II, 101, 2). As the incarnate Word and the Word according to which the world is created, Christ is simultaneously means and end, sign and signified. Apart from the Incarnation, the "union of the infinite and the finite can, at most, be presented dialectically as a self-abolishing process."[25] The Incarnation overcomes that destructive dialectic by joining "together what in human terms is eternally incompatible: love for one existent is conjoined with love for Being itself."[26]

That this lesson governs the entirety of philosophical theology is clear from the exordium to the *Contra Gentiles* (I, 1), where Thomas considers the office of the wise. Following Aristotle, he states that the duty of the wise is to consider the order of the universe. The ultimate Good of the universe is truth, and the unifying end of the speculative

[25] Urs von Balthasar, *Seeing the Form,* 171.

[26] Urs von Balthasar, *Seeing the Form,* 193.

and the practical orders is the vision of that primordial truth through which all other things are true. Divine wisdom, Thomas continues, became flesh specifically in order to manifest the truth. Christ is thus the middle term in the ascent from nature to grace, an ascent made possible by his descent.

PRUDENCE, CONTEMPLATION, AND CHARITY

Because grace perfects and elevates nature, the full import of the natural virtues, their efficacy in the moral life, can be had only from a supernatural perspective. In the *Summa Theologiae*, for example, the structure of moral teaching, which is determined by the theological virtues and by the gifts of the Holy Spirit, exhibits the transformation of nature by grace. Thomas links each gift with either a theological or a cardinal virtue. The gifts of knowledge and understanding are associated with faith; the gift of fear with hope; the gift of wisdom with charity; the gift of counsel with prudence; and the gift of fortitude with fortitude. Even though supernatural virtues and gifts transcend the natural order, they do not abolish the natural virtues. Instead, they presuppose and assist them. The prominence of virtue in Thomas's moral theology is instructive; it counters the supposition that the Christian notion of charity anticipates a Kantian view of the primacy of universal duties and its attendant construal of the moral life in terms of altruism and equal regard. Such a view is antithetical to the ancient and Thomistic understanding of the good life in terms of the virtues constitutive of human happiness. By denying the importance of the distinctions among persons constitutive of ordinary moral and political experience, this view is apt to underestimate the role of prudence in the moral life. Thomas makes no such mistake. For example, counsel, which corresponds to the virtue of prudence, is a gift through which God moves human beings to give counsel concerning singular acts (*ST,* II-II, 52, 1). As we shall see, Thomas's account of charity, which is the form of the virtues, reinforces the crucial role of prudence in the moral life.

The recovery of the theological role of prudence serves to free Thomas from the view of moral education as mere conformity to the moral law, with heroic self-denial as a moral paradigm. In the third book of the *Summa contra Gentiles,* Thomas considers numerous objections to voluntary poverty, three of which are *(a)* that poverty violates the mean of liberality, *(b)* that the renunciation of the activity of procuring goods necessary to sustain human life is unnatural, and *(c)* that begging is contemptible (*SCG*, III, 130). The indeterminacy of prudence—the impossibility of reducing it to an immutable set of rules—suggests a strategy for responding to the objections. The mean need not be construed quantitatively "according to the amount of exterior things" *(secundum quantitatem exteriorum)*, but rather according to reason, which "measures not only the quantity of the thing it uses, but the condition of the person, his intention, and the occasions of time of place . . . which are requisite in the acts of the virtues." If one embraces voluntary poverty for the right reason and with due regard to circumstances, it is not excessive. The deeper criticism of mendicancy is that it is unnatural and contemptible. Again, Thomas finds a response in the Aristotelian understanding of prudence. He grants that active power and rule are naturally superior to receptivity and obedience: "It is obvious that mendicancy involves a certain abjection. To suffer is more ignoble than to act, to receive than to give, and to be ruled and to obey than to govern and command; however, on account of the addition of some added circumstance, the appraisal can be reversed" (*SCG*, III, 135). Virtuous humiliation is not stupidity or unthinking toleration of any sort of deprivation. There may be circumstances where enduring certain evils or sacrificing certain natural goods is a means to attaining some greater good or to avoiding a greater evil. The counsels, then, are not for the weak, but for those who through a surplus of divine power and a proper exercise of prudence freely choose to "cast aside" other things for the sake of the highest Good. Renunciation and the discipline of the self are not ends in themselves, nor are they veils for the resentment rooted in the fragile nihilism of the many.[27] Thomas's novel application of the Aristotelian mean to the counsels involves nothing less than the articulation of Christian prudence.

Further support for the prominence of prudence in the life of faith can be garnered from the discussion of charity. The similarity between prudence and charity is evident in the statement that charity

---

[27] For the Dominican understanding of poverty and of the dualistic heresies that the Order of Preachers opposed, see Guy Bedouelle, O.P., *Saint Dominic: The Grace of the Word*, 138–54 and 171–79.

is the "mother of all the virtues." By commanding other virtues, it conceives the "acts of the other virtues, by the desire of the last end" (*ST*, II-II, 23, 8, ad 3). The differences are equally striking. The ordering principle in charity arises from the movement of the will toward God; in contrast to prudence, which presupposes rectified appetite, charity is essentially a matter of rightly ordered desire. In contrast to the moral virtues, it can be lost through the commission of one serious sin (*ST*, II-II, 24, 11–12). Because charity has God, who cannot be loved excessively, as its object, it does not consist in a mean as do the moral virtues (*ST*, II-II, 27, 6).

Charity is essentially relational and in this life inherently temporal. Thomas embraces Augustine's description of charity as the "movement of the soul towards the enjoyment of God for his own sake" (*ST*, II-II, 23, 2). It is a kind of friendship, founded on the communication of mutual love: "there is communication between us and God, insofar as he communicates his happiness to us" (*ST*, II-II, 23, 1). In the discussion of charity as friendship, Thomas borrows much from Aristotle, for whom friendship is much more than an instrumental good. It is partly constitutive of the good life and is the arena in which the virtues are most fruitfully exercised. Thomas goes further, not just in asserting the possibility of friendship between God and us. Charity is friendship—both between God and us and among us. Friendship is now the key to the good life. Charity, without which there is no true virtue, is the most excellent of the virtues, the form of all the virtues (*ST*, II-II, 23, 7–8). Thomas quotes Aristotle's assertion that " 'virtue is the disposition of a thing to that which is best,' " as the basis for an argument that true virtue directs humans beings to their principal good. Without such an ordering of our actions, there can be true but incomplete or imperfect virtue, as when an action is ordered to the common good of the community (*ST*, II-II, 23, 7).

In explicating the commandments of charity—love of God and neighbor—Thomas deploys Aristotle's principle that "each kind of friendship chiefly regards that good whose shared participation is the basis of the friendship" (*ST*, II-II, 26, 2). God is to be loved as the supreme Good and source of happiness, and the neighbor is loved as sharing in the happiness we receive from God. We are to love God more than we love ourselves because God is the source of our very nature and of the grace by which we participate in the highest Good

(*ST*, II-II, 26, 3). After love of God comes love of self. As is clear from the language of the great commandment to love our neighbor as we love ourselves, love of self is the "exemplar" for love of others (*ST*, II-II, 26, 4). Sinners, whose natures are divided and turned away from their true good, do not love themselves. They have a false estimation of themselves and thus love not what they are, but what they suppose themselves to be (*ST*, II-II, 25, 7). Grace perfects nature; charity does not eviscerate the order of natural associations. In the order of learning to love, there is a certain priority in the love of neighbor; according to Gregory, "the soul learns, from those things it knows, to love what it knows not" (*ST*, II-II, 26, 2, ad 1).

In defending our duty to love more those persons connected to us by blood, Thomas states that "we should measure the love of different persons according to the different kinds of union." He quotes Aristotle: " 'the love of different persons is determined by the diverse kinds of union proper to each' " (*ST*, II-II, 26, 8; *Ethics*, IX, 2, 1165a17). The order of love is based on nature and on the merit of virtue; those who are nearer to God merit greater love. Instead of eliminating our natural attachments, charity "commands each act of the other kinds of friendship, even as the art about the end commands the art concerning the means" (*ST*, II-II, 26, 7). Thus, charity is inherently prudential; it must consider not only the order of natural associations, but also the time and place of specific actions. In battle, for instance, one should obey an officer rather than one's father, although generally speaking the latter is more deserving of honor (*ST*, II-II, 26, 8, ad 3). Thomas even argues that it is more meritorious to love our friends than to love our enemies because the former are more closely united to us. The strength of our love for God, however, is more evident in the love of enemies; in that act, our affections are borne to what is furthest from us, as "the power of fire is proved to be stronger according as it spreads its heat to more distant objects" (*ST*, II-II, 27, 7).

The prominence of charity, of rectified desire, in the good life, is the distinctive feature of the Christian depiction of the good life. Given the dependence of will on reason, the objection to charity's being the most excellent of the virtues is patent. The response hinges on the different modes of operation of intellect and will. The operation of the intellect culminates with the presence of the thing understood in the intellect, whereas the operation of the will reaches its term in the "tendency of the appetite toward a thing as its goal" (*ST*, II-II, 23, 6, ad 1). The presence in the intellect through knowledge elevates things less perfect than the human soul, whereas things above the soul are contracted and reduced to conform to our mode of knowing. In relationship to things superior to the soul, then, love is more perfect; it reaches out and strives to adapt itself to the object of desire. In this respect, love is higher than knowledge. The priority of charity does not, of course, violate the general principle that love presupposes knowledge, for charity follows faith, an intellectual reception of revealed truths. Through faith, charity is "regulated, not by human wisdom, as the moral virtues are, but by God's wisdom," which "transcends the rule of human reason" (*ST*, II-II, 24, 1, ad 2). Like prudence, charity efficaciously orders the whole of human life and integrates cognition and affection.

The gift of understanding is a "supernatural light" *(lumen supernaturale)* that enables believers to penetrate revealed truths concerning divine things. The gifts of science and wisdom pertain to judgment, which is the second operation of reason, but understanding concerns simple apprehension, the first act of reason (*ST*, II-II, 8, 1). Because understanding seems incompatible with faith, Thomas notes that the understanding of divine things through faith is imperfect, ordered to the complete comprehension of the blessed (*ST*, II-II, 8, 2). The most striking feature of the gift of understanding is that it extends beyond speculative reason to practical matters. Understanding concerns all those things ordered to faith; because certain practical actions are ordered to faith, understanding extends to these actions (*ST*, II-II, 8, 3). Conversely, understanding presupposes purification of the passions and the intellect, the latter of which occurs when the intellect is freed from its attachment to misleading phantasms and erroneous opinions concerning God. The gift of understanding corresponds to the beatitude proclaiming the pure of heart blessed (*ST*, II-II, 8, 7). The gifts include an intimate link between cognition and affection, a link that is less pronounced in the intellectual virtues.

The gifts of science and wisdom complement the gift of understanding; the former judges of human things, the latter of divine things. To science corresponds the beatitude blessing those who mourn because a right judgment of creatures leads to the realization that they occasionally prompt us to turn from God (*ST*, II-II, 9, 4). In the discussion of the gift of wisdom, Thomas recurs to Aristotle's definition of wisdom as belonging properly to the individual who has the most comprehensive capacity to order and judge, and who does so in light of the highest cause: "he is called wise simply, who through divine rules is able to judge and order all things." The gift of wisdom thus reigns over the whole of human life, over both thought and action: "directing human acts through divine rules" (*per divinas regulas dirigens actus humanos; ST,* II-II, 45, 3). To the objection that there is an incommensurability between the objects of wisdom, which are universal and necessary truths, and the objects of the practical life, which are particular and contingent, Thomas responds that these necessary and eternal matters are "rules of contingent things" (*regulae contingentium; ST,* II-II, 45, 3, ad 2). The reference to eternal rules seems to raise once again the possibility of construing ethics as a crude *techne,* wherein abstract forms or rules are imposed on contingent matter. We have already seen, however, that even the universal principles regarding love of God and neighbor cannot issue in particular judgments without the decisive intervention of prudence. Our apprehension of these rules is not a matter of abstract knowledge, but of knowledge through the mode of inclination.

Obviously, Thomas uses neither contemplation nor action univocally in his comparison between the natural and the supernatural orders. The transformation of the theoretical life is evident from his depiction of wisdom as arising not merely from the use of reason, but from a "certain connaturality to those things of which it judges" (*connaturalitatem quamdam ad ea de quibus iam est iudicandum*). Thomas contrasts the knowledge of chastity gained through moral science with that afforded by rightly ordered inclination. The disanalogy between the gift and the intellectual virtue of wisdom is palpable in its description as a sort of "compassion or connaturality to divine things" that "arises from charity" and "unites us to God" (*compassio, sive connaturalitas ad res divinas fit per charitatem, quae quidem unit nos Deo; ST,* II-II, 45, 2). If the role of rightly ordered desire is peculiar to the life of Christian wisdom, so too is the transformed depiction of the practical life. To the objection that wisdom cannot be practical because the practical life is laborious and burdensome, Thomas responds: "burden or labor does not occur in human acts undertaken at the direction of wisdom; rather, burden for wisdom is converted into sweetness and labor into rest" (*ST,* II-II, 45, 3 ad 3). In fact, the gift of wisdom corresponds to the beatitude—blessed are the peacemakers, for they shall be called sons of God (*ST*, II-II, 45, 6). Peace is a consequence of due order, the effecting of which is proper to the wise. Peacemakers, moreover, are called sons of God. They "partake of the similitude of the only begotten Son, . . . who is begotten wisdom" (*inquantum participant similitudinem Filii unigeniti, . . . qui est sapientia genita; ST*, II-II, 45, 6).

The final section of the second part of the *Summa* supplies an account of the relationship between action and contemplation in the Christian life. The penultimate treatise argues for the superiority of the contemplative over the active life (*ST*, II-II, 179–82). The defense of the perfection of the contemplative life recalls the exordium of the second part, the treatise on the ultimate end, in which the contemplation of God is identified as the goal of human life. In the transition from the initial to the final examination of contemplation, Thomas's position has been enriched. The principal authority in the latter passages is no longer Aristotle, or even Augustine, but Gregory, whom Jean Leclerq calls the "doctor of desire."[28] On the authority of Gregory, for instance, Aquinas argues that the contemplative life has its roots in the affections: "from the love of God we are inflamed to behold his beauty" (*ex dilectione Dei aliquis inardescit ad eius pulchritudinem conspiciendam; ST*, II-II, 180, 1, and II-II, 180, 7, ad 1). Beauty encircles the contemplative life. The perception of the beautiful initiates desire; contemplation of spiritual beauty or goodness is the beginning of spiritual love (*ST*, I-II, 27, 2). Conversely, the experience of beauty is a consequence of contemplation. The role of the Incarnation in the contemplative life should not be overlooked. The Incarnation offers a perception, commensurate to the human mode of understanding, of the form of divine life. In Christ, we see the beauty of the divine life, and our desire to participate in that life is thus inflamed (*ST*, III, 1, 2).

The peroration of the second part is the treatise on the states of life (*ST*, II-II, 183–89). Thomas states that the contemplative life is intrinsically superior to the active life, yet the life devoted solely to contemplation is inferior to one given to both contemplation and instruction. The rhetorical structure and doctrinal content of the second part mirrors and points to the Dominican way of life. As Simon Tugwell notes in his introduction to *Early Dominicans*, a volume of

---

[28] Jean Leclerq, *L'Amour des lettres et désir de Dieu*, 30–39.

the Classics of Western Spirituality, both the Franciscans and the Dominicans aspired to the *vita apostolica*.[29] The two religious orders evinced strikingly different orientations, however. Tugwell explains the difference in the following way: whereas the Franciscans emphasized *vita* and sought to conform their apostolate to the paradigmatic way of life that Francis led, the Dominicans accentuated *apostolica* and saw their way of life as serving the needs of the apostolate. Although, as Tugwell notes, references to *utilitas* abound in early Dominican treatises, it is not clear that utility provides an adequate description of the Dominican life. Tugwell's accentuation of utility finds little support in Thomas's position on the mixed life. Thomas does indeed repudiate a univocal conception of religious life; he highlights the diversity of ends, corresponding to the various works of charity. Yet the accent is not on utility, but rather on the religious life as a "certain kind of training where one aims by practice at the perfection of charity" (*ST*, II-II, 188, 1). Thomas seeks to correct the pragmatic, pastoral tendencies in his order by placing moral theology within the full scope of speculative theology and by integrating the good with the beautiful in the very structure of his moral teaching. Similarly, he envisages the apostolic life as a participation in the activity whereby the superabundant beauty of the creator is manifested to creatures and whereby one angel communicates to another. As Guy Bedouelle, O.P., puts it, the Dominican purpose was to restore the "bond between the Word received and the Word given, and thus to incarnate it in a significant way of life."[30]

Thomas does not, then, justify the mixed life on the basis of its utility; an instrumental view of the good life is antithetical to his intent. The life of teaching and preaching is superior to the merely contemplative life only when the former *ex plenitudine contemplationis derivatur*. The notion of an abundance or plenitude of contemplation overflowing into the activity of teaching or preaching recalls Thomas's remarks about *claritas* as an irradiation of superabundant beauty and as a manifestation of splendor. Indeed, the phrase "to hand on to others things contemplated" (*contemplata aliis tradere*), which Thomas deploys in his defense of the mixed life and which has come to be the motto of the Dominican order, surfaces in other

---

[29] 23–26.
[30] *Saint Dominic: The Grace of the Word*, 245.

contexts. The phrase occurs in Thomas's affirmative response to the question whether one angel illuminates another and in his defense of the claim that it was fitting for Christ to converse or be familiar with men (*ST*, III, 40, 1). Christ took on human nature in order to manifest divinity through humanity (*ST*, III, 40, 1, ad 1). The basic argument on behalf of the mixed life runs thus: "The contemplative life is simply better than the active life, which is occupied with corporeal acts. But the active life in which, by preaching and teaching, one hands on to others things contemplated is superior to the life that is exclusively contemplative because the former presupposes an abundance of contemplation. Thus, Christ chose such a life" (*ST*, III, 40, 1, ad 2). The mixed life not only contemplates the source of beauty, but also imitates and participates in the creative act whereby that beauty is communicated to creatures (cf., *ST*, I, 106, 1). Indeed, Thomas follows Dionysius in describing the activity of contemplation according to a threefold motion (*ST*, II-II, 180, 6). The fact that motion can be attributed to contemplation indicates that this activity is not an inert stasis, but a higher sort of activity. We would thus misconstrue eternity were we to see it simply as a cessation of time and a negation of plurality and movement. Dionysius describes angelic contemplation in terms of a circular motion, which is the perfect beholding of God; a straight motion, which is the enlightening of lower angels and other creatures; and an oblique motion, which combines the previous two in such a way that the care for those beneath them accords with the love of God. Although we can never attain the degree of angelic integration in activities of contemplating and of assisting others (*ST*, II-II, 181, 4), the mixed life in a dim way reflects the angelic. Thus, a complicated pattern of ascent and descent, rather than a simple ascent from the things of the world to the transcendent good, characterizes the Christian understanding of the good life.

BEAUTY AND THEOLOGICAL PEDAGOGY

The good life, according to Thomas, is ultimately an imitation of the life of the second person of the Trinity, the incarnate Word of God, who manifests the splendor of the internal life of God. The motif of the manifestation of splendor and beauty pervades Aquinas's theological pedagogy, wherein the beautiful is the formality under which the good is made manifest to the rational appetite. The good life is much more than obedience to law; it integrates reason and passion. The role of the beautiful in the good life underscores the importance of human receptivity to the world and its creator. It also reveals the continuity, even in theological matters, between Thomas and the ancients. The Greek term *kaloskagathia* links the good and the beautiful as manifest concretely in human action and in noble ways of life. Thomas's depiction of Christ's life as the epiphany of the good life embraces and transforms the Greek notion.[31]

One of the difficulties in treating the topic of beauty in Aquinas is that the very notion of a Thomist aesthetics is suspect. Thomas never considered the issue systematically, and a collation of his remarks on beauty, which are scattered throughout the corpus, indicate the fragmentary character of his treatment of beauty. Even the famous division of the marks of the beautiful into proportion, integrity, and clarity does not find consistent support in Aquinas's texts.[32] A consideration of beauty, moreover, rarely surfaces in its own right; rather, it surfaces in the context of other issues upon which Aquinas brings to bear its relevant features. He provides no theory of the beautiful, and what he does say seems remarkably restrained, even by medieval standards.[33]

---

[31] Although interest in Aquinas's ethics has soared in recent years, his account of beauty appears doomed to only occasional and marginal attention. Among the more important studies are: Francis J. Kovach, *Die Aesthetik des Thomas von Aquin;* Armond A. Maurer, C.S.B., *About Beauty;* and Umberto Eco, *The Aesthetics of Thomas Aquinas.* All these works are helpful. Kovach makes a convincing case for the objectivity of aesthetics in Aquinas, even if he seems to import a modern understanding of the dichotomy between subject and object. Eco's text is an attempt to reach a more historically accurate understanding of Thomas's position. Eco is particularly successful in his criticisms of Maritain's project of grounding aesthetic experience in intellectual intuition, a notion that is positively repudiated in Aquinas's texts. Yet one detects a shift in Eco's attitude toward Aquinas in the conclusion to the 1970 edition of the book. In the revision, Eco lapses into a dogmatic historicism and is satisfied with certain facile criticisms of Aquinas's aesthetics. The revision mars what is otherwise perhaps the best book available on Thomas's aesthetics. Maurer's book is also close to the text, yet it exhibits a more irenic attitude toward the writings of Gilson and Maritain.

[32] See Mark D. Jordan, "The Evidence of the Transcendentals and the Place of Beauty in Thomas Aquinas."

[33] Umberto Eco suggests that Thomas sought to temper the Neoplatonic approach to beauty: "In a Dionysian universe, coruscating with beauty, mankind risked losing its place, of being blinded and then annulled" (*The Aesthetics of Thomas Aquinas,* 48).

Thomas never, of course, uses the term *aesthetics;* it is in fact a modern term, one that is associated with spontaneous feeling and creativity, and is often placed in opposition to or exalted above the true and the good.[34] The severing of the link between the good and the beautiful cuts the moral off from the natural inclinations of the agent. It thus eviscerates ethics and provides the impetus for the transformation of ethics into aesthetics. The supposed liberation of the beautiful from the good transforms the moral life into a *techne,* grandly conceived; the task of human life becomes autonomous self-creation. If one focuses, however, not on these modern accretions, but on the etymology of the term, then the notion of a Thomistic aesthetics is less objectionable. The Greek word *aisthesis,* from which *aesthetic* is derived, means "perception"—in particular, perception that is connected with feeling. As Thomas puts it, the beautiful is that which when seen pleases. What is more important, the understated but pervasive presence of the beautiful in premodern texts signals its unobtrusive integrative capacity. Without it, the true and the good are likely to become distorted and subject to precisely the sort of instrumentalization many contemporary thinkers detest. As Urs von Balthasar puts it, "If the *verum* lacks that splendor which for Thomas is the distinctive mark of the beautiful, then the knowledge of truth remains both pragmatic and formalistic. . . . If the *bonum* lacks that *voluptas* which for Augustine is the mark of its beauty, then the relationship to the good remains both utilitarian and hedonistic."[35]

In order to see how the function of the beautiful in Thomas forestalls the possibility of utilitarian and instrumental views of the true and the good, we need to have some handle on the relevant vocabulary. Of the well-known three marks of beauty, two appear most frequently: *claritas* and *proportio.* When Thomas identifies the good and the beautiful, he states that clarity and proportion are contained in the notion of the good. In his discussions of *claritas,* he often adduces the examples of light and color. Yet the scope of *claritas* is not limited to the sensible realm. He also refers to the *claritas* of intellect or spirit, and in these contexts the terms *illumination, manifestation,* and *splendor* figure prominently. In many places, Thomas

---

[34] In spite of Maritain's attempt to harmonize modern and Thomistic notions of the beautiful, these modern motifs find little support in Aquinas's texts.

[35] *Seeing the Form,* 152.

follows Dionysius in seeing *claritas* as an overflowing of an abundance of divine beauty. *Proportio* or *consonantia* has to do with a coming together of things necessary for an end; the terms surface in the explication of hierarchical ordering. Thomas often speaks of a diverse and fitting order of goods or beings. The third, less-prominent mark of the beautiful is *integritas,* which is translated as completeness or wholeness. The term *integritas* refers to the realization of a thing's proper perfection; it involves the judgment that something is what it ought to be. Although the good and the beautiful are identical in subject, they are distinct in notion. The beautiful is distinguished from the good in having a reference to the cognitive power, to perception. The connection between the beautiful and cognition underlies another of Thomas's best-known remarks about beauty: the beautiful is that which pleases when seen.

In *The Aesthetics of Thomas Aquinas,* Umberto Eco acknowledges that "beauty is grounded in the formal structure of the object of aesthetic *visio.*" He proceeds to argue that a grasp of the formal structure of natural things in an "aesthetic *visio*" requires "a deep and exhaustive knowledge of the object."[36] But this sort of knowledge is available only to the creator of natural forms. Hence, aesthetic *visio* is not possible for human beings, which Eco calls the "central *aporia*" in Thomas's aesthetics. There are a number of problems with Eco's objection. How damaging to Thomas's aesthetics is it for Thomas to deny that human beings can have the sort of experience of beauty that God has? Making Aquinas out to be a skeptic concerning human knowledge of nature would undermine his entire philosophy. Although Eco is right to note that Thomas stresses the limitations to our knowledge of natural forms, his claim that Thomas sees knowledge as either exhaustive or nonexistent is dubious. Thomas refuses to adopt either of these equally extravagant alternatives. He tends to depict human knowledge as existing for the most part between absolute certitude and utter doubt. The process of moving from the latter to the former can in itself be the source of delight and an occasion for the appreciation of the beautiful. In defending the position that wonder is a cause of pleasure, Thomas addresses the objection that wonder presupposes ignorance, which is not pleasant. He responds that wonder is pleasant insofar as it inspires the desire and the hope of

---

[36] 203.

gaining knowledge (*ST,* I-II, 32, 8). Appropriately, Thomas's pedagogical intent is to avoid foreclosing further inquiry and to foster
continual delight. Pleasure is a cause of thirst or desire, especially
when one possesses a perfect thing, yet not perfectly, obtaining that
possession little by little (*ST,* I-II, 33, 2).[37]

Because the appreciation of the beautiful is an appreciation of
goods congruent to human nature, there is a connection between
the good life and the beautiful. Two passages bring out connections
between the good and the beautiful. In the first, Thomas speaks of
the good as the cause of love, as that which draws desire to itself; in
the second, he notes that the Greek term *kalos* is derived from the
verb *kaleo,* to call or summon. In the *De Veritate,* Thomas writes
that "for the appetite to terminate at the good, the peaceful, and the
beautiful is not for it to terminate at diverse things. By the very fact
that someone desires the good, he also desires the beautiful and the
peaceful" (22, 1 ad 12).[38] There are, however, differences between
the good and the beautiful. The beautiful involves a reference to the
cognitive power, whereas the good involves the motion of the will
toward a desirable object. At times, Thomas brings the two together:
"the object moving the appetite is a good apprehended; whatever in
the apprehension itself appears beautiful is taken as fitting and good"
(*ST,* II-II, 145, 2, ad 1). These passages suggest that the beautiful
should be understood as the way the good manifests itself to the
rational creature.

Thomas's discussion of the rational creature is itself replete with
aesthetic language. The treatment of human nature follows the treatment of the order of creation, with its participated hierarchy of being.
The description of the created order, with its "consonant order of
diverse grades," calls to mind the essential features of Thomas's account of beauty. In his *Expositio super Dionysiam de Divinis Nominibus* (Commentary on the Divine Names), Thomas speaks of creation
as an overflowing of superabundant beauty. He refers to the human
soul as an irradiation of divine intelligence and speaks of human intelligence as a participation in the light of divine intelligence. I have
already noted that Thomas associates the term *claritas* with radiance

---

[37] In the passage, Thomas refers to our knowledge of God, which is presently faint
but which holds out the hope of further knowledge.

[38] *Quaestiones Disputatae,* vol. 1.

and brilliance, and that one of the principal examples of *claritas* is intellectual light, the manifestation of intelligibility. The entire created order is, of course, an example of *claritas*. It manifests the splendor of divine understanding. Yet human beings provide a particularly instructive instance of *claritas*. We are not simply parts of the created order; rather, we have a capacity to grasp that order, to understand and take delight in it. We have the ability to provide demonstrations, intelligible connections, and arrangements to themselves and to one another. The operation of human intelligence made sensible through speech is a manifestation of divine intelligence in the corporeal order.

Human beings are precariously situated at the juncture of the worlds of matter and intelligence or spirit: we are "placed between the things of this world and spiritual goods." Accordingly, Thomas emphasizes the limited capacity of the human soul: "The human soul is called intellectual through participation in the intellectual power, a sign of which is that it is not wholly intellectual, but only according to a part. It reaches an understanding of truth by argument with a certain discourse and movement" (*ST*, I, 79, 4). Human beings are not properly intellectual, but rational creatures, whose intelligence is the furthest removed from the divine. Thomas contrasts human with angelic understanding, wherein there is no movement from one thing to another. The very operation of the human intellect is discursive and mobile (*ST*, I, 79, 8).

The union of matter and intelligence in human nature makes human existence more complex than that of other creatures. Lower creatures attain limited goods by means of few movements, whereas superior creatures attain a perfect good by few movements. Human beings are peculiar in that we attain a perfect good through "many and diverse operations and powers" (*ST*, I, 77, 2). We exist "on the boundary of spiritual and corporeal creatures, and therefore the powers of both sorts of creatures converge in us" (*ST*, I, 77, 2). A consequence of the complexity of human life is that the attainment of the human good requires a *complicatio*, a convergence or coming together of many things: "The human soul is in the last level according to nature of those creatures capable of beatitude, and thus it needs many and diverse operations. Another reason why the human soul is replete with a multitude of powers is that it exists on the boundary of spiritual and corporeal creatures, and thus the virtues of both sorts of creatures converge in it" (*ST*, I, 77, 2). The discussion of the complexity of human life is reminiscent of the notion of proportion, which is a coming together of things necessary for an end.

The appreciation of the good as beautiful is rooted in the perception and attainment of goods suitable to one's nature (*ST*, I-II, 32, 1). Thomas identifies *honestum* with *decorum* or *pulchrum* and with *delectabile*. *Honestum* is "naturally convenient to man" (*naturaliter conveniens homini*) and is that in which a human being naturally delights, just as the philosopher has shown concerning the operation of virtue (*ST*, II-II, 145, 3). Because the result of such perception is pleasure or delight, the passages on pleasure in the *Summa* are directly relevant to the present topic. The effect of pleasure is expansion or dilation (*ST*, I-II, 33, 1). The effect can be seen with respect to both the apprehensive and the affective powers of the soul. With regard to the apprehensive power, the soul is said to be enlarged or dilated (*animus hominis dicitur magnificari seu dilatari*); and with regard to the affective powers, the powers of the soul are said to hand themselves over to continue within the object of delight (*sic dilatatur affectus hominis per delectationem, quasi se tradens ad continendum interius rem delectantem; ST*, I-II, 33, 1). Grace restores the note of the beautiful to the human apprehension of natural goods and expands the powers of the soul, rendering them increasingly receptive to its operation. The perception of the beautiful plays an important role in Thomas's understanding of the nature and efficacy of divine pedagogy. It fosters openness to the divine and docility to divine instruction.

I have already considered in some detail the revealed law of the Decalogue, the content of which partially overlaps with the natural law. Certain features of that discussion are germane to the present consideration. Grace closes the gap, introduced by sin, between the precepts of the natural law, which concern goods appropriate to human nature, and the apprehension of the suitability of the law to human nature. The "real ground" of virtue, according to Thomas O'Meara, is an "anthropology of grace."[39] "[A] kind of habitude . . . presupposed by the infused virtues as their principle and root" (*ST*, I-II, 109, 3, ad 3), grace restores beauty to the human soul but also makes possible an appreciation of the good as beautiful (*ST*, I-II, 109, 7, and III, 87, 2, ad 3). It reestablishes the connaturality of the

---

[39] "Virtues in the Theology of Thomas Aquinas," 256–57 and 269.

good, which is a precondition of love (*ST,* I-II, 27, 1), and restores the ability to perceive, take delight in, and appropriate the *claritas* or radiant beauty of the good, which is embodied in the virtues.

THE NARRATIVE SHAPE OF CREATION AND REDEMPTION

Another way of approaching the understanding of the beautiful and its link to the good is through a consideration of creation. As Josef Pieper has commented, "creation determines and characterizes the interior structure of nearly all the basic concepts in St. Thomas's philosophy of being."[40] According to Thomas, creation is an artifact reflecting the divine art, a manifestation of the wisdom and beauty of God. Throughout the consideration of creation and providence, he draws analogies to the work of artistic production. In his discussion of the eternal law, he writes, "Through his own wisdom God is the governor of the universe of things to which he is compared as an artist to his artwork. The pattern of divine wisdom, insofar as all things are created through it, has the character of art, exemplar, or idea" (*ST,* I-II, 93, 1). Such comparisons have led some commentators to assimilate Christian ontology to a productive conception of being. There are, however, important disanalogies between divine creation and artistic production. God does not make through some temporal process by inducing forms into preexisting matter, as the human artist does. The artist creates only by presupposing and in some measure by cooperating with nature. Because God creates from nothing, God is cause of the very being of things (*ST,* I, 44, 2). We have difficulty conceiving of creation because our mode of understanding is tied to the realm of sensible and temporal substances: "In creation, by which the whole substance of a thing is produced, the same thing can be taken as different now and before only according to our way of understanding" (*ST,* I, 45, 2, ad 2). Change presupposes the existence of the thing that becomes something other; creation presupposes nothing.

Whereas making involves a temporal struggle between mind and matter, creation is a bestowal of being, the sheer manifestation of

---

[40] *The Silence of St. Thomas: Three Essays,* 48.

form. It is what Cornelio Fabro calls "transcendental appearing."[41] Another essential feature of human artistic production—namely, the gap between who one is and the model according to which the arti- fact is made—is inapplicable to divine creativity. In God, there is no distinction between the artistic idea and the subsistent and unified perfection of God. The being of God is the model of created things. God is the exemplary cause of the order of creation, which reflects the creator's wisdom, beauty, and goodness. There is, then, a funda- mental disparity between the works of nature and art, on the one hand, and the work of creation, on the other. Divine creation of the whole from nothing undercuts the possibility of viewing any creature as possessing autonomous creative powers. God creates both the maker and that out of which something is made: "no created being can produce a being absolutely, except insofar as it causes being in this particular thing, and so it is necessary to presuppose that whereby a thing is this particular thing, prior to the action by which it makes its own likeness" (ST, I, 45, 5, ad 1).

The structure of Thomas's most important theological works re- flects the notion of God as an artist. The orders of the *Summa contra Gentiles* and the *Summa Theologiae* mirror the *exitus-reditus* struc- ture of creation. The works begin from God, turn to the procession of creatures from God, and culminate in the return of creatures to the first principle. In contrast to the Neoplatonic tendency to con- strue the procession and return of creatures as a necessary process, Thomas insists that creation is a result of divine freedom. Creation need not have occurred at all; indeed, because the possibility of cre- ation is not in the creature, one should reject the view that before created things existed, they were possible.[42] Contingency and free- dom play decisive roles in the Christian conception of creation.

Another feature of Neoplatonic construals of creation is the thesis that divine perfection requires God's distance from that which has emanated from God. Such a view of God's relationship to the world follows from a certain conception of God's perfection, transcen- dence, and independence. As a consequence, God could neither know nor care for individual creatures. Some thinkers in this tradition allow that God knows something about creation, but knows only the

---

[41] "The Problem of Being and the Destiny of Man," passim.
[42] See Kenneth Schmitz, *The Gift: Creation*, 126.

highest beings, those separate from matter, or only the universal natures of all things. Thomas counters that this view imposes onto God an account of perfection that is more appropriate to imperfect, finite beings. The very notion of "perfection," which literally and originally means "thoroughly made," is inapplicable to God, who undergoes no indigent process to achieve excellence. Our perfection consists in moving from particulars to universals, from the lowly to the exalted. But our inability to know individuals as individuals and our ability to be distracted from higher things by lower beings result from the imperfect order of human knowing. To attribute such a conception of perfection to God is anthropomorphic; it arises from a failure to make adequate use of the method of negation in transferring terms from created things to God, who knows low and high alike, effortlessly and in the same way. Thomas's discussion of God's knowledge of evil and vile things is pertinent: "It is better for us not to know evil and vile things, as they detract from our consideration of better things, for we cannot understand many things at once, and the thought of evil sometimes leads the will astray into evil. Such concerns are inapplicable to God, who beholds everything in one vision and whose will cannot be deflected toward evil" (*ST*, I, 22, 3, ad 3).

Those who suppose that it is unbecoming for God to know lowly creatures have an imperfect and anthropomorphic understanding of divine perfection. Pagan philosophy identifies the goal of philosophy with the divine. As Pierre Hadot puts it, "the description of this transcendent norm" of wisdom "ultimately coincides with the rational idea of God."[43] In this way, God would be the model of the philosophic life. But one also finds a subtle reversal of this ordering, wherein the divine life is seen simply as an extension of the philosophical life. Such a reversal constitutes a kind of philosophical idolatry, wherein God is, in Ortega y Gasset's apt description, a philosopher staring at himself in the mirror. By conflating their own life with the divine, philosophers fail to see that the transition from human to divine understanding involves a fundamental reversal in the relationship to things. Things are measures of the veracity of the human mind, whereas God is the measure of the truth of things.

God measures things as the model in the mind of an artist measures artifacts. The best analogy for understanding God's relationship

---

[43] "Forms of Life and Forms of Discourse," in *Philosophy as a Way of Life*, 57.

to the world comes from practical, not theoretical, knowledge. "Just as all things wrought by art are subject to the ordering of that art," so too all created things come under God's knowledge. "The causality of God . . . extends to every being, not only to the principles of species, but also as to the principles of individuals; not only to things incorruptible, but also to things corruptible" (*ST*, I, 22, 2). God knows as cause, as creator, and as the providential guide of the order of the universe. Were God to know only universals, not singulars, that knowledge would be imperfect, for created things have being only in singulars. Thomas's metaphysics of concrete actuality counters the possibility of seeing singulars as merely imperfect instantiations of what is truly real, the universal. The perfection of creation consists in the order of the parts to one another and to the whole. If God were not responsible for and knowledgeable about all created things, the order of the universe would fall under the sway of numerous concurring subordinate causes and thus result from chance. To attribute to created beings the order of creation is impossible, for such beings already exist within a predetermined order. A part cannot create the whole of which it is a part. The multitude, distinction, and order of things comes from God (*ST*, I, 47, 1). God's immediate providence over all created things removes any possibility of a dualistic metaphysics. There is no supreme evil; indeed, evil itself presupposes the good. Evil is only the lack of a perfection appropriate to a creature. Strictly speaking, evil is not.

God is not aloof, then, from the contingent order of time and space. Divine providence is understood chiefly in terms of prudence, which orders things to a suitable end. Thomas writes, "Providence is the chief part of prudence, to which the other parts are directed—namely, remembrance of the past and understanding of the present because from memory of past things and understanding present things we infer how to provide for the future" (*ST*, I, 22, 1). Without becoming temporal, God is present to and cares for the whole of time. Even after creating the natural order, God can intervene supernaturally through miracles in order to instruct creatures about themselves, their place within the whole, and their relationship to God. Both the natural and the supernatural plans of the universe are included within the one encompassing plan of divine providence, which orders the whole of time to a final transfiguration. The contrast between this view and the Neoplatonic construal of creation as a necessary process of emanation and return is palpable. The divine artwork is a historical narrative, which has as its centerpiece the dramatic encounter between God and us. The ethical itself falls under the rubric of providence.

Preparatory to the depiction of the interaction between God and us is a metaphysical consideration of creation, which focuses on human nature as a microcosm of the whole. Thomas's anthropology culminates in the consideration of the human being as an *imago Dei*, a discussion that recapitulates the teaching on the human soul as an irradiation of divine intelligence and on the necessity of a complication of goods in the human achievement of the end. The Platonic relationship of image to exemplar is crucial to theological pedagogy. In a question on the "end or term of the production of man," Thomas states that the *imago Dei* is present in human beings in only an imperfect manner. Following Augustine, he holds that the self-reflexive character of human knowledge dimly mirrors the internal, trinitarian life of God. He refers to the "procession of the word according to the intellect" and to the "procession of love according to the will" (*ST*, I, 93, 6). The act of knowing that one knows and of loving what one knows reflects the processions of and relations between the persons of the Trinity. In the account of the procession of the interior word, to know is to speak. There is no separation here between knowing and speaking or between either knowing or speaking and loving. Within this context, we should understand the account of the interior concept or intelligible species, which establishes not some utterly private realm of interiority, but an interior conversation that is ordered to exterior manifestation. The interior conversation is the term of our activity of knowing things. The word is thus not a speaking of an isolated self to itself. Recall Wilhelmsen's thesis, to which I previously adverted, that the ego or self exists only in the act of knowing the other-as-other. When we put that thesis together with the metaphysical doctrine of participated being, we see that we are "bereft of any internal ontological identity of our own." Instead, we are "constituted dynamically even as the selves we are through our marriage to the other." The failure to realize this connection leads to existential angst, the great discovery of late modernity—an awareness that our "cherished identity, our egocentricity, is grounded in the abyss of nothingness."[44] Thomas's doctrine of the interior word, the *verbum cordis,* precludes any possible dichotomy between reason and speech, between the two senses of logos he inherits from Aristotle. Once again, Thomas makes explicit the connections among reason, speech, and the social order and between self-knowledge and friendship that he established somewhat indirectly in his reading of Aristotle.

The human soul is but an image of the Trinity, and the perfection of the image consists not in any self-reflexive act, but in the conversion of the soul to God. There is an "image of the divine Trinity in the soul only through a comparison with its object, which is God" (*imago divinae trinitatis in anima solum per comparationem ad obiectum quod est Deus; ST,* I, 93, 8). The authority is, of course, Augustine: "There is an image of God in man not because he is able to remember, love, and understand himself, but because he can remember, love, and know God, by whom he was made." There are three senses in which an individual can be said to be an *imago Dei:* first, on account of natural aptitude to know and love God; second, through habitual and actual, although imperfect, knowledge and love of God; and, third, according to the similitude of glory. The three ways are arranged hierarchically and historically; they correspond to the states of *creatio, recreatio,* and *similitudo.* Thomas's moral pedagogy offers an account of the human movement from *creatio* through *recreatio* toward *similitudo.*

Marie Dominique Chenu's famous reading of the structure of the *Summa Theologiae* in terms of the Neoplatonic motif of the *exitus-reditus* focuses on the second part as marking the transition from the *exitus* to the *reditus.* As we have seen, the *exitus-reditus* captures the structure of the work at only a very general level. According to Chenu, the *secunda pars* articulates the objective and necessary order of moral theology, an order that is not conceptually tied to the contingent, historical fact of Christ's incarnate life.[45] One should not search the *secunda pars* looking for evidence of its Christocentric character. Admittedly, the work does not follow a strictly historical order; indeed, the structure resists characterization in terms of any

---

[44] Wilhelmsen, "Modern Man's Myth of Self-Identity," in *Being and Knowing,* 208–11.

[45] See *The Scope of the "Summa"* and *Introduction à l'étude de Saint Thomas d'Aquin,* 259–76.

one model of theological pedagogy. The purported dichotomy, however, between the necessary and the contingent, the moral and the
historical, is foreign to Thomas's thought.[46] My previous discussion
of the dialectical character of divine pedagogy shows the dichotomy
to be a false one. In the treatise on law, the notion of a divine pedagogy, operating in a historically discernible order, undergirds Thomas's discussion of the hierarchy of the laws. Thomas considers the
time, mode, intent, and consequences of the revelation of the moral
law in the Decalogue. The *prima secundae* culminates in the considerations of sin, law, and grace. Thomas thus locates human self-
understanding within a historical and dramatic narrative.

Given dominant contemporary notions of narrative, which are
often allied to an antimetaphysical epistemology, the application of
narrative to Thomas's teaching might appear to be misleading. An
appreciation, however, of the role of narrative in that teaching arises
not from a neglect of Thomas's metaphysics but from a proper understanding of it. His theocentric metaphysics prepares the way for an
understanding of God as present and active in history. As we have
already seen, Thomas repudiates the view that God is ignorant of and
indifferent to contingent singulars. He also argues that reason cannot
determine one way or another whether the world has always existed.
He quotes Aristotle's statement from the *Topics* that "there are dialectical problems, of which we do not have proofs, such as, 'whether
the world is eternal' " (*ST*, I, 46, 1). Philosophy thus presents no
obstacle to the revealed teaching concerning the beginning of the
world, which cannot be known by reason (*ST*, I, 46, 2). Conversely,
it presents no impediment to the teaching that the world will come
to an end. The limitations to natural reason provide an opening for
the Christian view of created being, which has a narrative shape to it,
with a beginning, middle, and end. Because God can intervene in
history, the gift of creation is open to divine initiative, to an encounter

---

[46] Given Thomas's account of the dialectical status of the law, its subordination to
virtue, and its ordinability to the Incarnation, it is difficult to agree with Chenu's
reading: "The Old Law, the law par excellence, is located logically after the general
treatise on law; there is thus necessarily a certain reduction of its historical role to
abstract categories" (*Introduction à l'étude de saint Thomas d'Aquin*, 272). For a
corrective that establishes the link between Thomas's cognitional theory and his
metaphysics, on the one hand, and myth and history, on the other, see Wilhelmsen,
"Existence and History," and "The Philosopher and the Myth," in *The Paradoxical
Structure of Existence*, 109–47.

between God and human beings in the contingencies of time and space. As Kenneth Schmitz eloquently puts it, "the term *gift* is rooted in a domain of significance that is charged with discontinuity and contingency, with risk, vulnerability, and surprise. Moreover, the gift points beyond itself to its source, to a more or less definitely apprehended giver."[47]

Thomas's theological metaphysics is precisely an articulation of the gift whose source is the triune God. Every important theological discussion culminates with the Trinity, with the manifestation of the internal and communal life of God. We have seen that the Verbum is the source and summit of the laws and the archetype of the virtues.[48] Thomas identifies the beautiful with the Verbum, the exemplary cause of the created order and of the moral life.[49] Following Damascene, Thomas calls the Verbum a manifestation of the beauty of the life of God, the light and splendor of the divine understanding (*ST*, I, 19, 8). The three marks of the beautiful—namely, *claritas, proportio,* and *integritas*—are appropriately said of the second person of the Trinity. The accentuation of manifestation in the discussion of the Verbum is instructive for two reasons (*ST*, I, 34, 1). First, it undercuts the supposition that the life of contemplation necessarily entails isolation from others, considering that the life of God, whose knowing is simultaneously a speaking and a loving, is the paradigm of the contemplative life and God's life is inherently communal. Second, as Augustine puts it, the term *verbum* signifies "not only relation to the Father, but also relation to those beings made through the Word by his operative power" (*ST*, I, 34, 3). Quoting Psalm 32.9, "He spoke and they were made," Thomas states that the "Word implies the operative idea of what God makes."

Of course, the divine Word is not just the perfect image of the creator and the model of all created things, but it is also the incarnate Word, upon whose entrance into history the narrative of divine providence pivots. Thomas links the Incarnation and the contingent needs and possibilities of the human condition in the first article of the

---

[47] *The Gift: Creation,* 44.

[48] The Verbum is the exemplary cause of the created order. See *ST*, I, 34, 3, and I, 44, 3 and 4.

[49] The unification of cosmology and psychology can be seen in Thomas's response to the question of the fittingness of the Second Person's assuming human nature (*ST*, III, 3, 8).

third part, which asks whether the Incarnation was necessary for the restoration of the human race. Although he concedes the logical possibility of an Incarnation had we not sinned and of God's saving humankind by other means, he highlights the anodyne purpose of the Incarnation. The authority is Augustine, who suggests that "there was not a more fitting [*convenientior*] way of healing our misery" (*ST*, III, 1, 2). The *convenientia* argument highlights the compatibility of the Incarnation with the conditions and needs of human nature. The uses of the term *conveniens* echo two previous sets of remarks: first, concerning the necessity of a coming together of many things for the attainment of the end of human life, and, second, concerning the nature of proportion or consonance as a mark of the beautiful. The plethora of references to *convenientia* in the sections on the Incarnation support the view that the Incarnation is the key to the wholeness and proportion of revealed truth.[50]

As we have already seen, in his discussion of the beautiful Thomas frequently deploys the term *conveniens*, which means a "coming or bringing together," a "convergence." Something is fitting to a certain end when in or through it many things concur that are expedient for the end. *Conveniens* and its cognates take on the meanings of agreement, harmony, and suitability. The context of these comments is the question whether liberation from sin occurs in a more convenient way through the passion of Christ than through other means. Thomas responds that beyond the liberation from sin, many things useful for salvation accrue to human beings through Christ's passion: *(a)* we know how much God loves us; *(b)* it offers an example of obedience and other virtues; *(c)* we receive justifying grace and the glory of beatitude; *(d)* because we have been redeemed by the blood of Christ, we see more clearly the necessity of maintaining our freedom from sin; and *(e)* redemption through human nature reveals our dignity. *Conveniens* seems to be a vehicle of the intelligibility of theological truths, which lie beyond the scope of rational demonstration.

Thomas depicts Christ as *the* moral exemplum. Christ possesses the virtues "most perfectly beyond the common mode." Christ has, in the words of Plotinus, the "virtues of the sublime soul." Christ

---

[50] See, for instance, Thomas's argument at *ST*, I, 39, 8, that the term *species* or *pulchritudo* is most fittingly applied to the Second Person.

offers examples of right conduct and teaches human beings to live according to the virtues of faith, hope, and charity. In depicting Christ as a model of the moral life, Thomas is continuing a classical line of argument. Following Aristotle, he holds that the good person is the measure of all things. One way of reading the account of the virtues in the *Ethics* is as a series of narrative descriptions, which provide concrete examples of the good life. By identifying the good and the beautiful as embodied in the life of Christ, Thomas recalls the Greek notion of *kaloskagathia*. His discussion of the life of Christ and account of the virtues, gifts, and beatitudes complete and correct the Aristotelian discussion of the good and the beautiful. In the contingent historical event of the Incarnation, there is an epiphany of the good life. The pedagogy of the Incarnation locates human nature and its aspiration for happiness within a comprehensive narrative of the whole cosmos.

There is ample basis in the *Summa Theologiae* for seeing Christ as the epiphany or *claritas* of the good life; this epiphany involves a transformed understanding of the good and the beautiful in Aristotle and points to a distinctively Christian aesthetics, one that has redemptive suffering as its centerpiece. Evidence of the transformed understanding can be had from the discussion of Christ's resurrected body. That it was a glorified body signifies that glorification occurs through humility (*ST*, III, 54, 3). Thomas argues, moreover, that it was appropriate for Christ's resurrected body to retain the wounds of crucifixion. In response to the objection that these wounds are inappropriate signs of corruption or defect, Thomas says that they pertain "not to corruption or defect, but to a greater accumulation of glory, in that they are signs of virtue" (*ST*, III, 54, 4, ad 1). Unlike those who see in the image of a crucified God an inversion of all standards of beauty and a celebration of deformity and weakness, Thomas sees the splendor of abundant love and beauty. As Urs von Balthasar has put it, "Death, too, belongs to the form in which immortal beauty becomes manifest, and it is dying which in the end truly impresses immortal beauty on the spirit that contemplates it."[51]

The narrative structure of the Christian account of divine providence is clear. Can we describe that narrative in more precise terms, perhaps in terms of the genres of tragedy and comedy? The role of

---

[51] *Seeing the Form*, 198.

suffering in the Christian narrative has led some to align it with tragedy. As Thomas More writes, "For to prove that this life is no laughing time, but rather the time of weeping we find that our savior himself wept twice or thrice, but never find we that he laughed as much as once."[52] On this passage, Leo Strauss reposes a contrast between religion and philosophy: "If we compare what More said about Jesus with what Plato tells us about Socrates, we find that 'Socrates laughed twice or thrice, but never find we that he wept as much as once.' A slight bias in favor of laughing and against weeping seems to be essential to philosophy. For the beginning of philosophy . . . is not the fear of the Lord but wonder."[53] The philosophy of Plato and Aristotle eclipses the tragic vision. The Socratic understanding of the contemplative life and its approach to the vision of the Good transcends the order of tragedy. This is one outcome of the debate between poetry and philosophy. As previously noted, Aristotle repudiates the view, underlying much of tragic poetry, that the gods are jealous.[54] The emphasis on the intelligibility of nature, the openness of human nature to the eternal, and the aspiration for and hope in immortality are all characteristics of philosophy's eclipse of tragedy.

Aristotle's discussion of tragedy is noteworthy for the meager attention it gives to the role of the gods, fate, and necessity. Amélie Rorty writes, "The argument of the *Poetics* is intended to show that the best effects of tragic drama derive from its representational truthfulness rather than from ecstasy: that the turn of the plot depends on human agency rather than on demonic or divine forces. . . . It is a person's character *(ethos),* as determining his actions and choices, rather than any cosmic justice *(dike)* or vengeance *(nemesis)* that determines his fate."[55] Aristotle praises certain types of tragedy: those that highlight the onerous task of coming to self-knowledge and of achieving the mean in action, and those that focus on the noble response of moral agents to bad fortune.[56] These themes are, of course,

---

[52] *Dialogue of Comfort against Tribulation,* chap. 13, quoted by Leo Strauss in "On the Euthyphron," 206. The discussion of tragedy and comedy restates the concluding chapter of my book *Dialectic and Narrative in Aquinas: An Interpretation of the "Summa contra Gentiles,"* 167–77.

[53] "On the Euthyphron," 206.

[54] *Metaphysics,* I, 2, and XII, 7.

[55] "The Psychology of Aristotelian Tragedy," 3.

[56] In "Aristotle's Favorite Tragedies," Stephen A. White argues that Aristotle favors tragedies that underscore the protagonist's "overcoming moral luck."

important in Aristotle's *Ethics*.[57] There is a disparity, nonetheless, between the *Poetics* and the *Ethics* because the latter attempts to describe the man of perfect virtue. Despite these differences, both works evince the gap between aspiration and achievement of excellence and happiness, the *Poetics* by depicting the way contingent features of character and circumstance can conspire against human agents and the *Ethics* by failing to provide any concrete examples of the man of excellence.

Although Thomas did not comment on the *Poetics* and has little to say about the connection between tragedy and ethics, his consideration of the pedagogy of the natural and revealed law addresses some of the themes just mentioned. In fact, a number of features of Thomas's ethics accentuate the possibility of tragedy. The difficulty of hitting the mean, of rectifying the passions, and of meeting the requirements of the moral law, even in those individuals who grasp and want to live in accordance with the life of virtue, can occasion conflicts between what one ought to do and what one does, as well as between one's aspirations for happiness and the assaults of fortune. The Christian narrative in no way ignores those features of human experience that are the source of tragedies. Indeed, the prominence of suffering in the Christian life embraces, rather than circumvents, those features. Much of Christian moral education rightly consists in a preparation for tragedy. Stanley Hauerwas puts the relationship between tragedy and the Gospel thus: "We believe, on the basis of the cross, that our lives are sustained by a God who has taken the tragic into his own life. . . . we are thus freed from the obsession of securing our significance against death."[58]

For the Christian, tragedy cannot be the dominant narrative of the moral life. According to many contemporary writers on tragedy, the metaphysics underlying tragic narrative involves the assertion of "ontological violence" at the foundations of things.[59] Paul Ricoeur states that tragedy reflects a "primordial incoherence."[60] The metaphysics of creation repudiates the possibility that "ontological violence" or "primordial incoherence" are woven into the foundations of reality.

---

[57] *Nichomachean Ethics*, I, 6; I, 9; and I, 10.

[58] *Truthfulness and Tragedy*, 12.

[59] John Milbank, *Theology and Social Theory: Beyond Secular Reason*, 278–325.

[60] *The Symbolism of Evil*, 219. See also René Girard, *Violence and the Sacred*, 287–91.

Instead, creation reflects the goodness, wisdom, and beauty of the divine perfection. Evil is a privation of the good, not a positive force in opposition to the good; evil is parasitic, contingent, and temporary. As Ricoeur puts it, "guilt must be distinguished from finiteness" (219) and ontology from the historical origins of evil in order to overcome the tragic vision.[61]

Sometimes tragedies present the gods as the sources of fate, inimical and inscrutable to humans. The counsel to obey an inexplicable fate is not part of the Christian narrative. The accusation occasioned by the revelation of the law is not an end in itself; it prompts humans to hope for a redeemer. The virtue of hope, Thomas writes, is a mean between "presumption and despair" (*ST*, I-II, 64, 4, ad 3). The author of the whole does not remain a detached spectator; rather, God enters into the story and embraces its tragic features so as to overcome them. As Ricoeur observes, the "divine abasement completes and annihilates tragedy." The suffering servant reverses the tragic pattern and makes it possible that the "evil undergone is an action redeeming the evil committed."[62] Divine mercy also reverses a key pattern in tragedies, wherein the recognition serves to bring about the downfall of the tragic hero and exacerbates his suffering. In Christianity, the moment of recognition, of self-appropriation, is an occasion for repentance and the reception of forgiveness.

The dominant features of the Christian narrative render it more akin to comedy than to tragedy.[63] Comedies usually culminate with union overcoming isolation, with agents receiving more than what they are owed or expect. In contrast to tragedies, which typically conceal their artificial character, comedies make explicit reference to the artificial means by which the happy ending is procured. They even go so far as to introduce the author into the drama. The central event in the Christian narrative is the Incarnation, the entrance of the Word, in accordance with which the world was created, into the order of time and space. The role of time is also peculiar in comedy.

---

[61] *The Symbolism of Evil*, 219.

[62] Ricoeur, *Symbolism of Evil*, 324 and 328. Ricoeur fails to explore the role of comic narrative in the Judeo-Christian Scriptures, and thus he can speak of that narrative only negatively in terms of its eclipsing or undermining tragedy.

[63] I use the vague term *features* to avoid the claim that there is one "theory" of comedy to which all comedies must conform. I thus wish to distance my view from Frye's construction of a cosmic genre theory, unifying the whole of literature.

As Northrop Frye puts it, "In comedy time plays a redeeming role: it uncovers and brings to light what is essential to the happy ending."[64] Thomas's discussion of the appropriate time of the revelation of the Old Law and of the coming of Christ in the fullness of time indicates that time has an intelligible order to it and that it need not be a nemesis.[65]

The Christian emphasis on redemptive suffering, on the pattern of Christ's passion and crucifixion, underlies Thomas More's reference to this life as a "time of weeping" and Strauss's association of Christianity with tragedy. But the latter classification is simplistic; it overlooks what Northrop Frye describes as a "kind of comedy where the complications in front of the happy ending become tragic, so that the comedy contains a tragedy instead of avoiding one."[66] Scripture is a " 'divine comedy' in which the two greatest tragedies, the fall of man and the Crucifixion, are episodes."[67] Strauss's reference, moreover, to fear of the Lord as the beginning of Christian wisdom is accurate, but incomplete. As Thomas notes, fear is the foundation of the gifts of the Holy Spirit, not "as though it were more excellent than the other gifts," but "in the order of generation," so that we might "depart from evil on account of fear" (*ST*, I-II, 68, 7, ad 1). In the order of excellence and nobility, the gifts of knowledge, understanding, and wisdom are superior to the gifts of piety, fortitude, and fear. Finally, Strauss's contrast between philosophic laughter and religious sorrow is not exactly to the point. Christian comedies typically follow a narrative pattern that begin in misery and end in joy, which is "an act or effect of charity" (*ST*, II-II, 28, 4). To the objection that joy does not result from charity because in this life we are apart from God, the source of joy, Thomas responds that "even in this life, he is present to those who love him, by the indwelling of his grace" (*ST*, II-II, 28, 1, ad 1). He proceeds to distinguish between rejoicing in the divine good in itself and rejoicing in it insofar as we partake of it. In the latter sense, joy admits a mixture of sorrow, for we rightly grieve over what hinders our participation in the divine good. Nonetheless, the

---

[64] *Anatomy of Criticism*, 213.

[65] As Frye puts it, "comedy normally attains its happy ending through some mysterious and unexpected twist in the plot" (*The Great Code: The Bible and Literature*, 156).

[66] *T. S. Eliot: An Introduction*, 89.

[67] Frye, *T. S. Eliot*, 90.

comic features of the Christian narrative are not relegated to the state of the soul after death. Anticipations of it occur even here and now.

In light of the previous development of the image of God as artist and as author of the narrative of providence, we can now consider the role of art in Thomas's moral theology. His most famous comments about art, specifically about poetry, are quite pejorative. In the opening question of the *Summa*, Thomas calls poetry the lowest of teachings *(infima doctrina)* and distinguishes sharply between its pedagogical poverty and the power and intelligence of scriptural instruction *(ST,* I, 1, 9). What marks the superiority of Scripture over poetry is its author, who makes not only words but things signify and who elevates the understanding of the believer beyond the mere image. When Thomas goes on to argue that it is appropriate for Scripture to use metaphors and sensible images, he makes clear both that Scripture replaces poetry and that it reinstates some of the features of poetic discourse. From Thomas's supposition that the images in Scripture are means of understanding intelligible realities, we might expect him to prefer more exalted images of God. He does not. Following Dionysius, he defends the appropriateness of Scripture to show forth divine realities "under images of base bodies rather than noble ones" *(sub figuris vilium corporum quam corporum nobilium; ST,* I, 1, 9, ad 3). The use of images from lowly things corrects our tendency to confuse God with exalted but inadequate images. It also underscores how great the distance is between our language and thought and the divine reality. Scripture not only deploys vile and multiple images, but it also contains many senses *(ST,* I, 1, 10). According to the allegorical sense, individuals and events of the Old Testament figuratively anticipate those of the New Testament. Not even the New Testament is an end in itself; according to the anagogical sense, the events of the life of Christ and the early Christian Church anticipate the life of the blessed with God in eternity. Thus, Scripture divides and organizes the whole of time.

Sripture's use of images and its multiple senses reveal the dramatic and inherently temporal character of divine artistry. Insofar as we are not mere pawns or passive subjects in the plan of divine providence, we can actively participate in the divine artistry. We must be clear about what this participation does not entail. We have already noted the absence in Thomas's aesthetics of anything like the modern aesthetics of self-creation or the cult of the genius. When Thomas argues, moreover, that it is proper to God alone to create, he defines the act of creation as the production of being absolutely, a production that presupposes nothing (*ST,* I, 45, 5). Creatures cannot bring things into being in an absolute sense, but they can produce a superadded perfection in an already existing creature (*ST,* I, 45, 5, ad 1). In this context, it is helpful to recall the various stages of the perfection of the *imago Dei* in us: creation, re-creation, similitude. Obviously, we had nothing to do with our original creation, but we can play a role in the re-creation of ourselves and others. We are, as Dionysius puts it, cooperators with the divine plan, conscious and free instruments of the divine art. When our contemplative love for God overflows into teaching and acts of charity, we dimly mirror the relationship of God to the world and of higher angels to lower ones. In this way, the divine art is central to the theological teaching on the relationship between contemplation and action.

CONCLUSION: THE GOOD LIFE AS THE PRACTICE OF TRUTHFULNESS

There are, then, a number of connections among contemplation, prudence, and art in the Christian moral thought of Aquinas. We find Thomas inheriting, clarifying, and extending the categories of *theoria, phronesis,* and *techne.* As noted in the discussion of theory and practice in Aristotle's political teaching, all three play an important role in communal pursuit of the good life. Aquinas's doctrine of the divine art and of our participation in it also entails the cooperation of art, theory, and prudence. Contemplation overflows into a life of action, a life that attends prudentially to the concrete circumstances of persons and actions, and that seeks to refashion the world in light of the intentions of its original artist. In theology, there is a more explicit development of and a greater emphasis on the cooperative endeavor of theory, art, and prudence. Thomas's dialectical encounter with the philosophical understanding of the virtues highlights both the overlap and the disparities between theology and philosophy.

In his discussion of the ultimate end of human life, for example, Thomas presses certain Aristotelian premises about happiness to an end unknown to Aristotle. The unresolved difficulty *(aporia)* concerning happiness in Aristotle's corpus provides an opportunity for the dialectical engagement of philosophy by theology. Instead of the deployment of a crude conception of hierarchy as the superimposition of one view on another, one authority on another, or one discipline (theology) on another (philosophy), we have a subtle dialectical reformulation of positions in light of the very problems that these positions sought to resolve. A similar strategy is at work in the discussion of the overlap of portions of the Decalogue with the natural law. For all the likenesses between philosophical and theological pedagogy, there are crucial differences. The clearest sign of a certain incommensurability between philosophy and revelation is that the latter locates the human condition within a comprehensive historical narrative of creation, fall, redemption, and final transformation. Contingent historical events, unknowable by philosophy, are the keys to the good life. In my discussion of narrative, I focused on creation and redemption. I noted Thomas's repudiation of some Arabic theses concerning the necessity of God's distance from the world and the impossibility of God's knowing and caring for lowly singulars. I also noted the etymological and substantive link between providence and prudence. In the Incarnation, furthermore, time and eternity, finite and infinite, divine and human are united, as God enters the creator's own story to invite human cooperation in bringing about a comic resolution to the apparently tragic features of the human condition. Both of these Christian teachings counteract the tendency to see concrete singulars as faded images of abstract, pristine universals and to dissolve the integrity of finite creatures in the sea of eternity. Instead, Thomas's theological account of beauty highlights the manifestation of infinite wisdom, goodness, and beauty in and through a finite, embodied form. As Urs von Balthasar puts it, "Aesthetic experience is the union of the greatest possible concreteness of the individual form and the greatest possible universality of its meaning or of the epiphany within it of the mystery of being."[68]

In the encounter with God, we do not simply recover and rightly order our natural capacities of knowing and loving. Admittedly, the first moment in the moral pedagogy of revelation involves not alienation from nature, but the recovery of the order of natural inclina-

---

[68] Seeing the Form, 234.

tions. The dialectical engagement of nature by revelation evinces the reasonableness of revelation as it shows reason where it went wrong and why. This is not, however, the primary focus of revelation. In the act of faith, we believe not merely or primarily in a pedagogy that clarifies our natural potentiality, but in the authority of God and in the unified and concrete whole of God's revelation. In the encounter with God, we are discovered rather than discovering. Instead of a dichotomy between rational autonomy and submission to authority, there is an interpenetration of trusting and knowing, a knowing that is experiential and connatural and thus akin to the kind of knowing appropriate to prudence and the moral virtues. Faith, the first of the theological virtues, has both an intellectual dimension, concerning the first truth, and an affective dimension, concerning the first truth as ultimate end and final good. Hope accompanies faith, both of which are ordered to charity, which unites us to the end and orders all things in light of and toward the love of God. The Christian practice of contemplation is rooted in and overflows into charity.

As noted in the discussion of Aristotle, there is reason to think that prudence governs the whole of human life, including that portion of it devoted to contemplation. Aristotle does not, however, develop this point, and some commentators have interpreted his silence as countenancing an amoral and radically individualist conception of the intellectual life. The link between charity and the gift of wisdom integrates the contemplative and the practical, and renders individualism unthinkable. From Augustine, Thomas derives the virtue *studiositas,* a moral virtue that moderates and rightly orders our natural desire for knowledge. Knowledge is a good, an object of the intellectual appetite. Given that we take delight in knowing, just as we do in the goods of the body, there is need for temperance. It is important that we not misconstrue temperance as curbing an excessive desire for pleasure on particular occasions and thus as being characterized by pain or inertia. The temperate person's desires have been transformed so as to take delight in the enjoyment of appropriate pleasure and to find both excess and deficiency painful. Similarly, the virtue of *studiositas* does not eliminate or merely curb our intellectual eros because the virtue is defined both positively and passionately as a "vehement application of the mind" *(vehemens applicatio mentis).* In response to the objection that *studiositas* cannot be a part of the moral virtue of temperance because it concerns cognitive matters,

Thomas observes that the acts of the intellect are commanded by the appetitive power and that these acts can be ordered variously "in one way or another and to this or that" (ST, II-II, 166, 1, ad 2). Precisely the ordering of these acts is subject to the moral virtue of *studiositas*, a part of temperance.

Thomas proceeds to describe the opposed vice, *curiositas*, which involves the inordinate application of the mind (ST, II-II, 167, 1). He cites four examples of inordinate intellectual appetite: (a) the pursuit of less-useful and less-noble knowledge; (b) the attempt to derive knowledge from a source forbidden by divine law—for example, the desire to gain knowledge of the future from demons; (c) the desire to know truths about creatures without referring that knowledge to its due end—namely, knowledge of God; and (d) the desire for knowledge that exceeds one's intellectual capacity. Although philosophers may acknowledge some of these sorts of disorder, theological considerations are clearly prominent. This impression is confirmed by Thomas's nearly exclusive reliance on Christian authorities, especially Augustine. How important are the virtues and vices of the intellect to Thomas's moral theology? Their importance can be gathered from related remarks about the capital vice of pride (*superbia*), an instance of which constituted our original sin against God. Pride is a desire for a spiritual good beyond our natural level or measure, an inordinate desire for excellence. We must be careful not to conclude from this definition that any desire to be like God or to have a knowledge of God is vicious; such a desire is sinful only when it is inordinate or when we suppose that we can attain beatitude by our own efforts, unaided by God (ST, II-II, 163, 2, ad 2). To avoid pride, we must pair magnanimity, which urges us to pursue great goods and thus curbs our tendency to despair of achieving them, with humility, which tempers excessive ambition for elevated goods and thus curbs presumption.

Thomas's discussions of *studiositas* and *curiositas* often trace the misuse of the intellect to pride or see pride as a result of that misuse. The failure to restrain and rightly order the natural desire for knowledge can be allied to the vice most damaging to our pursuit of the beatitude to which we are called. The potential link between pride and the desire for knowledge is not a critique of philosophy itself, but rather a critique of an excessively rationalistic view of philosophy as constituting the sufficient good for human beings. Such a view is presumptuous and idolatrous.

The need for a virtue to temper and guide the acts of speculative reason evinces our tendency to be so captivated by the objects of knowledge that we are oblivious to other relevant goods and to the way any particular activity must fit into the whole of our life. No particular action or set of actions can constitute a good life. Thomas's ethical appraisal of the intellectual virtues shifts our attention from the object or content of the acts of knowing to their nature as acts of a human being and even more broadly to the way these acts contribute to a way of life. It underscores what Linda Zagzebski calls the "self-implicating" character of acts of knowing.[69]

Thomas's philosophical and theological writings are at once reflections on, contributions to, and enactments of a specific way of life. Although he makes philosophical arguments, his life is not that of the philosopher in the ancient sense—that is, in the sense that he takes as his highest authority the communally embodied tradition of philosophical inquiry, with its texts, methods, and exercises. Instead, in his work, philosophy is decisively subordinated to the authoritative teaching of the Gospel. Thus, Hadot is perhaps right in his observation that in the Middle Ages "philosophy is no longer a way of life," but he is wrong to suppose that philosophy must consequently be reduced to a "purely theoretical and abstract activity."[70] Aquinas's careful appraisal of—indeed, immersion in—philosophy seeks to keep alive the aspiration to the life of wisdom as a desire natural to human beings. The pursuit of wisdom remains the inspiration for the practice of the virtues—speculative and practical, natural and infused. Hadot also thinks that the professionalization of education in the medieval university narrows and ossifies intellectual pursuits, stripping them of their connection to a way of life. As student and teacher, Thomas participated in the education of the university and appropriated the forms of debate prevalent in its curriculum, but he subsumed all of this within a specific way of life. I have already had occasion to refer (in references to the studies by the Dominicans Boyle and Tugwell) to the specifically Christian and Dominican way of life in the context of which Thomas's thinking developed.

---

[69] See *Virtues of the Mind.*
[70] "Philosophy as a Way of Life," in *Philosophy as Way of Life*, 270.

That way of life locates the pursuit of truth within a communal context of the practice of a host of virtues. There is in fact a moral virtue of truth and even a truth of life *(veritas vitae)*. The moral virtue consists in speaking the truth when it is necessary and insofar as it is necessary *(ST,* II-II, 109, 1). We do not, of course, owe a revelation of all truth to everyone; our duties in matters of truth telling vary in both degree and kind, from person to person and circumstance to circumstance. Although truthfulness refers primarily to speech, its scope is broader and includes deeds and signs, all of which must be disposed in a due order *(ST,* II-II, 109, 2). The shift from the content or objects of knowledge to the acts of knowing, speaking, and doing does not involve a retreat to some subjective and private arena. Rather, it locates the appraisal of these acts within a communal context. Truthfulness is a part of justice arising from our social nature, in light of which we owe to others all those things without which the constitutive goods of human society cannot be preserved *(ST,* II-II, 109, 3, ad 1). One of these things is the "manifestation of the truth." We manifest truth in the broadest sense when we reveal ourselves in "life and speech to be such as we in fact are" *(aliquis et vita et sermone talem se demonstrat, qualis est; ST,* II-II, 109, 3, ad 3). Because the truth of life is measured by our conformity to the model of the divine life, which is embodied in the virtues, we should not only exhibit ourselves to others as we are, but also understand ourselves in light of and strive to realize the natural and the theological virtues. Of course, we are apt to find ourselves and our communities regularly falling short of the standards of the virtues; the Christian corrective to the temptation to despair is to locate mercy and forgiveness at the heart of our pursuit of the truth of life. There is thus perhaps no more apt or succinct formulation of Thomas's view of the good life than to say that it consists in the practice of the manifold virtue of truthfulness.

BIBLIOGRAPHY

ANCIENT AND MEDIEVAL AUTHORS

Aquinas, Thomas. *Expositio super Dionysiam de Divinis Nominibus.* Turin and Rome: Marietti, 1950.

————. *Expositio super Librum Boethii* De Trinitate. Leiden: Brill, 1955.

————. *In Aristotelis* De Anima *Commentarium.* Edited by Angelus Pirotta. 4th ed. Turin and Rome: Marietti, 1965.

————. *In Aristotelis Libros* Peri Hermeneias *et* Posteriorum Analyticorum. Turin and Rome: Marietti, 1955.

————. *In Decem Libros* Ethicorum *Aristotelis ad* Nichomachum *Expositio.* Edited by R. Spiazzi. Turin and Rome: Marietti, 1964.

————. *In Libros* Politicorum *Aristotelis Expositio.* Rome: Marietti, 1951.

————. *In Octo Libros* Physicorum *Aristotelis.* Edited by P. M. Maggiolo. Turin and Rome: Marietti, 1965.

————. *Lectura super Johannem.* Rome: Marietti, 1952.

————. *Quaestiones Disputatae: De Veritate.* Rome: Marietti, 1949.

————. *Scriptum super Libros Sententiarum.* Edited by P. F. Mandonnet. Paris: Lethielleux, 1929–33.

————. *Sententia super* Metaphysicam. Turin and Rome: Marietti, 1950.

————. *Sententia super* Peri Hermeneias. Turin and Rome: Marietti, 1955.

————. *Sententia super* Posteriora Analytica. Turin and Rome: Marietti, 1955.

————. *Summa contra Gentiles.* The Leonine edition. In *L'édition bilingue de la Summa contra Gentiles.* Paris: Lethielleux, 1961. Corrigenda to the Leonine edition by R. A. Gauthier in his introduction, in *Somme contre les Gentiles.* Collection Philosophie Européenne dirigée par Henri Hude, 45–57. Paris: Éditions Universitaires, 1993.

————. *Summa Theologiae.* Torino: Marietti, 1948.

Aristotle. *The Complete Works of Aristotle.* 2 vols. Edited by J. Barnes. Revised Oxford translation. Princeton, N.J.: Princeton University Press, 1984.

————. *Ethica Nichomachea.* Edited by Ingram Bywater. Oxford: Clarendon, 1980.

————. *Metaphysics.* Edited by David Ross. Oxford: Clarendon, 1924.

————. *Physica.* Edited by David Ross. Oxford: Clarendon, 1950.

————. *Topica.* In *Organon Graece.* Vol. 2. Edited by N. A. Weitz. Leipzig, 1846. Reprint, Aalen: Scientia, 1965.

Suarez, Francisco. *De Legibus ac Deo Legislatore.* In *Corpus Hispanorum de Pace.* Madrid: Instituto Francisco de Vitoria, 1971.

Modern Authors

Ackrill, J. "Aristotle on Eudaimonia." In *Essays on Aristotle's* Ethics, edited by Amélie Rorty, 15–34. Berkeley: University of California Press, 1980.

Aertsen, Jan. *Nature and Creature: St. Thomas Aquinas's Way of Thought.* Translated by H. D. Morton. Leiden: E. J. Brill, 1988.

Ambler, Wayne H. "Aristotle's Understanding of the Naturalness of the City." *Review of Politics* 47 (1985): 163–85.

Arendt, Hannah. *The Human Condition.* Chicago: University of Chicago Press, 1958.

Auerbach, Erich. *Mimesis: The Representation of Reality in Western Literature.* Translated by Willard R. Trask. Princeton, N.J.: Princeton University Press, 1953.

Bacon, Francis. *The New Organon.* Edited by Fulton H. Anderson. Indianapolis: Bobbs-Merrill, 1960.

Barnes, Jonathan. "Aristotle's Theory of Demonstration." *Phronesis* 14 (1969): 123–52.

————. "Proof and Syllogism." In *Aristotle on Science: The* Posterior Analytics, 17–59. Padua: Editrice Antenore, 1981.

Barth, Karl. *Church Dogmatics.* Translated by G. T. Thomson. 8 vols. Edinburgh: T. & T. Clark, 1936–77.

Bedouelle, Guy. *Saint Dominic: The Grace of the Word.* San Francisco: Ignatius, 1987.

Beer, Samuel. "The Rule of the Wise and Holy: Hierarchy in the Thomistic System." *Political Theory* 14 (1986): 391–422.

Berns, Laurence. "Rational Animal—Political Animal: Nature and Convention in Human Speech and Politics." *Review of Politics* 38 (1976): 177–89.

Berquist, Duane. "Descartes and the Way of Proceeding in Philosophy." Ph.D. diss., Laval University, 1964.

Blanchette Oliva. *The Perfection of the Universe according to Aquinas: A Teleological Cosmology.* University Park: Pennsylvania State University, 1992.

Bodéüs, Richard. *The Political Dimension of Aristotle's* Ethics. Translated by E. Garrett. Albany: State University of New York Press, 1993.

Boyle, Leonard, O.P. *The Setting of the* Summa Theologiae *of St. Thomas.* Toronto: Pontifical Institute of Mediaeval Studies, 1982.

Brock, Stephen. *Action and Conduct: Thomas Aquinas and the Theory of Action.* Edinburgh: T & T Clark, 1998.

Burnyeat, Miles. "Aristotle on Understanding Knowledge." In *Aristotle on Science: The* Posterior Analytics, edited by Enrico Berti, 97–139. Padua: Editrice Antenore, 1981.

———. "Is an Aristotelian Philosophy of Mind Still Credible?" In *Essays on Aristotle's* De Anima, edited by Amélie Rorty and Martha C. Nussbaum, 1–26. Oxford: Clarendon, 1992.

Burrell, David. *Aquinas: God and Action.* Notre Dame, Ind.: University of Notre Dame Press, 1979.

———. *Knowing the Unknowable God: Ibn-Sina, Maimonides, and Aquinas.* Notre Dame, Ind.: University of Notre Dame Press, 1986.

Caputo, John D. *Heidegger and Aquinas: An Essay on the Overcoming of Metaphysics.* New York: Fordham University Press, 1982.

Carls, Maria. "Law, Virtue, and Happiness." *The Thomist* 61 (1997): 425–47.

Cessario, Romanus, O.P. *Christian Satisfaction in Aquinas: Toward a Personalist Understanding.* Washington, D.C.: University Press of America, 1982.

———. *The Moral Virtues and Theological Ethics.* Notre Dame, Ind.: University of Notre Dame Press, 1991.

Chenu, Marie Dominique. "Création et histoire." In *St. Thomas*

Aquinas, 1274–1974: Commemorative Studies, vol. 2, 391–400. Toronto: Pontifical Institute of Mediaeval Studies, 1974.

———. *Introduction à l'étude de saint Thomas d'Aquin.* Paris: J. Vrin, 1954.

———. *The Scope of the* Summa. Washington, D.C.: Thomist, 1958.

Cleary, John. "On the Terminology 'Abstraction' in Aristotle." *Phronesis* 32 (1985): 13–45.

Cooper, John. "Aristotle on Friendship." In *Essays on Aristotle's Ethics,* edited by Amélie Rorty, 301–40. Berkeley: University of California Press, 1980.

Corbin, M. *Le chemin de la théologie chez Thomas d'Aquin.* Paris: Beauchesne, 1972.

Coulter, Gregory. "Aquinas on the Identity of Mind and Substantial Form." *American Catholic Philosophical Quarterly* 64 (1990): 161–79.

Crane, Michael. "Synderesis and the Notion of Law in St. Thomas." In *L'homme et son destin.* Paris: Beatrice-Nauwelaerts, 1960.

Crisp, Roger, and Michael Slote, eds. *Virtue Ethics.* Oxford: Oxford University Press, 1997.

De Koninck, Charles. "Abstraction from Matter." *Laval Théologique et Philosophique* 13 (1957): 133–96; 16 (1960): 53–69, 169–88.

———. "In Defense of St. Thomas: A Reply to Fr. Eschmann's Attack on the Primacy of the Common Good." *Laval Théologique et Philosophique* 1 (1945): 9–109.

De Lubac, Henri. *Surnaturel.* Paris: Aubier, 1946.

Descartes, René. *Meditations.* Translated by Donald Cress. Indianapolis, Ind.: Hackett, 1993.

Dewan, Lawrence, O.P. "St. Thomas, Aristotle, and Creation." *Dionysius* 15 (1991): 81–90.

Doig, James C. "The Interpretation of Aquinas's Prima Secundae." *American Catholic Philosophical Quarterly* 71 (1997): 171–95.

Donagan, Alan. *Theory of Mortality.* Chicago: University of Chicago Press, 1977.

Donnelly, Phillip J. "Discussions on the Supernatural Order." *Theological Studies* 9 (1948): 213–49.

Dunne, Joseph. *Back to the Rough Ground.* Notre Dame, Ind.: University of Notre Dame Press, 1993.

Eco, Umberto. *The Aesthetics of Thomas Aquinas.* Cambridge, Mass.: Harvard University Press, 1988. Originally published as *Il problema estetico in Tommaso d'Aquino.* 2d ed. Milan: Bompiani, 1970.

Fabro, Cornelio. "The Intensive Hermeneutics of Thomistic Philosophy." *Review of Metaphysics* 27 (1974): 449–91.

———. *Participation et causalité selon St. Thomas d'Aquin.* Paris: Éditions Béatrice Nauwelaerts, 1961.

———. "The Problem of Being and the Destiny of Man." *International Philosophical Quarterly* 1 (1961): 408–36.

———. "The Transcendentality of Ens-Esse and the Ground of Metaphysics." *International Philosophical Quarterly* 6 (1966): 389–427.

Farrell, Walter. *The Natural Law according to St. Thomas and Suarez.* Sussex: St. Damian's, 1930.

Finnis, John. *Natural Law and Natural Rights.* Oxford: Clarendon, 1980.

Fortin, Ernest. Review of *Natural Law and Natural Rights,* by John Finnis. *Review of Politics* 44 (1982): 590–612.

Freddoso, Alfred J. "Medieval Aristotelianism and the Case against Secondary Causation in Nature." In *Divine and Human Action,* edited by Thomas Morris, 74–118. Ithaca, N.Y.: Cornell University Press, 1988.

Frei, Hans. *The Eclipse of Biblical Narrative: A Study of Eighteenth- and Nineteenth-Century Hermeneutics.* New Haven, Conn.: Yale University Press, 1974.

Frye, Northrup. *Anatomy of Criticism.* Princeton, N.J.: Princeton University Press, 1957.

———. *The Great Code: The Bible and Literature.* New York: Harcourt, Brace, Jovanovich, 1981.

———. *T. S. Eliot: An Introduction.* Chicago: University of Chicago Press, 1963.

Funkenstein, Amos. *Theology and the Scientific Imagination: From the Middle Ages to the Seventeenth Century.* Princeton, N.J.: Princeton University Press, 1986.

Gadamer, Hans-Georg. *Truth and Method.* 2d ed. Translated by J. Wiensheimer and D. Marshall. New York: Continuum, 1989.

Gahl, Robert A. "From the Virtue of a Fragile Good to a Narrative Account of Natural Law." *International Philosophical Quarterly* 37 (1997): 457–72.

Garrigou-Lagrange, H. "Du caractère métaphysique de la théologie morale de Saint Thomas." *Revue Thomiste* 30 (1930): 341–55.

Gauthier, R. A. *La morale d'Aristote.* Paris: Presses Universitaires de France, 1958.

Geach, P. T. "Good and Evil." In *Theories of Ethics,* edited by Philippa Foot, 64–73. Oxford: Oxford University Press, 1967.

Geiger, Louis B. "L'homme, image de Dieu: À propos *Summa Theologiae,* Ia, 93, 4." *Rivista Filosofia Neo-Scolastica* 60 (1974): 511–32.

Gilson, Étienne. *Being and Some Philosophers.* Toronto: Pontifical Institute of Mediaeval Studies, 1952.

―――. *The Christian Philosophy of Thomas Aquinas.* Translated by L. K. Shook. New York: Octagon, 1983.

―――. *The Elements of Christian Philosophy.* Garden City, N.Y.: Doubleday, 1960.

―――. *The Spirit of Medieval Philosophy.* Translated by A. H. C. Downes. London: Sheed and Ward, 1936.

―――. *Le Thomisme: Introduction à la philosophie de saint Thomas d'Aquin.* Paris: J. Vrin, 1944.

Girard, René. *Things Hidden Since the Foundation of the World.* Translated by S. Bann and M. Metteer. Stanford, Calif.: Stanford University Press, 1987.

―――. *Violence and the Sacred.* Baltimore: Johns Hopkins University Press, 1977.

Goerner, E. A., and W. J. Thompson. "Politics and Coercion." *Political Theory* 24 (1996): 1–28.

Guindon, Roger. *Béatitude et théologie morale chez saint Thomas d'Aquin.* Ottawa: Éditions de l'Université d'Ottawa, 1956.

Haakonssen, Knud. *Natural Law and Moral Philosophy: From Grotius to the Scottish Enlightenment.* Cambridge: Cambridge University Press, 1996.

―――, ed. *Enlightenment and Religion.* Cambridge: Cambridge University Press, 1996.

Habermas, Jürgen. "A Review of Gadamer's *Truth and Method.*" In *Understanding and Social Inquiry,* 335–63. Notre Dame, Ind.: University of Notre Dame Press, 1977.

Hadot, Pierre. *Philosophy as a Way of Life.* Edited by A. I. Davidson. Translated by M. Chase. Oxford: Blackwell, 1995.

Hall, Pamela. *Narrative and the Natural Law: An Interpretation of*

Thomistic Ethics. Notre Dame, Ind.: University of Notre Dame Press, 1994.

Harré, Rom, and E. H. Madden. *Causal Powers: A Theory of Natural Necessity.* Oxford: Basil Blackwell, 1975.

Hauerwas, Stanley. *Character and the Christian Life: A Study in Theological Ethics.* San Antonio, Tex.: Trinity University Press, 1975.

————. *Truthfulness and Tragedy.* Notre Dame, Ind.: University of Notre Dame Press, 1977.

Hibbs, Thomas. "Against a Cartesian Reading of *Intellectus* in Aquinas." *Modern Schoolman* 66 (1988): 55–69.

————. *Dialectic and Narrative in Aquinas: An Interpretation of the Summa contra Gentiles.* Notre Dame, Ind.: University of Notre Dame Press, 1995.

————. "Divine Irony and the Natural Law: Speculation and Edification in Aquinas." *International Philosophical Quarterly* 30 (1990): 419–29.

————. "The Hierarchy of Moral Discourses in Aquinas." *American Catholic Philosophical Quarterly* 64 (1990): 199–214.

————. "*Imitatio Christi* and the Foundation of Aquinas's Ethics." *Communio* 18 (1991): 556–73.

————. "Interpretations of Aquinas's Ethics Since Vatican II." In *Essays on the Ethics of Thomas Aquinas,* edited by Stephen Pope. Washington, D.C.: Georgetown University Press, forthcoming.

————. "Kretzmann's Theism vs. Aquinas's Theism: Interpreting *Summa contra Gentiles* I." *The Thomist* 62 (1998): 603–22.

————. "MacIntyre's Post-Modern Thomism: Reflections on *Three Rival Versions of Moral Enquiry.*" *The Thomist* 57 (1993): 277–97.

————. "MacIntyre, Tradition, and the Christian Philosopher." *Modern Schoolman* 68 (1991): 211–23.

————. "Moral Crisis and the Turn to Narrative." In *Freedom, Virtue, and the Common Good,* edited by Curtis L. Hancock and Anthony O. Simon, 194–211. Notre Dame, Ind.: University of Notre Dame Press, 1995.

————. "Principles and Prudence." *New Scholasticism* 61 (1987): 271–84.

————. Review of *Reading Aristotle's Ethics,* by Aristide Tessitore. *Review of Politics* 59 (1997): 939–41.

————. Review of *Virtues of the Mind,* by Linda Zagzebski. *The Thomist* 61 (1997): 485–88.

————. "A Rhetoric of Motives: Thomas on Obligation as Rational Persuasion." *The Thomist* 54 (1990): 293–309,

————. "Transcending Humanity." *Proceedings of the American Catholic Philosophical Association* 66 (1992): 191–213.

Hobbes, Thomas. *Leviathan.* Edited by Edwin Curley. Indianapolis, Ind.: Hackett, 1994.

Hoenen, P. "De Origine Primorum Principiorum Scientiae." *Gregorianum* 14 (1993): 153–84.

Hoose, Bernard. *Proportionalism: The American Debate and Its European Roots.* Washington, D.C.: Georgetown University Press, 1987.

Husserl, Edmund. *Crisis of the European Sciences.* Translated by David Carr. Chicago: Northwestern University Press, 1970.

Jaffa, Harry. *Thomism and Aristotelianism: A Study of the Commentary by Thomas Aquinas on the* Nichomachean Ethics. Chicago: University of Chicago Press, 1952.

Jenkins, John. "Expositions of the Text: Aquinas's Aristotelian Commentaries." *Medieval Philosophy and Theology* 5 (1996): 36–62.

————. *Knowledge and Faith in Thomas Aquinas.* Cambridge, Eng.: Cambridge University Press, 1997.

John Paul II. *Veritatis Splendor.* Boston: St. Paul Books and Media, 1993.

Jordan, Mark. *The Alleged Aristotelianism of Thomas Aquinas.* Gilson Lecture, no.15. Toronto: Pontifical Institute of Mediaeval Studies, 1992.

————. "The Evidence of the Transcendentals and the Place of Beauty in Thomas Aquinas." *International Philosophical Quarterly* 29 (1989): 393–406.

————. "The Names of God and the Being of Names." In *The Existence and Nature of God,* edited by Alfred Freddoso, 161–90. University of Notre Dame Studies in the Philosophy of Religion, vol. 3. Notre Dame, Ind.: University of Notre Dame Press, 1983.

————. *Ordering Wisdom: The Hierarchy of Philosophic Discourse in Aquinas.* Notre Dame, Ind.: University of Notre Dame Press, 1986.

Kant, Immanuel. *The Metaphysics of Morals.* Translated by T. K.

Abbot. In vol. 42 of *Great Books of the Western World*, 253–90. Chicago: Encyclopaedia Britannica, 1952.

Kass, Leon. *Toward a More Natural Science.* New York: Free Press, 1985.

Keenan, James F. *Goodness and Rightness in Thomas Aquinas's* Summa Theologiae. Washington, D.C.: Georgetown University Press, 1992.

Kenny, Anthony. *Aquinas on Mind.* London: Routledge, 1993.

Keys, Mary M. "Personal Dignity and the Common Good: A Twentieth-Century Thomistic Dialogue." In *Catholicism, Liberalism, and Communitarianism*, edited by Kenneth Grasso, Gerard Bradley, and R. Hunt, 173–96. Lanham, Md.: Rowman and Littlefield, 1995.

Klein, Jacob. *A Commentary on Plato's Meno.* Chapel Hill: University of North Carolina Press, 1965.

Kosman, A. "Explanation and Understanding in Aristotle's *Posterior Analytics.*" In *Exegesis and Argument: Essays in Greek Philosophy Presented to Gregory Vlastos*, edited by Edward N. Lee, Alexander Mourelatos, and Richard Rorty, 44–68. Assen, Netherlands: Van Gorcem, 1973.

Kovach, Francis J. *Die Aesthetik des Thomas von Aquin.* Berlin: De Gruyter, 1961.

Kraut, Richard. *Aristotle on the Human Good.* Princeton, N.J.: Princeton University Press, 1989.

Kretzmann, Norman. *The Metaphysics of Theism: Aquinas' Natural Theology in* Summa contra Gentiles I. Cambridge: Cambridge University Press, 1997.

Kupperman, Joel. *Character.* Oxford: Oxford University Press, 1991.

Lachtermann, David. *Ethics of Geometry: A Genealogy of Modernity.* New York: Routledge, 1989.

Lafont, Ghislain. *Structures et méthode dans la* Somme théologique *de saint Thomas d'Aquin.* Paris: Édition du Cerf, 1961.

Laporta, Jorge. *La destinée de la nature humaine selon Thomas d'Aquin.* Paris: J. Vrin, 1965.

Leclerq, Jean. *L'amour des lettres et désir de Dieu.* Paris: Éditions du Cerf, 1957.

Lesher, James. "The Meaning of Nous in the *Posterior Analytics.*" *Phronesis* 18 (1973): 44–68.

Lonergan, Bernard. *Verbum: Word and Idea in Aquinas.* Edited by

David Burrell. Notre Dame, Ind.: University of Notre Dame Press, 1967.

Lottin, Odon. *Le droit naturel chez saint Thomas d'Aquin et ses predecesseurs.* Bruges: Beyaert, 1931.

Louden, Robert. "On Some Vices of Virtue Ethics." In *Virtue Ethics,* edited by Roger Crisp and Michael Slote, 201–16. Oxford: Oxford University Press, 1997.

MacDonald, Scott. "Theory of Knowledge." In *The Cambridge Companion to Aquinas,* edited by Norman Kretzmann and Eleonore Stump, 160–95. Cambridge: Cambridge University Press, 1993.

Machiavelli, Niccolò. *The Prince.* Translated by Leo Paul De Alvarez. Dallas: University of Dallas Press, 1980.

MacIntyre, Alasdair. *After Virtue.* 2d ed. Notre Dame, Ind.: University of Notre Dame Press, 1984.

———. "The Magic in the Pronoun 'My.'" *Ethics* 94 (1983): 113–25.

———. "Plain Persons and Morality: Virtues, Rules, and Goods." *American Catholic Philosophical Quarterly* 66 (1992): 3–19.

———. *Three Rival Versions of Moral Enquiry.* Notre Dame, Ind.: University of Notre Dame Press, 1990.

Manent, Pierre. *The City of Man.* Princeton: Princeton University Press, 1998.

———. *Modern Liberty and Its Discontents.* Lanham, Md.: Rowman and Littlefield, 1998.

Maritain, Jacques. *Existence and the Existent.* Garden City, N.Y.: Doubleday Image, 1956.

Maurer, Armond A., C.S.B. *About Beauty.* Houston: Center for Thomistic Studies, 1983.

McInerny, Ralph. *Aquinas against the Averroists: On There Being Only One Intellect.* West Lafayette, Ind.: Purdue University Press, 1993.

———. *Being and Predication.* Studies in Philosophy and the History of Philosophy, no. 16. Washington, D.C.: Catholic University of America Press, 1986.

———. *Ethica Thomistica.* Washington, D.C.: Catholic University of America Press, 1982.

———. *The Logic of Analogy: An Interpretation of St. Thomas.* The Hague: Martinus Nijhoff, 1961.

———. *The Question of Christian Ethics.* Washington, D.C.: Catholic University of America Press, 1998.

Milbank, John. *Theology and Social Theory: Beyond Secular Reason.* Oxford: Basil Blackwell, 1990.

Modrak, Deborah K. W. *Aristotle: The Power of Perception.* Chicago: University of Chicago Press, 1987.

———. "The Nous-Body Problem in Aristotle." *Review of Metaphysics* 44 (1991): 755–74.

Murphy, Mark. "Consent, Custom, and the Common Good in Aquinas's Account of Political Theory." *Review of Politics* 59 (1977): 323–50.

Nelson, Daniel Mark. *The Priority of Prudence: Virtue and Natural Law in Thomas Aquinas and the Implications for Modern Ethics.* University Park: Pennsylvania State University Press, 1992.

Nussbaum, Martha. *De Motu Animalium: Text with Translation and Interpretive Essays.* Princeton, N.J.: Princeton University Press, 1978.

———. *The Fragility of Goodness: Luck and Ethics in Greek Tragedy and Philosophy.* Cambridge: Cambridge University Press, 1986.

———. *Love's Knowledge.* Oxford: Oxford University Press, 1990.

Nussbaum, M., and H. Putnam. "Changing Aristotle's Mind." In *Essays on Aristotle's* De Anima, edited by Amélie Rorty and Martha C. Nussbaum, 27–56. Oxford: Clarendon, 1992.

O'Callaghan, John. "The Problem of Language and Mental Representation in Aristotle and St. Thomas." *Review of Metaphysics* 50 (1997): 499–541.

O'Connor, Daniel. *Aquinas and Natural Law.* London: Macmillan, 1967.

O'Connor, David. Review of *Finding the Mean,* by Stephen Salkever. *Ancient Philosophy* 15 (1995): 251–56.

O'Meara, Thomas. *The Moral Virtues and Theological Ethics.* Notre Dame, Ind.: University of Notre Dame Press, 1991.

———. "Virtues in the Theology of Thomas Aquinas." *Theological Studies* 58 (1997): 256–87.

O'Rourke, Fran. *Pseudo-Dionysius and the Metaphysics of Aquinas.* Leiden: E. J. Brill, 1992.

Owens, Joseph. "The Inseparability of the Soul from Existence." *New Scholasticism* 61 (1987): 249–70.

Pasnau, Robert. *Theories of Cognition in the Later Middle Ages.* Cambridge: Cambridge University Press, 1997.

Peghaire, J. *Intellectus et Ratio selon S. Thomas d'Aquin.* Ottawa: n.p., 1936.

Pegis, Anton. "Nature and Spirit: Some Reflections on the Problem of the End of Man." *Proceedings of the American Catholic Philosophical Association* 23 (1949): 62–79.

———. "The Separated Soul and Its Nature in St. Thomas." In *St. Thomas Aquinas 1274–1974: Commemorative Studies,* vol. 1, 131–59. Toronto: Pontifical Institute of Mediaeval Studies, 1974.

Pieper, Josef. *The Cardinal Virtues.* New York: Harcourt, Brace, and World, 1965.

———. *Happiness and Contemplation.* Translated by Richard Winston and Clara Winston. New York: Pantheon, 1958.

———. *Leisure: The Basis of Culture.* Translated by A. Dru. New York: Pantheon, 1952.

———. *Prudence.* Translated by Richard Winston and Clara Winston. London: Faber and Faber, 1959.

———. *The Silence of St. Thomas: Three Essays.* Translated by J. Murray and D. O'Connor. New York: Pantheon, 1957.

Pinches, Charles. *Christians among the Virtues.* Notre Dame, Ind.: University of Notre Dame Press, 1997.

Pinckaers, Servais, O.P. *The Sources of Christian Ethics.* Translated by Sr. Mary Thomas Noble. Washington, D.C.: Catholic University of America Press, 1995.

Porter, Jean. *The Recovery of Virtue: The Relevance of Aquinas for Christian Ethics.* Louisville, Ky.: Westminster, John Knox, 1990.

Pritzl, Kurt. "Aristotle: Ways of Truth and Ways of Opinion." *Proceedings of the American Catholic Philosophical Association* 67 (1993): 241–52.

Rawls, John. *A Theory of Justice.* Cambridge, Mass.: Harvard University Press, 1971.

Ricoeur, Paul. *The Symbolism of Evil.* Translated by E. Buchanan. New York: Harper, 1967.

Rorty, Amélie. "The Place of Contemplation in Aristotle's *Nichomachean Ethics.*" In *Essays on Aristotle's* Ethics, edited by Amélie Rorty, 377–94. Oxford: Clarendon, 1980.

———. "The Psychology of Aristotelian Tragedy." In *Essays on Aristotle's* Poetics, edited by Amélie Rorty, 1–22. Princeton, N.J.: Princeton University Press, 1992.

Rorty, Richard. *Philosophy and the Mirror of Nature.* Princeton, N.J.: Princeton University Press, 1979.

Rosen, Stanley. *The Question of Being: A Reversal of Heidegger.* New Haven, Conn.: Yale University Press, 1993.

————. "Thought and Touch: A Note on Aristotle's *De Anima.*" *Phronesis* 6 (1961): 127–37.

Rousseau, Jean-Jacques. *Discourse on the Origin of Inequality,* pt. 1. Translated by Donald Cress. Indianapolis: Hackett, 1987.

Salkever, Stephen. *Finding the Mean: Theory and Practice in Aristotelian Political Philosophy.* Princeton, N.J.: Princeton University Press, 1990.

Sandel, Michael. *Liberalism and the Limits of Justice.* New York: Cambridge University Press, 1982.

Sartre, Jean-Paul. *Existentialism and Human Emotions.* Secaucus, N.Y.: Philosophical Library, 1957.

Schmitz, Kenneth. *The Gift: Creation.* The Aquinas Lecture. Milwaukee: Marquette University Press, 1982.

Schneewind, J. B. "The Divine Corporation and the History of Ethics." In *Philosophy in History,* edited by Richard Rorty, J. B. Schneewind, and Quentin Skinner, 173–91. New York: Cambridge University Press, 1984.

————. "The Misfortunes of Virtue." In *Virtue Ethics,* edited by Roger Crisp and Michael Slote, 178–200. Oxford: Oxford University Press, 1997.

Sherman, Nancy. *The Fabric of Character.* Oxford: Clarendon, 1989.

————. *Making a Necessity of Virtue: Aristotle and Kant on Virtue.* Cambridge, Eng.: Cambridge University Press, 1997.

Simon, Yves R. *The Definition of Moral Virtue.* New York: Fordham University Press, 1986.

————. *Freedom of Choice.* New York: Fordham University Press, 1969.

————. *Moral Virtue.* New York: Fordham University Press, 1986.

————. *The Tradition of Natural Law.* 1965. Reprint. New York: Fordham University Press, 1992.

Simpson, Peter. "St. Thomas and the Naturalistic Fallacy." *The Thomist* 51 (1987): 51–69.

Staley, Kevin. "Happiness: The Natural End of Man?" *The Thomist* 53 (1989): 215–34.

Strauss, Leo. "An Introduction to Heideggerian Existentialism." In

The Rebirth of Classical Political Rationalism, edited by Thomas L. Pangle, 27–46. Chicago: University of Chicago Press, 1989.

———. "On the Euthyphron." In *The Rebirth of Classical Political Rationalism*, edited by Thomas L. Pangle, 187–206. Chicago: University of Chicago Press, 1989.

———. *What Is Political Philosophy?* Chicago: University of Chicago Press, 1991.

Taylor, Charles. "Philosophy and Its History." In *Philosophy in History*, edited by Richard Rorty, J. B. Schneewind, and Quentin Skinner, 17–30. New York: Cambridge University Press, 1984.

———. *Sources of the Self: The Making of the Modern Identity*. Cambridge, Mass.: Harvard University Press, 1989.

Tessitore, Aristide. *Reading Aristotle's* Ethics: *Virtue, Rhetoric, and Political Philosophy*. Albany: State University of New York Press, 1996.

Thompson, Walter Jay. "Aristotle: Philosophy and Politics, Theory and Practice." *Proceedings of the American Catholic Philosophical Association* 68 (1994): 109–24.

Tierney, Brian. "Hierarchy, Consent, and the 'Western Tradition.'" *Political Theory* 15 (1987): 646–52.

Tugwell, Simon. Introduction to *Early Dominicans: Selected Writings*, 1–47. Classics of Western Spirituality. New York: Paulist, 1982.

Urs von Balthasar, Hans. *Seeing the Form*. Vol. 1 of *The Glory of the Lord: A Theological Aesthetics*. Translated by E. Leiva Merikakis. San Francisco: Ignatius, 1982.

Veatch, Henry. "Variations, Good and Bad, on the Theme of Right Reason in Ethics." *The Monist* 66 (1983): 57–70.

Weisheipl, James. *Friar Thomas D'Aquino: His Life, Thought, and Works*. Washington, D.C.: Catholic University of America Press, 1983.

Westberg, Daniel. *Right Practical Reason*. Oxford: Clarendon, 1994.

White, Stephen. "Aristotle's Favorite Tragedies." In *Essays on Aristotle's* Poetics, edited by Amélie Rorty, 221–40. Princeton, N.J.: Princeton University Press, 1992.

Wians, William. "Aristotle, Demonstration, and Teaching." *Ancient Philosophy* 9 (1989): 245–53.

Wilhelmsen, Frederick. *Being and Knowing*. Albany, N.Y.: Preserving Christian Publications, 1995.

————. *The Paradoxical Structure of Existence.* Irving, Tex.: University of Dallas Press, 1970.

Williams, Bernard. "Ought and Moral Obligation." In *Moral Luck,* 114–23. Cambridge, Eng.: Cambridge University Press, 1981.

Wolterstorff, Nicholas. *John Locke and the Ethics of Belief.* New York: Cambridge University Press, 1996.

————. "The Migration of the Theistic Arguments: From Natural Theology to Evidentialist Apologetics." In *Rationality, Religious Belief, and Moral Commitment,* edited by Robert Audi and William Wainwright, 38–81. Ithaca, N.Y.: Cornell University Press, 1986.

Zagzebski, Linda. *Virtues of the Mind.* Cambridge, Eng.: Cambridge University Press, 1996.

INDEX OF NAMES